P9-CZV-808

"NO ONE CAN
HURT HIM
ANYMORE"

"NO ONE CAN HURT HIM ANYMORE"

CAROL J. ROTHGEB
AND
SCOTT H. CUPP

PINNACLE BOOKS
Kensington Publishing Corp.
http://www.kensingtonbooks.com

Some names have been changed to protect the privacy of individuals connected to this story.

PINNACLE BOOKS are published by

Kensington Publishing Corp.
850 Third Avenue
New York, NY 10022

All Kensington Titles, Imprints, and Distributed Lines are available at special quantity discounts for bulk purchases for sales promotions, premiums, fund-raising, and educational or institutional use. Special book excerpts or customized printings can also be created to fit specific needs. For details, write or phone the office of the Kensington special sales manager: Kensington Publishing Corp., 850 Third Avenue, New York, NY 10022, attn: Special Sales Department, Phone: 1-800-221-2647.

Pinnacle and the P logo Reg. U.S. Pat. & TM Off.

First Printing: May 2005

10 9 8 7 6 5 4 3 2 1

Printed in the United States of America

This book is dedicated to Dr. Richard Zimmern . . .
A.J.'s guardian angel . . .

Acknowledgments

First of all, I would like to thank my editor of *Hometown Killer*, Gary Goldstein, for recommending me to Miles Lott, the editor of *"No One Can Hurt Him Anymore"*—and for his confidence in me—making it possible for me to be a part of this project.

And Scott Cupp—not only for being a joy to work with but, more important, for everything he's done in his career to bring justice to those who would do harm to the youngest and most vulnerable in our society.

My love and gratitude to my children—Jeanne, David, and Dana. Once again, I had their unwavering support, love, and encouragement.

And, as always, my love to my granddaughters—Mallory, Chelsea, Miranda, and Sarah. My hope is that they will know that their dreams can come true.

Most of all, I want to thank with all my heart F. Peter "Pete" Dixon, retired homicide prosecutor, for supporting me, encouraging me, and loving me through this difficult project. If it hadn't been for his guidance and honesty, I don't know if I would have made it. He is truly *The Wind Beneath My Wings*.

—Carol J. Rothgeb

To my brother, George, the smartest and bravest man I know.

For my children—Kaitlin, Elizabeth, and Scotty—and the wonderful future that awaits them.

I want to specifically acknowledge three people: Judge Joe Marx, without whom the cases would never have been won; State Attorney Barry Krischer, who supported me before the filing of the charges, during the time it took to get the cases tried, and has supported me as this book made its way to print. This case is also a testament to the fine police work of the men and women of the Palm Beach County Sheriff's Office, which was exemplified by the hard work, dedication, and persistence of lead detective Michael Waites.

—Scott H. Cupp

PROLOGUE

His name was A.J.

He loved Ninja Turtles and Steven Seagal movies.

He was ten years old and small for his age. He had tousled brown hair, watchful brown eyes, and a look of perpetual apology on his baby face, as if everything he did—or thought—required one. A.J. had a sixth sense about anger and aggression. He could see it in the twitch of an eye or the tilt of a head. He had mastered "body language." He had endured. Scars—psychological and physical—were his constant companions.

This was as happy and secure as it ever got for A.J.: He was walking his dog. To be sure, the animal was truly a mutt, but no ordinary dog—not to A.J. The peaceful look on his face revealed that they had a bond. Neither of them had anywhere else to look to for friendship—much less love.

In truth, the dog had it better.

It was 1:30 in the morning and cool outside—almost cold. A.J. wore a stained T-shirt and pants a size too small. He laughed out loud as he tried to keep up with the dog.

The neighborhood was veiled in darkness, but A.J. wasn't afraid. At least, not of walking his dog at such strange hours. Going back home—that's what he feared more than anything.

The dog took him full circle around the neighborhood and they finally ended up in front of their residence—nearly indistinguishable in the row of look-alike houses. The dog stopped, sharing A.J.'s reluctance.

Maybe if he used the patio door, they wouldn't notice him coming in. . . .

CHAPTER 1

No more pain . . . no more humiliation . . . no more fear . . . it was finally over. No one could ever hurt him again. In the cold, still water, in the middle of the spring night, he had finally found peace.

David Schwarz struggled to wake up enough to understand what his wife was saying to him—and why she was shaking him. After a moment, he realized that Jessica was telling him that his ten-year-old son, A.J., was missing. Now wide-awake and alarmed, he stumbled to the kitchen, with his wife right behind him—insisting that she had already looked everywhere and he was nowhere to be found.

As he passed by the patio door—still trying to comprehend what was happening—he glanced outside and noticed that the ladder was hanging on the side of their aboveground swimming pool. Could it be? Was it possible that A.J. had gone swimming? At this hour? It was barely daylight—the sun had just come up.

David rushed to the side of the pool, which was located about five feet from the patio door, and saw the boy under the water about halfway down. But something was terribly wrong. He quickly jumped into the pool and lifted his son out of the water.

It was heartbreakingly obvious that A.J. was dead. David shouted at Jessica to call 911, and then gently laid his son's cold, stiff body on the ground. Disbelieving—and stunned—

he went into the house to get a sheet to cover him. Then he sat down in a chair at the patio table—a few feet from his son's body—to wait.

The beautiful Sunday morning of May 2, 1993, was clear and dry with the promise of becoming very hot, with the temperature already in the low seventies. Within minutes of the 911 call, sirens screamed in the distance as paramedics and law enforcement officials approached the area from different directions. Their destination was a residence on Triphammer Road in the Concept Homes Development, a low-to-medium-income neighborhood near Lantana, Florida.

As soon as the officers from the Palm Beach Sheriff's Office (PBSO)—who were working the graveyard shift—arrived, they cordoned off the ranch-style house with yellow crime-scene tape. Neighbors started filtering out of their homes—some still in their nightclothes—trying to find out what had happened.

Corporal Bobbie Hopper, the responding officer, walked around the house and entered the backyard through a wooden gate located on the west side of the house. A six-foot-high privacy fence surrounded the entire area.

The octagon-shaped swimming pool was centered in— and completely dominated—the small yard. It was no more than four feet deep and there was a white plastic ladder on the outside of the pool and another on the inside.

The victim was lying on the grass under a flowered bedsheet next to the north side of the pool. When the officer removed the sheet, she saw that the young boy was on his back and was naked.

His right arm was bent at the elbow and lying across his chest, and his left arm was bent at the elbow near his side— his forearm outstretched. The tips of his fingers on both hands were bent inward, not quite—but almost—balled into fists, therefore suggesting a struggle might have taken place.

Both his legs were bent at the knees and the heels of both feet rested on the ground with his toes pointed upward.

And he was covered with bruises. They were everywhere, on his arms, his legs, his neck, and his face. A deep abrasion scored the right side of his nose. Another feathered away from his mouth. The underside of his chin was clearly bruised. The neck, chest, and abdomen were nicked and abraded. A patchwork of bruises ran down his hips and his legs.

Oddly enough, there was a blue-and-green-colored stain—along with some sparkles in his hair—on the left side of his hairline.

Detective Michael Waites was awakened by the shrill ringing of the telephone at 6:25 that morning. The police dispatcher on the other end of the line requested that he respond to an apparent drowning. After being informed that the victim was a child, he was in his car and on the road within minutes.

Sergeant Ken Deischer, of the PBSO's Homicide Unit, met him in front of the house and briefed him: The victim was a ten-year-old white male. He had been discovered floating facedown in an aboveground swimming pool in the backyard. Nude. And covered with bruises.

Michael Waites would be the lead investigator. He had been a homicide detective since 1987 and a member of the SWAT team since 1985. Quiet, easygoing, and thorough, he listened more than he spoke.

Several detectives, including Jimmy Restivo and Chris Calloway, were en route to conduct a canvass of the neighborhood. They could only hope that if there had been child abuse—or anything suspicious—that the neighbors would be willing to talk to the investigators.

Deischer and Waites circled around to the backyard and Waites examined the body. He anticipated that the cause of death was drowning. The manner of death, on the other hand—

whether it was from natural causes, suicide, accident, or homicide—was something he hoped the medical examiner would be able to determine.

Corporal Hopper provided him with the victim's name and date of birth: Andrew J. Schwarz, born April 24, 1983. She added, "But everyone called him A.J. He lives . . . lived here with his father, stepmother, and two stepsisters." They would later learn that the older one was A.J.'s stepsister and the younger one was actually his half sister.

Waites entered the house through the patio door that led into the extremely cluttered kitchen. Among other things, there were empty beer cans everywhere.

David Schwarz, a big man with an untamed beard and a look of disbelief and shock on his face, was seated at the kitchen table. It was easy to see why everyone—as the detective would later learn—called him "Bear."

Waites introduced himself and immediately began assessing the father's state of mind, searching for signs of shock: the onset of grief, anger, and loss.

David, struggling to speak, said that A.J. went to bed around 9:00 the night before and was fine. He said that he had stayed up, watching TV, until around midnight—maybe 12:30—and that Jessica had gone to bed sometime prior to that. Before he went to bed, he had checked on the kids. All three of them were sound asleep in their bedrooms—including A.J.

The next thing he remembered was his wife waking him up with the news that A.J. was missing. She informed him that A.J. wasn't in his bedroom or anywhere else in the house.

Waites asked him what time that was and Bear said it was around 6:00—maybe a little after. He went on to say that he was standing in the kitchen when he noticed that the ladder was in the pool, and he remembered removing the ladder from the pool late the previous evening. When he stepped into the backyard to investigate, he saw his son's body in the pool.

David Schwarz was seriously shaken. He could have been

acting, but Waites didn't think so. The detective asked what A.J. had been wearing when he went to bed, and Bear replied, "Ninja Turtle sweatpants and a T-shirt."

And now he was naked next to the swimming pool.

Waites asked David Schwarz to sign a "consent to search" for the house and curtilage and he agreed.

When Detective Doreen Schoenstein, of the Crime Scene Unit, returned to her vehicle to obtain the items necessary for the investigation and the search, she noticed that several of the neighbors who had gathered outside their homes were very upset and speaking in hostile tones about Jessica and David Schwarz.

When Schoenstein went into the house, Detective Waites told her that he was attempting to speak with A.J.'s stepmother. Due to the suspicious circumstances surrounding the child's death, Jessica and David had been kept separated until they could be questioned.

Hopper and Schoenstein accompanied Detective Waites to the other side of the house and found Jessica, along with her daughters, in the younger girl's bedroom. It was a cheerful room with posters and pictures on the walls and cluttered with dolls and toys.

When Hopper knocked on the open door, Jessica was stretched out on the bed and looked ill when they entered the room. Waites wondered silently if she was hungover and made a mental note to inquire about the couple's drinking habits.

Jessica Schwarz was a heavyset woman—5' 2" tall and weighing 175 pounds. Her state of mind was not as easy to read as her husband's. She appeared to be dazed and the first thing she said was that she couldn't believe this was happening. The next was that she felt sick to her stomach.

Detective Waites asked for some time alone with her and Hopper took Jessica's two daughters, four-year-old Jackie Schwarz and ten-year-old Lauren Cross, to another bedroom.

Schoenstein left the room to continue her investigation. First she went to the backyard to examine the pool and found that the water was fairly clean—except for a few leaves in the bottom—and cold to the touch. After collecting a water sample, she returned to the house through the patio door. She examined and photographed the sliding door and noticed that the lock was broken. She determined that the Schwarzes were in the habit of securing the door by placing an old cane in the track.

David Schwarz told her he couldn't remember whether the sliding door was open or not, prior to finding A.J.'s body.

Her next stop was A.J.'s bedroom: a dungeonlike room on the northeast corner of the house, directly off the kitchen, and attached to the garage. There was no doorknob. Instead, there was a piece of cloth—or rag—pulled through the knob hole and tied. And a lock—on the outside of the door.

On the inside of the door was a note from A.J.'s teacher—a progress report dated "4-2-93" that indicated that he and his teacher had had a very good day.

"Bleak" was the word that came to mind when she entered A.J.'s room. There was a simple twin bed along one wall and, on the opposite wall, a dresser that appeared to be used for storage with boxes—marked "Christmas decorations"—stacked on top of it. The window covering was a floral sheet, and there was a door leading to the attached garage.

And, on a desk, there was a piece of notebook paper with a child's handwriting on it. "I have a big stupid mouth, I don't know when to shut up" was written over and over again.

Black trash bags filled with clothing were on the floor, and several socks were scattered around.

Poorly lit. The room smelled of stale urine. There were no posters on the walls. No photographs. No Nintendo. No stereo or radio. No books. On a bookcase under the window, there were a few toy action figures and toy cars. In the center of the room—on the floor—were a turquoise sleeping bag, a dark T-shirt, and a pair of Ninja Turtle sweatpants. And inside the pants, a pair of boy's underwear.

The clothes A.J. had worn to bed the night before.

On a small table, Schoenstein found two bottles of Easter-egg coloring—blue and green—but both of them were empty.

When she went back through the kitchen and entered the living room, she saw several pictures of the girls displayed, but did not see any photographs—not even one—of A.J. anywhere in the room. Or anywhere else in the house.

Next she went to Lauren's room and—like Jackie's—it was bright and cheerful with pictures and posters on the walls and dolls and toys scattered around. A color television. A Nintendo game. And a stereo system.

Meanwhile, after everyone else had left the room, Waites asked Jessica, "How was it that you found out that A.J. was missing?"

"I just woke up out of the blue. I never wake up that early on a Sunday. But I was thirsty. So I went to the kitchen for a drink of water and there was A.J.'s door open. I mean, he always sleeps with it closed, so I looked in his room and he wasn't there. I even looked under the bed. Uh-uh. I checked everywhere, in the garage—in the bathroom—in the family room—everywhere. . . . When I couldn't find him, I figured I better wake up Bear. And he found him in the pool a couple of minutes later."

Without prompting, she began to describe the abuse that A.J. had suffered at the hands of his natural mother, Ilene Logan (who had—after her divorce from David Schwarz—married and then divorced a man named Timothy Logan). It was that abusive situation, Jessica told him, that led to A.J.'s placement with her and Bear.

If Jessica had seemed upset when Waites first came into the room, she didn't now. She appeared agitated and aggressive, but not overwhelmed with the grief or disbelief that Bear had demonstrated.

She went on to tell him that A.J. had been treated for hyperactivity—and also received therapy for the past abuse—at South County Mental Health. He also had spent six weeks at the mental institution, located in Vero Beach, the previous year. She explained that he had presently been "in between counselors."

Detective Waites later informed Doreen Schoenstein that

A.J. had been under the care of a psychiatrist and had been in protective custody. He had also been taking a medication known as imipramine, a drug used to relieve symptoms of depression.

Jessica had told him that she was the one who personally administered the medication to A.J., but now she couldn't find it. Nor could she find it the day before. She claimed she did not know "what happened to it."

Schoenstein searched the residence, but she was unsuccessful in locating the medication.

It was after 8:00 when Waites returned to the backyard. Before the body was removed, he studied it again. What about an errant dive into the pool? Could A.J. have gone for a swim and knocked himself out? He examined A.J.'s forehead, looking for the full bruising that is consistent with such a hypothesis, and couldn't detect it.

Could A.J. have gone swimming, cramped up, and gone under? Possible, but the pool wasn't that deep. As he looked from the body to the pool, he realized that A.J. was tall enough to stand up, no matter how severe the cramps. That led to another question: do ten-year-old boys go swimming naked?

As he looked at A.J.'s face, he wondered if the boy could have inexplicably decided to go snorkeling in the middle of the night. Gotten up, taken off his Ninja Turtle pants, gone outside, and put the ladder up next to the pool? Could he have taken in water through the snorkel, panicked, and wrenched off the mask with enough force to cause such lacerations and bruising? Not likely. Still, he walked back to the swimming pool and searched the bottom. There was a mask, but no snorkel.

Could he have been electrocuted? Doubtful, given the condition of the body, but he made a note to check any electrical problems around the house. Could he have been climbing the ladder, slipped, and hit his head against the wood railing that framed the pool? That was a real possibility, but it didn't explain the abrasions on his neck and shoulders—or the bruises on his chest and legs.

No one from the medical examiner's office had arrived

and Waites was informed that they wouldn't be coming. Forensic investigator Doug Jenkins had been contacted and he advised that he would not respond to the scene, but would send Professional Removal Service (a body removal service contracted by the county) to transport the corpse to the Palm Beach County Medical Examiner's Office.

The attendants, David Grant and Don Scott, finally arrived at 8:35 and—after checking for signs of recent trauma—removed the body. An autopsy was scheduled for the next afternoon; Detective Waites would be there.

An extraordinary scene had developed in front of the house. Besides the official vehicles, investigators, and neighbors, members of the press and curiosity seekers now had converged. The detectives who had been conducting the neighborhood canvass began to check in.

Jimmy Restivo—a huge, burly man—was a transplant from New York, and his twenty-two years with NYPD had done as much to solidify his cynicism as it did to sharpen his skills. He consulted the scribbles on his notepad and said, in his heavy New York accent, "Wait'll you hear this. The kid was out walking his dog at one-thirty last night. One-thirty this morning! Guy next door saw him. Name's Ron Pincus Junior. He's pulling in from work and here's A.J. wandering the streets with his dog."

Waites looked at Restivo. "He sure it was one-thirty?"

"Positive. He'd just gotten off work."

Waites responded, "Mr. Schwarz says the boy was sound asleep when he went to bed at twelve-thirty."

Restivo shook his head. "Uh-uh. That doesn't fit either. Pincus says he noticed a light on in the Schwarz living room and the TV on. Same time—one-thirty.

"Two weeks ago, Pincus overheard the stepmom shouting at the kid that if he 'doesn't straighten up,' she's going to 'tie him up and run him over.' Heard her say she hates him. Pincus says it goes on all the time. Guess what the stepmom calls the kid? She calls him 'Jeffrey Dahmer.' You believe that?"

Another detective added: "She's been heard calling Andrew everything from a 'stupid loudmouth' and a 'slut' to a 'piece of shit' and a 'bitch.' "

"You've got names and addresses on all these people?" Waites asked.

"Every one."

Chris Calloway, of the Special Investigations Unit, dealt—on a daily basis—with sex crimes, child abuse, and neglect. He had at least a dozen pages of notes to follow up on, all of them indicating that Andrew Schwarz had been subjected to physical and emotional abuse for years—up to and including the day before his death.

Waites asked, "Was HRS ever involved?" HRS—Health and Rehabilitative Services—is Florida's version of social services, and their handling of child abuse cases had been under intense scrutiny for almost a year.

Calloway replied, "They were regular visitors. The last time was when A.J. showed up at a neighbor's house with a broken nose and two black eyes. Very suspicious.

"The story was that A.J. had cracked his face against the handlebars of his sister's bike. This neighbor, an Eileen Callahan, doesn't believe it. She thinks Jessica threatened the kid to get him to tell that story and to stick with it.

"I talked to him myself. If someone hit him, he wouldn't say."

Detective Waites requested that David and Jessica Schwarz, along with Jackie and Lauren, come to the sheriff's office to be interviewed. Detective Calloway would conduct a joint investigation into the allegations of the abuse.

The investigation into his death—and life—would reveal that by no stretch of anyone's imagination had A.J. Schwarz lived anything even close to a happy life—or even a normal one.

CHAPTER 2

Please, for the kids' sakes, give them both to us and I promise we will comply with everything you want us to do. Give them a break, and David and myself a chance to prove we can make a difference and change their lives for the best.

—Jessica Schwarz

Andrew J. "A.J." Schwarz was born to David Schwarz and his first wife, Ilene, on April 24, 1983. Ten years and eight days later he was dead.

When David met Ilene Spence in 1980, she already had a baby girl named Patsy. There was no father's name listed on Patsy's birth certificate, only the notation that he had "left before she was born." Therefore, her last name was Spence—her mother's maiden name. David and Ilene were married in 1982 and their son was born the following year.

According to David, Ilene kept the children—and the apartment—clean. But after she "kicked him out" and they were divorced in 1986, she "worked nights as a stripper, had many lovers, and abused drugs and alcohol."

He saw A.J. and Patsy every weekend. Even though Patsy was not his own child, he loved her and did not want to separate the two children.

David lived alone for a short time until he met Jessica. A

former truck driver, traveling from New York City to Miami, she had sold her truck and moved to Florida.

A.J. was three years old when he first visited with both Jessica and David. Jessica would later say that the children were "malnourished, dirty, and dressed poorly." She also claimed that A.J. could not talk, was shy or frightened, that he would hide his face, and was totally inarticulate. She also said that he did not use tableware and acted like a sick animal.

David's words were similar: The children were "kept poorly, dirty, thin, and ragged." The children told him that Ilene's lovers had beaten them.

In 1987, A.J. became ill and was hospitalized. HRS was called in because A.J. had bruises on his back and claimed he had been beaten "with a stick."

Shortly after that, Ilene, along with the children, disappeared, and David did not see them again until November 1989, when he—by chance—met them on the street. They again disappeared and he did not see them until HRS called him in 1990.

At the initial HRS medical exam, A.J. was diagnosed as hyperactive. He also could not hear well, suffered from asthma, and his front teeth were rotten. He was a mess.

Jessica and David were given temporary custody of the children—although they remained under protective custody of the state. Both of them were sickly when they arrived and had lice and ringworm.

Jessica had sent a letter to HRS, which read in part:

Please, for the kids' sakes, give them both to us and I promise we will comply with everything you want us to do. Give them a break, and David and myself a chance to prove we can make a difference and change their lives for the best.

Shortly before noon on Sunday, May 2, Michael Waites interviewed thirty-six-year old David Schwarz at the sheriff's office. Still quite distraught, his voice echoed the genuine disbelief and shock that he was feeling:

Waites: I just need to—real quickly—go over what happened this morning. Start with dinnertime last night—how A.J. was acting up until he goes to bed.

David: He was fine. He ate dinner with everybody else. No, he ate in his room. Uh, chicken—just like everybody else. Fine. Offered to do the dishes. So he did the dishes. Fine. Girls were in playin' Nintendo. And, uh, he finished up the kitchen. Did some schoolwork in his room. 'Cause he hadn't been to school—he hadn't been feelin' good. And around nine o'clock or so, he came in and said "good night." Went to the bathroom and went to bed. I watched TV until about midnight. Checked on all the kids and I went to bed. This morning the wife said, "A.J.'s gone." I said, "What?" The door was open. The garage door was locked. Front door was locked. She was looking in the backyard. I looked in the backyard. Saw him in the pool. I noticed the ladder was up on the pool.

Waites: Uh-huh.

David: Ladder was up. I said, "Oh, shit!" I looked in and there he was. Jumped in and carried him out. Arm was stiff. . . . I told the wife, "911." Came in while she was on the phone and I said, "He's stiff. I don't think there's any way they're gonna revive him. Paramedics came. I covered him with a sheet. That's the extent . . .

Waites (after a slight pause): You were saying earlier that there had been some problems with the neighbors?

David: From what my wife's been sayin' . . . I have, myself, no problems with the neighbors. I'm not there during the week. I work twelve, thirteen hours a day. I come home. I eat there and I'm in the house. Just from what the wife says . . . I mean . . . I don't have any problems myself with any of the neighbors.

Waites: Have the neighbors ever called HRS or anything like that?

David: Someone has.

Waites: In the past?

David: Yeah. They don't tell us who does it. I forget how many times, but it's been cleared each time.

Waites: Uh-huh. Okay.

David: With no problems.

Waites continued after a long silence: And when—either you or your wife—aren't out by the pool . . . the ladder's normally kept away from the pool, so that your kids or neighborhood kids don't get into it?

David: Right. The ladder's only put up when they're going in to swim. That was our thought for safety—along with the fence. The ladder was kept on the ground against the house till we got this puppy and he likes to chew things. So we put it up on that table.

Waites: The door that was open that you talked about—that was his bedroom door?

David: Yes.

Waites: He normally sleeps with that closed?

David: Yeah. The kids do sleep with their doors closed, because I like to watch TV at night and Jessica gets up once in a while to get something to eat. And this way, they don't get bothered. The dogs can't go in their rooms. The dogs sleep with us in our room.

Waites: One of the neighbors told one of the detectives standing out there that they saw A.J. out walking the dog—after midnight last night. Is that any way possible? I mean, you just said the dogs sleep with you.

David: Yeah. The dogs weren't out after midnight.

Waites: Okay. That's just what one of them said as one of the detectives was walking to his car and it kind of struck me as odd because I can't see—

David: What? We don't walk the dogs.

Waites: I'm just telling you what someone said. I'm just trying to make sure I've got everything cleared up.

David (exclaiming): Lord Almighty!

Waites: I mean, once you're in at night—unless the dogs wake you up—they're in with you, right?

David: If they wake me up, I put them out the back.

Waites: The back? Okay.

David: Once in a while, the girls would walk them around the block.

Waites: Uh-huh. But that's going to be daylight hours—it's not going to be after midnight. . . .

David (distressed): Yeah! Good God! I'm gonna be sick. He was not out walking the dog after midnight!

(The detective waited several moments before continuing the questioning, allowing David to regain his composure.)

Waites: The problems that your wife had with the neighbors . . . ?

David: Uh-huh.

Waites: And I realize again that you're not home during the day with the hours that you're putting in working. Do you think it could have been—normally, she talks kind of in a loud voice . . . ?

David: Yeah.

Waites: Well, I don't have a problem with that. Did you ever think, like, if she may have been just yelling at one of the kids or something—just with her being naturally loud-natured—that they may have misinterpreted it? That it may have resulted in HRS being called? Or people may have seen her out yelling at the kids not to do something and just thought something else?

David: She doesn't yell unless she's out the back door or in the house. She doesn't go out front yelling.

Waites: Okay.

David: But, yeah, she does raise her voice. I raise my voice. The neighbors raise their voice.

Waites: It's normal? Well, normal to kids.

David: Yeah. Well, Jessica has a loud voice to begin with.

Waites: But there was never anything that someone might consider excessive punishment? That's ever gone on?

David: All right, on Thursdays, A.J. would get up early and go out and collect cans. And someone thought that was punishment.

Waites: Because he went out and collected cans?

David: Yeah.

Waites: Would he do this before school?

David: Yeah. And HRS came and asked about this shit. Punishment? Punishment is taking away the TV; not letting him go in the pool.

Waites: HRS just came out because someone called and said you had your kid out collecting cans on Thursdays?

David: No, they didn't come out for that. The guardian ad litem brought that up—that someone called him on it.

Waites: Did he say if there was anything else said other than just out picking up cans or . . . ?

David: Yeah. They (HRS) come over, woke all the kids up, looked at their bodies . . . nothing—nowhere. They get spanked—of course.

Waites: Yeah.

David: We can't do much more than that because they can call on us. The kids themselves can call on us.

Waites: Yeah. True.

David: I mean, excessive punishment would be grounding—can't go out and play. That may be excessive.

Waites: But nothing excessive, as far as physical? I mean, I agree with you. A slap across the butt is a slap across the butt. Every once in a while a kid's going to get one.

David: I've used my belt on them a few times.

Waites: Now . . . and again. . . . I mean, I was raised that way, you know?

David: I was too. But you can't do that—well, you're not supposed to do that nowadays.

Waites: It's not like you're standing over them—over one of the kids and hitting on them for five or six minutes. I mean—

David: They'd be in the hospital if I did that.

Waites: Exactly.

David: I'm not a little guy.

Waites: The cans—he just liked collecting them? Is there any particular reason that he told the guardian when they asked him about it?

David: Just collecting them for Mommy (Jessica), that's all. He might've said something. He's—he was a little A.D.D. His mama (Ilene) hit him in the head with a frying pan—deaf in one ear. Had him carrying drugs and stuff—and he was molested. So he's—was not completely straight in his head. He'd give you the shirt off his back—he was a good kid.

Waites: If somebody asked him—saw him one morning and asked A.J., "Why are you out collecting cans?" would he make up something? Exaggerate something?

David: More than likely. I can't say. The neighbors came over and said some stuff he said and then he denies it. He'd tell a lie quicker than the truth—that's for sure.

Waites: But that all relates back to the stuff he went through with his natural mother?

David: I'm sure of it. It has to. One thing we did expound on with the kids—tell us the truth. He just had a very hard time doing that.

Waites: Was he a fairly good swimmer?

David: Yeah. From what I seen . . . in the pool . . . at the beach. . . .

Waites: Your wife told me he's been going to counseling and had a guardian and so forth for some period. And, I guess, he even was when he was still in Fort Lauderdale, before he came up to live with you—from the problems that he'd had down there.

David: Right.

Waites: Do you think this all could have resulted just in finally being too much pressure from all that?

David: I don't know. The psychiatrists have all said that he's got a lot of hurt inside. And I don't know. I can't say. I have no idea. Like I said, he wasn't depressed or nothing that I saw, in the last couple days. So I don't know what happened. I don't know what happened. Wife woke me up—found him in the pool. I can only speculate. I don't know. The water was awful cold.

That afternoon, HRS workers removed A.J.'s stepsister, Lauren, and half sister, Jackie, from the Schwarz home and put them in protective custody. They were placed in the home of their grandparents—Jessica's mother and father.

Records showed that sheriff's deputies had been called to the Triphammer Road residence fourteen times since May 1990—for such incidents as battery, petty theft, and "neighbor trouble."

In June 1991, deputies arrived at the house—after being called about a fight—and found Jessica Schwarz being pinned down in their driveway by her husband. David Schwarz explained that she had been drinking at a neighbor's house and when he tried to take her home, she started hitting him, then broke the windshield on his car.

Jessica informed the deputies that if they did not take her away, there would be more fighting. She was arrested, pleaded guilty to battery, and was sentenced to time served.

On Monday, there was a guidance counselor and a school psychologist present at Indian Pines Elementary School to help students deal with their feelings about their classmate's sudden and tragic death.

That morning, Detective Restivo studied his notes from the interviews with David and Jessica's neighbors. It was all too clear that there was something terribly wrong in the Schwarz home.

First he had interviewed Eileen Callahan, the neighbor who had told him that A.J. was severely abused—to the point that she had called HRS and made a complaint. She had seen

A.J. with two black eyes and what appeared to be a broken nose. Even though he told everyone who asked him that he had fallen off his bicycle, Callahan had found that hard to believe, since the child was never seen riding a bicycle.

In fact, it seemed that A.J. wasn't allowed to play at all, and was "constantly cleaning the garage" and had even been seen washing his father's truck—with a toothbrush.

Callahan also told the detective that every Thursday morning for the last couple of months—between 5:00 and 6:00—she saw A.J. collecting aluminum cans from the garbage in front of each residence on the street. She further claimed that this was a provision (community service) for a probation of some type that was imposed on Jessica Schwarz—but she wasn't sure what the charges had been.

Another neighbor, Jim Ebenhack, had also seen A.J. collecting cans very early on Thursday mornings and taking them back to his house. He also told Restivo that the stepmother was constantly verbally abusing the child, including—but not limited to—calling him "a useless piece of shit."

Louis Steinhauer—yet another neighbor—had seen the boy's black eyes and possibly broken nose. A.J. was in the company of his sister Jackie when Steinhauer asked what had happened. Jackie turned to A.J. and warned, "Remember what Mom told you to say!" A.J. replied, "Yes. I fell off my bike."

Although the parents drove Lauren to school, Steinhauer stated that A.J. was made to walk. He had actually seen the parents drive away with the girls in the car while A.J. started walking to school.

About two weeks earlier, Jessica had gone to school, taken A.J. out, and brought him home where "she beat him because he forgot to feed the cat."

The weekend before his death, A.J. was seen walking back and forth, in the front yard of his house, saying, "I'm no good; I'm a liar." Steinhauer said he could hear the stepmother and father from inside the dwelling, shouting, "Can't hear you!" And A.J. would then scream the words even louder.

He had also seen the young boy being made to edge the lawn with regular household scissors.

As Detective Restivo was canvassing the neighborhood, a thirteen-year-old girl approached him and asked if she could speak with him. Jamie Falk explained that she was a friend of A.J.'s sister Patsy. She told the detective that Jessica was "always mean to A.J. and would not let him play." One day when she was over there—a very hot day—Jessica made A.J. go to his room, where there was no air conditioner—with the windows closed. She made him stay there for hours at a time.

That same day, Michael Waites contacted South County Mental Health and verified that the victim, Andrew Schwarz, had indeed been treated there.

At 12:30 that afternoon, Waites, along with Detective Calloway and Sergeant Deischer, met with several members of the Florida Department of Health and Rehabilitative Services. Terry Neuenhaus, Sandra Owen, Sandy Warren, Richard Lyles, and Jim Koubla met with the investigators at the PBSO Crimes Against Persons Unit.

On May 19, 1992, the reports indicated that Jessica Schwarz had been the subject of an HRS investigation involving crack cocaine use, sale of crack cocaine, and physical abuse on Andrew Schwarz. The case was closed by HRS without classification. Detective Ole Olsen, of the PBSO, had also investigated the charges, which were determined to be "unfounded."

On January 25, 1993, Jessica Schwarz was again investigated by HRS and the PBSO because of the injuries Andrew Schwarz had suffered to his nose, which caused both of his eyes to swell. It was feared that Jessica Schwarz had broken the child's nose. HRS closed the investigation without classification. Detective Chris Calloway had closed the criminal investigation as "unfounded."

HRS had ordered a psychological evaluation for both Jessica and Andrew Schwarz at the conclusion of their investigation.

* * *

At 3:30 in the afternoon, Detectives Waites and Schoenstein were in attendance as Dr. James Benz, the chief medical examiner for Palm Beach County, performed the autopsy on Andrew Schwarz.

On A.J.'s head, Dr. Benz found a large area—about 5 inches long and 1¾ inches wide—covered with "a bluish-green dye containing glitter." And he found recent mild scratches behind each of his ears and a long recent abrasion on the right side of his nose, mild recent abrasions on the inside of his upper lip, the corner of his mouth, and his face. There were recent abrasions on his right elbow, a recent scratch on his left forearm.

He found multiple old, discolored bruises under his chin, on his torso, on his buttocks, and on his thigh. He also observed brown, yellow, and purple bruises of various sizes and age on almost every part of A.J.'s body.

Dr. Benz's opinion was that the cause of death for Andrew Schwarz was the result of drowning—the manner of death undetermined.

CHAPTER 3

The next thing I saw was David carrying him out and then I went to the bathroom and threw up.

—Jessica Schwarz

Scott H. Cupp, of the state attorney's office, chief of the Crimes Against Children Unit, was assigned to oversee the legal aspects during the investigation of Andrew Schwarz's death. Michael Waites met with him on Tuesday, May 4, to review what they had learned to date and to request subpoenas for various medical records.

Cupp, originally from Pittsburgh, Pennsylvania, was the youngest of three children in a middle-class family. His father was a production planning engineer for U.S. Steel and his mother was a housewife. Before deciding, at the age of twenty-four, to go back to school, Cupp drove a cab, worked in a steel mill, sold cars and insurance.

Having already decided he wanted to be a lawyer, he enrolled at Duquesne University and—much to his father's disappointment—majored in English instead of one of the sciences.

After graduating from Western New England College School of Law in Springfield, Massachusetts, he promptly moved to Florida, where he became a prosecutor with the state attorney's office in Fort Myers.

Prior to arriving in West Palm Beach in January 1993,

Cupp was prosecuting child abuse and adult sex crimes in Florida's Third Circuit. The Third Circuit consists of seven counties—Suwanee, Columbia, Lafayette, Madison, Hamilton, Dixie, and Taylor. The area is sparsely populated and beautiful. The towns of Live Oak, Lake City, Madison, Jasper, Mayo, Cross City, and Perry are reminiscent of the Old South.

The Third Circuit boasted some of the finest prosecutors that Cupp had ever met. State attorney Jerry Blair and ASA Bob Dekle had tried and convicted Theodore Bundy. And, although Bundy was convicted of other homicides—committed in other jurisdictions—his death warrant was carried out for the Third Circuit conviction for the murder of twelve-year-old Kimberly Leach.

The Third Circuit was where Cupp "cut his teeth," prosecuting crimes against children, and it was an eye-opening and rewarding 3½-year experience.

Cupp listened to Detective Waites's audiotaped interview with Jessica Schwarz, conducted in an interrogation room at the sheriff's office at 10:50 the previous Sunday morning, May 2—immediately before the detective had questioned David Schwarz.

Cupp would have given anything for a video accompaniment, but he was forced to rely on his imagination. Maybe that was for the best. He listened to the voice—the inflections—the tonality. He pictured her posture—her expressions—her body language.

On the tape, Waites asked her about the previous night. About A.J.'s routine. About his state of mind.

Jessica: He was acting fine. He . . . he ate all his dinner. Ate everything. He was talking. As a matter of fact, he was singing. I don't remember why. He was fine.
Waites: What did he do throughout the evening?
Jessica: Umm . . . he was reading a book and brought it in and asked me what a word was and I told him. He was out in the living room with the girls. They were doing their hair. And that's about it. I mean, then he . . .

everybody . . . the kids went to the bathroom, brushed their teeth, and went to bed.

Waites: Okay, what time would A.J. normally go to bed?

Jessica: On a Saturday, normally between nine and ten, but last night it was closer to nine than ten. They all went to bed at the same time last night.

Waites: Do you remember what A.J. was wearing when he went to bed?

Jessica: Ninja Turtle pants and uh . . . uh, a T-shirt . . . a dark T-shirt.

Waites: Did you see him after he went to bed? Did he wake back up at all before you went to bed?

Jessica (hesitantly): I fell asleep watching *Bonanza* and, uh . . . and I didn't wake up until I got up to . . . uh . . . I was going to have a piece of cheese and I was thirsty and he usually shuts his door when he goes to bed and it was opened. . . .

Waites (patiently): Okay.

Jessica: And I called him, and there was no answer.

Waites: Then what happened after that?

Jessica (answering with more confidence): I searched the house and the garage, and then I woke my husband up.

Waites: And after you woke your husband up?

Jessica: Well, he wasn't really awake, you know; I got him out of a sound sleep. And he sees A.J. in the pool and says, "Oh, my God," and jumped in the pool.

Waites: Uh-huh.

Jessica: I didn't look. . . . I . . . I caught a . . . I don't know where he was in the pool or what position or anything. I didn't get that close.

Waites: Hmmm.

Cupp thought it was an interesting answer. A qualification that wasn't necessary. Why would she do that?

Jessica: The next thing I saw was David carrying him out and then I went to the bathroom and threw up.

(Waites then took her through the rules of the pool, when the kids were allowed to swim and when they weren't. Were they allowed to swim naked? Were they allowed to dive?)

Waites: When A.J. was found, he didn't have any clothing. Had he ever before gone in the pool without clothing?

Jessica: Yes. They all had.

Waites (surprised): They had?

Jessica: Yeah.

Waites: So that's nothing that would be . . .

Jessica: Well, it wasn't a practice. . . . They made a game out of it and, you know, they got thrown in with their clothes on. And I've turned around and—all of a sudden—their clothes were off—bathing suits were off—and . . . I mean, it wasn't a habit, but they made a game out of it a few times.

Waites shifted gears and asked her about the counseling A.J. was receiving, about his guardian ad litem, and about the intervention of the Department of Health and Rehabilitative Services.

In the guardian ad litem program, the court assigns guardians to individual children who—for whatever reason—have their young lives brought before a judge. Divorce, abuse, delinquency, the distribution of a trust—many matters can lead to the need for a guardian. The guardian was to work for one overriding concern: the best interest of the child.

Cupp was intrigued by the way Jessica answered the questions: the incessant rambling as she jumped from one thought to the other, as if every question were an attack. The lack of sorrow—it was absent from her words and indiscernible in her voice—and the defense mechanisms as she fended off questions about A.J.'s numerous interactions with psychologists and social workers.

Waites: You told me earlier that A.J. was in counseling. And that was at South County in Delray?

Jessica: Yeah.

Waites: How often would the guardian [ad litem] come?

Jessica: Every two weeks and he'd call a lot and he'd stop by. He came over and gave all the kids Easter baskets.

Waites: How did it come about? The guardian ad litem?

Jessica: He was court-appointed. To follow up on, uh, how he was doing in school. To talk to him—how he was, um, how he was at home, how he was at school—if he had any problems. I mean, he'd take him out for walks, you know, just. . . . He talked to us, but it was mainly A.J.

Waites: You also said earlier that HRS had been out to the house before—is that associated with the guardian?

Jessica: Yes, the social worker would talk to the guardian. The social worker would come and check on the kids— A.J.—and talk to us. And she was trying to help him be back on Medicaid because we couldn't afford the counseling.

Waites: How long has A.J. been going to counseling?

Jessica: Over a year, but his counselor went on to a different job—so they were short a counselor—so he hadn't been in a couple of weeks. But two weeks ago, he went to the psychiatrist and he said he would call this week coming up—with, hopefully, they would have hired another counselor.

Waites: Okay. The psychiatrist—is that down in Delray? South County?

Jessica: There's only one down there, yeah, that takes care of all of them.

Waites: Have there been problems in school?

Jessica: Not that I . . . no.

Cupp sensed that she wanted to answer quickly, but her voice suggested she knew that straight-out lying wasn't a good idea.

Jessica: A.J. had problems on and off.

Waites (encouraging her): Uh-huh.

Jessica: Now, um, I'm going to tell you that for a long time I didn't get along with his teacher. Then we all had a meeting.

Cupp made a mental note to have Waites contact A.J.'s teacher as soon as possible.

Jessica (continuing): The guardian, the teacher, me, David, HRS, and we came to a very good understanding. What was happening was that A.J. was leaving for school at seven-thirty and not getting there until eight-thirty. And nobody told me right off the bat—like it wasn't important that I know. They waited till, like, report card day to write it [up], and I had no idea. And then, um, we set up [this meeting]. He was eating his snack on the way to school. I finally got a note home saying, "Please send him with a snack," and I wrote a note back saying, "I do send him with a snack—every day." And he had his name on the board a couple of times . . . nothing . . . nothing serious, and his grades were okay.

The words rolled off her tongue. Cupp had to remind himself that this was a woman whose stepson had been found dead less than five hours ago.

Jessica: He could concentrate. . . . I mean, he could hold his concentration long enough to get his grades, study. . . . [They were] a little up and down, but nothing . . . so the teacher and I were writing notes back and forth five days a week. I would write [her]. . . . She would write a note on Monday, seal it in an envelope, and [have him] bring it to me. A.J. didn't like that.

Jessica didn't want to let go of school and snacks, but Waites finally diverted her when he asked about A.J.'s guardian ad litem, a gentleman named Richard Zimmern.

Richard Zimmern was a retired pediatrician, who was originally from Stamford, Connecticut. He left his practice in 1989, after thirty-five years, and retired to Florida. He volunteered time to the guardian ad litem program in Palm Beach County. A.J. was fortunate to have the doctor assigned to him during the summer of 1992—for the last eleven months of his short life.

> Jessica: A.J. came [to us] equipped with a guardian ad litem. He had one in Fort Lauderdale because—
> Waites: Oh, okay.
> Jessica (adding quickly): That's where it all started.

Scott Cupp was still listening for the smallest morsel of grief, and wondered if what came next passed for it.

> Jessica: I don't believe we're sitting here talking about him [in] the past [tense]. Um, anyway, everything started in Fort Lauderdale.

Cupp tried to judge the quality of the brief reference to A.J.'s passing. He wanted to give the woman the benefit of the doubt.

> Waites: Okay. What type of problems had there been in Fort Lauderdale?
> Jessica: Sex. He was sexually abused, physically abused, mentally abused. . . . Um, the mother was—she had both of her kids dealing crack. She'd stuff their pockets and tell them where to go and she trained them to lie. A.J. could lie just like his mother. He could look you right in the eye and lie, and swear to God on it, and cry on it, and insist on it. And it was like trying to deprogram somebody. And her husband—her second husband— is in jail for the sexual abuse. I don't know why she never went—but she got out of it.
> Waites: This is A.J.'s natural mother?

Jessica: Right.

(Waites told her about the interviews conducted that morning with some of her neighbors and asked if there were any problems that could have been misinterpreted by anyone.)

Jessica (exasperated): If I was gonna do something that shouldn't have been seen, I would have done it in the house, I guess.

After a while, she admitted—almost proudly—that, yes, she sure was loud and, yeah, pretty much always yelling at someone or another. But other than that, well, no, she couldn't think of anything.

Waites rephrased his question, wanting to make certain that Jessica had the opportunity to admit that maybe her behavior, on occasion, might be the kind that a neighbor could possibly misunderstand.

Cupp could almost see her shrugging.

Jessica: Right now, I really don't think so.

Jessica may have been crude and loud, but she wasn't—Cupp decided—dumb. She made certain that Waites was aware that she and David had inherited damaged goods three years earlier.

According to Jessica, when A.J. came to live with them, he was hyper, abused, inattentive, mischievous, untrustworthy, and conniving.

But none of that went very far toward explaining why A.J. was dead. Or perhaps it did.

"What about chores?" Waites asked. "I mean, was he made to, like, say, do the yard or . . . ?"

Jessica answered eagerly, "Yeah, he did the yard. Last time, we all did the yard. Time before that the lawn mower broke. He did trim—trimmed the garden."

Cupp listened closely, remembering the neighbors' comments about A.J. trimming the lawn with scissors.

Jessica continued, "David would borrow somebody's lawn mower, you know. The grass wasn't that, well . . . We've only been doing the lawn for . . . A.J. would do the garden. The girls did the back garden until the dogs ripped them up, and…"

Rambling, dodging, searching. Scott Cupp knew that Waites was waiting her out.

Eventually, knowing better, Waites asked, "As far as the trim, it's something he would do with a weed-eater?"

Jessica: Yeah.
Waites: Or a small pair of hand shears or . . . ?

Cupp leaned closer to the tape recorder.

Jessica: Okay, he'd start out with the weed-eater, and he'd run around the yard with the weed-eater for maybe ten minutes; then he'd put it away, and none of it was done. So then he'd go out with the clippers, and it still wasn't done. And then one time, he went out there and weed-eated the whole backyard to where there was no grass. I mean, no grass. The trim wasn't done, but the yard was all whacked down, and he was very proud of that. He . . . he . . . he [said], "Look what I did! Look what I did!" And I looked and there was nothing but dirt.

Cupp had listened to hundreds of witness interviews and conducted a hundred more himself. Guilty parties, invariably, shared a common trait. Either they don't say a word, or the words just roll off their tongues—out of control. Jessica was a poster child for the latter. Guilty of what was the question.

Waites: Was he fairly well coordinated? Accident prone?
Jessica: No, he was . . . He'd trip over his own feet a couple of times a day, but nothing serious. I mean—
Waites (prodding): "I mean" . . . ?
Jessica: Oh . . . I got called on child abuse two months

ago because I was in the house—Jackie and him were outside. He was putting Jackie's bike away, and he must have tried to ride it, and he smashed his nose into the handlebars. When he came into the house, there was no bruises. There was no blood, but his nose was growing. And it sounds horrible right now, but I laughed because his nose was growing right in front of my face. And I gave him some ice, and it was fine. I said, "Does it hurt?" And he said, "No." And he went on playing.

Waites: Okay.

Jessica: And then the next day when he woke up . . . well, I woke him up for school . . . and when I went into his room . . . when I shook him a little and he turned over, his eyes were black. His nose was black and blue, and I had to wash his eyes out to open them. I mean they were swollen shut—just about. So I kept him home from school. We went to JFK (hospital). I couldn't even park in the parking lot—I had to park on the side street. That's how busy this place was. So I spoke to a doctor and I said, "Here's what happened. Here's the child. If I sit here and wait for five hours, are you gonna do anything?" He went, "No, just take an X ray." So I took him home. Took him to the doctor. The doctor set up the X ray. He got an X ray taken, and that was it. Put ice on it. And that was it.

Waites: Had you ever noticed any bruises that—

Jessica: He showed me a few bruises on his legs and his arms.

Waites: I mean, things that wouldn't be normal for a ten-year-old? Like, if he'd fallen off the bike or fallen on the playground or, you know, maybe look like he'd been in a fight with another kid or . . . ?

(Jessica answered that she had only seen him fighting once, on the way home from school, and that he had had a few bruises on him.)

Jessica: I think the last time I saw that boy naked was well over a year ago. Um, he showed me one or two

bruises. He'd get them here on his legs. He showed me
a wicked one on his leg once, and I . . . I said, "How'd
that happen?" He said, "I don't know."

Waites: But, I mean, like on the forearms and maybe
the chin area, the knee area? Those type bruises.

Jessica: And his thigh, you know; when he was wearing shorts, I saw it.

Waites: The front part of the thigh? The back part of
the thigh?

Jessica: The side.

Waites: Okay. You were telling me you found him in
the garage a couple of weeks ago?

Jessica: Last week.

Waites: Last week?

Jessica: Yeah, he was making noise in the garage and
hit himself in the head with the cane. I had a cane left
over from my knee surgery.

Waites: He was hitting himself on the top of the head or—

Jessica: Just banging.

Waites: All over?

Jessica: Yeah, he was just . . . and I've never seen that
behavior on him before, so I guess I should have
smartened up right then. (She paused and continued
after a moment.) I noticed he didn't get angry when he
should have. He didn't talk. He didn't know he was allowed to get angry. I told him, "If you have a problem
with me, or the girls, or at school, or kids, let us know.
And if you have to yell, you have to yell." He was
never allowed to do that.

Scott Cupp made a note to have Waites talk to the natural
mother as soon as possible, even though he was sure the detective already had that on his agenda.

Waites: How was A.J.'s attendance at school?

Jessica: On and off. When he first came, it was bad—

then it got good. Then he got bad again. He kept getting earaches. And he's so skinny that when you gave him medicine, he'd get sick. So we went to the doctor's a lot of times and then you get him home, give him the medicine, and he'd throw up. And then he never got a temperature of hundred and one—it was always a hundred and three. It was either normal or very high.
(After they discussed several of A.J.'s friends, Waites brought the interview back to the neighbors.)
Waites (as if it were the first time): Have you ever had any problems with your neighbors?
Jessica (sounding surprised): Oh . . .
Waites: Have they ever called HRS or anything like that?

Cupp had battled long and hard with Health and Rehabilitative Services over the years. They were notorious for letting cases slip through the cracks. And A.J.'s was most assuredly shaping up to be one of those.

Jessica: Yes, uh, one time they came to the house. First time . . .

Cupp noticed that she immediately contradicted herself.

Jessica: A.J.'s mother used to call HRS. Patsy, her daughter, she used to call HRS even from Fort Lauderdale. I mean, I was on the abuse line so much it was ridiculous. And they'd come out every time. It started when Jackie was still in diapers. They checked all the kids, and they'd keep the investigation going for a while; then they'd drop it, and then it would happen again.
(Jessica nonchalantly referred—once again— to the broken nose and black eyes that A.J. had suffered.) The last time, it was with the nose. Somebody said I did it to him, so they came. A cop with a gun and the HRS

investigators took Jackie away—I mean fast—into A.J.'s room and talked to her and looked at her. But Lauren wouldn't go. She was pissed. Very pissed, asking why we always have to go through this. She wouldn't talk to anybody. She just sat there and said, "I'm not going to talk to anybody. You have no right to come into my house and talk to me, and I'm not saying a word." So she was just pissed off.

Cupp wondered if Waites could hear the distinct difference in the attitude and tone she exhibited toward her two girls, Lauren and Jackie. Cupp heard pride, affection, and involvement. As Jessica rambled, Cupp tried to put words to her feelings about A.J. Even though A.J. was dead, all Cupp could hear was irritation, exasperation, and a general feeling of distaste and disapproval. He wondered if he was being too cynical or judgmental.

Jessica: She was very pissed off. She said to A.J., "Why does this always happen? Why do we always have to go through this?"

Cupp could hear just how much Jessica liked the fact that her ten-year-old daughter was "pissed" at the cops and the HRS investigators.

Jessica: And Jackie just babbled everything to the cop. I mean, she just yapped her mouth off. . . .

Cupp listened to this part again. A complete reversal of feeling. Here she was angry and disgusted with her younger daughter for "babbling everything" to the investigator, as if she were betraying her mom with every word. Now he couldn't wait to watch the videotape that Detective Calloway had made of Jessica alone with her daughters in the police interview room. All Calloway had told him about the tape was, "You've got to watch it. Amazing."

Jessica continued—without prompting from Waites—to talk about the incident involving A.J.'s broken nose. By all accounts, including his own, A.J. had fallen against the handlebars of Jackie's bicycle. None of the neighbors seemed to believe it. A.J.'s guardian ad litem didn't believe it.

Jessica (ranting): They (the HRS investigator and the detective) brought A.J. into the garage and made him show them how it happened, because I didn't even see. . . . His hair was longer then, and he had a bruise here, under his bangs. I didn't even see it. And the cop, you know, said to the HRS people, "Let's go. He did it. He did it. She didn't do it." So then I got called in to talk to HRS. They said it was a neighbor who called them. And a girlfriend of mine who lives over on the next block, she said HRS had called her about me. And I said to her, "I'm so sick of HRS! You tell them— the next time they call you—that I watched *Silence of the Lambs*, and that I'm that crazy doctor, that crazy man that eats people. You tell them that I'm eating my children because I'm so sick of all the accusations. It's ridiculous." And she . . . it was . . . you know . . .

Jessica hesitated, as if suddenly becoming aware of what she had just said. All Waites said was "Yeah." He was leading her.

Jessica gushed something about A.J.'s half sister, Patsy, and his natural mother, Ilene, and how "that family is whacked." Then she ran out of steam.

Waites gave her one last chance, asking, "Okay, is there anything else you can think of right now?"

Scott Cupp wasn't expecting anything worthwhile, and he was sure Waites wasn't either. They were both surprised.

Jessica mumbled, "No. When we do . . . when we do find out about A.J. . . . all I know . . . oh, all I know is, it's gonna be a zoo at my house, and I know I'm gonna react. I know I'm gonna end up in jail for hitting somebody."

"Damn!" Scott listened to a stretch of silence and tried to picture the expression on Waites's face. Eventually he heard him say, "Well, let's conclude the interview at this time."

Cupp rewound the tape, staring at the spools as they spun around. Now the work started.

CHAPTER 4

I believe Jessica probably did throw up, but the cause wasn't remorse—it was the combination of committing murder with her bare hands on a belly full of beer, and then having half of PBSO pouring through her house on a Sunday morning when she's usually sleeping it off.

—Scott Cupp

After the initial investigation on Sunday morning, the whole Schwarz family—David, Jessica, Lauren, and Jackie—had been asked to come to the sheriff's office to be interviewed. While Detective Waites conducted his interview with Jessica, Detective Calloway took Lauren to a room in the Juvenile Unit to wait while he questioned Jackie.

Jackie was two months shy of being five years old and had long, dark hair pulled back in a ponytail that reached past her waist. Calloway gently told her that maybe she could answer some questions for him about what had happened earlier in the day. The little girl told him that she "didn't know any questions," and that she "only knew her ABC's."

He then spoke briefly with her about telling the truth and telling a lie. It was apparent to him that she knew the difference between the two.

Jackie revealed that A.J. had been grounded the day before his death. So while the rest of the family attended Sunfest, an annual celebration held in nearby West Palm Beach, A.J. spent the day confined to his home. When Calloway quizzed Jackie about why A.J. had been grounded, she said that he had been playing with some green dye or paint near the family's dryer.

When Jessica found some of the dye on the dryer, Jackie said her mother became "very mad." Jessica had poured the dye over A.J.'s head, and then she "spanked him with a strap."

According to Jackie, both her mother and her father spanked A.J. a lot—with a strap and a belt.

Later in the interview, Jackie told the detective that earlier that morning she heard a splash in the swimming pool that woke her up. She went outside to the pool, climbed up the ladder, and saw A.J. in the pool underneath the water. Upon further questioning about this story, it became clear to Calloway that she was not telling the truth. He noticed many inconsistencies in her story, and when he pointed them out to her, she admitted that it wasn't true. When he asked her why, she replied, "Because I have to lie." Again he asked her why, and she replied, "Somebody doesn't get in jail."

He then asked Jackie to just tell him what really happened. Crying, she told him, "I'm going to get in trouble. I just don't want anybody to get hurt."

He tried to soothe her and told her that nobody would get hurt. She said, "Somebody already did get hurt."

When he asked her who had gotten hurt, she replied, "My brother."

He learned that Jackie had no idea how A.J. had gotten into the pool, and when he tried to question her further about her brother, she stated, "I'm going to run away."

From time to time, during the course of the interview, Calloway noticed that Jackie was looking behind him and laughing. When he turned to see what she was laughing at, he heard footsteps running away from the interview room. He got up and looked out the window and saw Lauren running down the hall, back to the waiting room, where he had stationed her prior to his interview with Jackie. Lauren had been watching her little sister as she was being questioned.

He asked Jackie if her mother had told her what to tell him—in reference to the fabricated story she had told him earlier. She said, "Yes." He asked her exactly what her mother had told her to tell him, and she replied, "The whole story I just told you."

The detective said, "But that's not the truth, is it?"

She said, "Yes."

It was obvious to Calloway that the child was confused as to what exactly she was supposed to tell him in reference to the questions he was asking her regarding A.J. He asked her if she was afraid of something and she said yes. When he asked what she was afraid of, she replied, "A.J. died."

After he concluded his interview with Jackie, Calloway attempted to question ten-year-old Lauren. It was quite apparent that she did not want to speak to him about A.J.'s death. She did admit, however, that her mother poured green dye over A.J.'s head, the day before he died, because he had been playing with the dye around the dryer.

She refused to answer any of the other questions that he asked.

When Detective Waites finished questioning Jessica, she was allowed to join the girls until his interview with David Schwarz was completed. Detective Calloway watched the reunion from the television room located directly across the hall from the interview room. He turned the television set on and it activated the camera located in the room where Jessica and her two daughters were waiting.

Jessica sat in a hardback chair in the center of the room, with her sunglasses propped gingerly on top of her head. Lauren, pouting and irritable, was seated off camera during most of the tape.

Jackie was anxious and clearly confused. She paced. Her mother wanted to know what they had told the police. It was obvious that Jackie knew she was in trouble—even before

she told her mom that she had told the police about A.J.
being grounded and the green dye and the spanking.

As she listened, Jessica became furious. She jumped out
of her chair, grabbed Jackie roughly by the shoulders, and
lifted her off the ground. She held her face-to-face with her
and snapped, "Do you want Mommy to go to jail?"

Shaking, Jackie said, "No."

Jessica was livid. "If you tell these people anything,
Mama's gonna go to jail. Now, what did you tell them?"

Tears welled up in Jackie's eyes. Jessica shook her, and
said, "I'll never see you again."

Upon hearing that, Jackie started sobbing.

Referring to the green dye and the spanking, Jessica
asked, "Why did you tell them that?"

Jackie didn't answer.

Jessica insisted, "You can't tell these people anything.
Okay?"

Through her tears, Jackie replied, "I'm not going to say
anything else."

Jessica's face was only inches away from her daughter's:
"Just say, 'I don't know. I don't know.'"

Finally Jessica released her daughter and returned to the
chair. She said impatiently, "Jackie, they can throw me in
jail."

Jackie exclaimed, "I don't want you to go to jail!"

Jessica, playing on the child's fears, asked, "Do you want
me to go to jail?"

Jackie paced nervously. "No. I just don't want A.J. to
die."

Jessica, as cold as ice, answered, "Well, he did."

A few minutes later, Jackie told her mother, "I had to tell
him a lie."

Jessica responded, "Oh, God, my own daughter's going to
put me in jail!"

Lauren told her mother that she had been standing on the
other side of the window while the detective was interview-
ing Jackie, and that she had heard Jackie telling him things.

Jessica said to Jackie, "You got a big mouth. You don't talk to anybody anymore. You just say, 'I don't know.' "

Lauren added, "I was telling him lies, and he said, 'Your sister has a whole different story.' "

Jessica replied flippantly, "So? She's four—you're ten."

Investigators would later learn that Jessica Schwarz had been fired from her job—as a day care worker—the previous March. Her employer had been so intimidated by Jessica's temper that she had called the sheriff's office to have a deputy present while she gave Jessica the news.

Scott Cupp's initial involvement with A.J.'s death came with an impromptu meeting at the PBSO with Detectives Waites and Deischer, along with their lieutenant Steve Newell. Waites reported to them that Dr. Benz expressed reluctance—during the postmortem—to classify A.J.'s death as a homicide. They decided there should be a meeting with Benz at the medical examiner's office.

The purpose was to find out what questions he needed answered and to find out what they needed to do—from an investigative standpoint—in order to make him comfortable classifying A.J.'s death as a homicide.

It was decided that Scott Cupp, Lieutenant Newell, and Detectives Waites, Deischer, Calloway, and Restivo would meet with the medical examiner. Additionally, Cupp suggested that they have Dr. Philip Colaizzo there. He was the medical director of the Child Protection Team (CPT). CPT was an entity established by Florida law to assist the Department of Health and Rehabilitative Services in carrying out their responsibilities in investigating reported cases of child abuse and neglect.

The team included a medical director who performed examinations on children who had been physically and sexually battered and rendered opinions in court. A psychologist conducted interviews and evaluations of children and their caregivers. There was a host of others with specialized training who conducted forensic interviews with children. The interviews were videotaped. The purpose of the interview was to document and record exactly what had happened to a child. The information was then available for law enforcement, HRS, the state attorney, and, ultimately, a criminal and/or dependency court proceeding.

Having Dr. Colaizzo present turned out to be disastrous. Dr. Benz seemed to be offended by his mere presence. Their purpose, in gathering all these people together, was to show Benz that they were willing to do whatever he suggested needed to be done as to follow-up, and also to show him respect. But he apparently decided he was being pressured and second-guessed.

Dr. Colaizzo asked him a few medical questions, which was the beginning of the end. Benz's responses to Colaizzo's questions were—at the very least—condescending.

The net result of the meeting was that Benz—clearly—was going to be headstrong in his decision to classify A.J.'s manner of death as "undetermined."

To say that Cupp was disheartened would be an understatement, but it quickly gave way to an overwhelming sense of determination.

Attempting to prosecute someone for homicide, without first having a medical examiner's opinion that there was one, is next to impossible. Benz was highly qualified as the chief medical examiner in Palm Beach County and was held in high esteem among his peers throughout North America. Cupp was well aware of situations in which prosecutors had obtained second opinions from other medical examiners in difficult cases—but it was always to confirm the initial findings.

Cupp was faced with the task of finding someone to perform a full second autopsy and hope the result would be different. He knew that it would be next to impossible. Even if it could be accomplished—in order to convict Jessica Schwarz of killing A.J.—he would have to cross-examine Dr. Benz, who would surely be the defense's star witness.

A.J.'s death occurred just four months after Cupp's boss, Barry Krischer, took office for his first term as state attorney for the Fifteenth Judicial Circuit of Florida—in and for Palm Beach County. Krischer hired Cupp to come in with him in January when he took office, specifically to run the Crimes Against Children (CAC) Unit.

There were those outside the state attorney's office that questioned the wisdom of pursuing the case. That was not surprising. What was startling was that many within the office thought the case was political suicide for those prosecutors naive enough to go against Benz.

But Cupp never questioned going forward. He was scared at times—many times—but his resolve to go forward never wavered.

On Tuesday, May 4, Detective Calloway returned to the Concept Homes Development to gather additional information about the Schwarz family.

There he interviewed Ida Falk, who told him that she and her family had lived on Triphammer Road for about 2½ years. Her thirteen-year-old daughter, Jamie, had talked to Detective Restivo on Sunday. Ida Falk had seen A.J. early every Thursday morning collecting aluminum cans from the neighborhood recycling bins. She believed Jessica Schwarz had been court ordered to perform community service and that one part of that community service was collecting aluminum cans. A.J. was made to gather them to assist his stepmother, she thought.

She heard Jessica swearing at A.J. on a daily basis. Even though she couldn't recall the exact words that were used, she said they were "dirty and vulgar." Also, Jessica was "always" referring to A.J. as stupid.

About a year earlier, she had seen A.J. in the front yard—for an hour or two—with his mouth taped shut. She, too, had seen him edging the lawn with regular household scissors.

Mrs. Falk told the detective that two or three months earlier her husband, Jarrell, had seen A.J. walking to school in the rain. Mr. Falk had slowed down to pick him up, but when he glanced in his rearview mirror, he saw that Jessica was right behind him. Assuming that she would pick the boy up, he continued on down the road. However, Jessica did not pick him up; she just passed him by.

After talking with Mrs. Falk, Detective Calloway spoke with her son, Troy, a fifth-grade student at Indian Pines Elementary School. Troy told the detective that, not long after they moved to Triphammer Road, he started going over to A.J.'s house to see if he could play—but most of the time, he was grounded and wasn't allowed. On one occasion, he saw A.J. with "brownish" tape over his mouth. Jessica had explained to Troy that A.J. was "being bad."

More recently—a month or so earlier—he had seen A.J. running down Triphammer Road naked.

At the house next door to the Schwarz home, Ron Pincus Jr. repeated the story to Detective Calloway that he had told Detective Restivo on Sunday: When he arrived home from work—about 1:30 in the morning—he had seen A.J. walking his dog. A.J. had asked him what he doing home so late. Pincus was tired and simply replied, "I have to get to bed." The boy told him good night and Pincus continued up the walk. He glanced over at the Schwarz house and noticed that the blinds were up in the living room and the lights and television were on.

About two weeks before that, he had seen A.J. edging his yard with scissors. Pincus said he felt sorry for him, so he went over and edged the Schwarz yard with his own edger. While he was there, he heard Jessica tell A.J. that he had a new nickname—"Jeffrey Dahmer." For the last two weeks of the young boy's life, that was what his stepmother called him.

He had seen A.J. swim on several occasions, but he was not allowed while the girls were swimming. A.J. was only allowed to go into the pool to clean it—before the girls got in—so they could have a clean pool to swim in.

Jessica had told Pincus a few weeks earlier that she hated A.J.—that she had always hated him. And that she could never bring herself to love him.

After the detective left, Pincus thought about how he had come home from work that previous Saturday night, bone-tired and looking forward to bed, and had been startled when he heard a rustling in the bushes next door. When he saw A.J. holding a leash, he realized that the noise he heard was the dog nosing around in the shrubbery.

A.J. seemed to want to talk, but Pincus was just too tired for chitchat.

Calloway then went to interview another neighbor whom Detective Restivo had talked to on Sunday—Eileen Callahan. She had only lived on Triphammer Road for about a year, but she had seen and heard a lot. She was a stay-at-home mom with three children and lived across the street and one house up from the Schwarzes.

Callahan's pregnancy with her third child had been a difficult one and she had spent much time resting on her living-room couch. From that location in her home, she couldn't help but notice the strange and bizarre behavior of her loud and obnoxious neighbor. She also witnessed the special wrath that Jessica seemed to have for her stepson.

Unfortunately for Eileen—and what she wouldn't find out for quite some time—was that her first name, though spelled differently, was the same as A.J.'s biological mother—Ilene. That fateful coincidence eventually caused her untold anguish, fear, and unwanted attention.

Not long after she and her family moved to Triphammer Road, Callahan had seen A.J.—on his hands and knees in the rain—edging the grass with a pair of scissors.

In October 1992, she had heard Jessica tell A.J. that she was "taking Halloween away from him," and asked him if he wanted her to take Christmas away too. And—in fact—Callahan had seen him cleaning out the garage on Christmas Day.

She had become so concerned about A.J. not being in school on Thursdays—due to the fact that he was collecting aluminum cans, and then later crushing them in his drive-way—that Callahan had called Child Protective Services to report it. She claimed that she was "put off" and told to call Indian Pines Elementary School—which she did. An employee at the school told her that they were aware of A.J.'s absenteeism.

About a month before his death, A.J. had told Eileen's husband, Rich, that he had to do chores from the time he woke up in the morning until the time he went to bed. And that his stepmother punished him by not allowing him to go to school.

In January 1993, when she saw A.J.'s black eyes and bruised nose, Eileen had seen enough. She called Florida's hot line, which had been set up for the public to report children who are known to be—or suspected to be—abused, neglected, or abandoned. As the public-service announcements promised, she called anonymously.

Well, not quite—she gave her first name, Eileen.

HRS protective investigator Barbara Black was assigned to the call and—as per local protocol—she called the sheriff's office to have them assign a detective from CAC to accompany her.

She and Chris Calloway went to the house on Triphammer Road and the detective spoke with A.J. The young boy adamantly maintained that he had fallen against the handlebars of his sister's bicycle as he was walking it into the garage to put it away.

Black detailed A.J.'s denial—and Jessica's ranting—in her report, including Jessica's complaint that she had had at least five abuse complaints against her and that she'd "had enough."

Jessica went on and on to Black about how the neighbors hated her and that Ilene was always calling in complaints against her and harassing her.

Barbara Black closed the investigation the same day she started it. Considering the information she apparently based her decision on, it is impossible to overstate how incredibly tragic her decision turned out to be. She placed a call to Joan Wyllner, A.J.'s protective supervision worker. It was Wyllner's responsibility to monitor A.J.'s placement in the Schwarz home. One must keep in mind, while reading the report, however, that Eileen Callahan left only her first name when placing the call to the hot line.

"Worker Joan Wyllner said she does not feel [Jessica] would hurt the child and fail to get medical care. She is very attentive to the child's medical needs. She had asked Broward [County] about closing the case last week. Joan feels natural mom (Ilene) somehow knows that this was asked. She always seems to throw a monkey wrench in when things go smooth.

"Joan saw the child January 4, 1993. No problems noted. (Joan did not wish to accompany this [protective investigator] and detective to the residence.)"

It appeared—even though the phone conversation with Joan Wyllner was put near the end of the narrative—that Black spoke to her prior to going to the scene.

As if that weren't tragic enough, what Eileen Callahan reported to Calloway left Scott Cupp truly speechless and incredibly sad. As he looked back, the overwhelming sense of hopelessness—of being trapped—that A.J. must have felt became clear to him.

Detective Calloway informed Eileen Callahan that he had been the one who had accompanied the woman from HRS to investigate the incident.

Eileen Callahan told the detective that, the day before the investigation, Jackie had come out of the house and went over to where A.J. was sitting on the driveway. She heard Jackie say, "What did Mommy tell you to say?" A.J. replied, "That I fell and hit my nose on the bicycle."

The day after the HRS/PBSO investigation was conducted at the Schwarz home, Mrs. Callahan received a phone call from the HRS investigator who had been with Calloway the day before. Unbeknownst to Eileen Callahan, her phone number had been recorded on the report of the complaint she made—which was now in the hands of Barbara Black.

Black told Mrs. Callahan to leave the Schwarzes alone and that she was not to call or make up any stories of abuse, and that if she did in the future—she could be prosecuted.

"She instructed me that she had spoken to me on a prior occasion, which I denied. She told me that if I continued to call, that they would slap a harassment charge on me, and that she would take my children instead. And that A.J. was lucky to be having a roof over his head. And gave me the supervisor's name and phone number—if I had a problem with the phone call."

At that time, Eileen Callahan was still unaware that her first name sounded the same as A.J.'s biological mother's—and she didn't know Barbara Black's name.

She was, of course, very upset by the phone call, so she called Joan Wyllner to make a complaint.

"I did tell her it was the woman that showed up at the [Schwarz] house because Barbara Black addressed herself as that. Ms. Wyllner said there was nothing she could do to find out who the person was that called me because there were so many people in that office. That there was 'no way' she could track it down. And then she went into great length explaining A.J.'s past.

"She was telling me that they had put him there so that he would be safe. The house that he grew up in or was living in—in Broward County—he was being abused there. Supposedly, he was sexually abused.

"She told me that Palm Beach County was looking into this as a favor to Broward County, that this was not Palm Beach County's problem. She told me if I wanted to file a complaint, that I could write a letter to H.G. Holley [state offices] complex. But she couldn't give me an address or a phone number, or her supervisor, or [whose] attention that I should mail the letter to."

Eileen Callahan told Joan Wyllner that A.J. was "going to end up dead" if HRS didn't do something about the situation.

There would be no more "harassing" phone calls to the

hot line complaining about A.J.'s treatment at the hands of his stepmother—save one last anonymous call, on May 2, in the afternoon, after his body was found.

At eight o'clock on Tuesday evening, May 4, Detectives Restivo and Waites, along with Sergeant Deischer, met with Mary Idrissi—A.J.'s third-grade teacher—at her home. She told them that A.J. was very wanting of attention—constantly wanting to be hugged and shown other signs of bonding. She further stated the he often talked about his home and appeared to be happy and, in fact, often referred to being happy living with his natural father and his two sisters [*sic*].

Idrissi described A.J. as being open and intelligent and able to cope with problems very well. She related a disturbing incident—which had taken place during the first week of school—involving the child and Jessica, in which Jessica spoke very demeaningly about him and recited his faults to her. Jessica continued to belittle him while he was standing right there beside her.

Idrissi sent weekly progress reports home with A.J. and often received belligerent replies from Jessica. He was not allowed to have school supplies or participate in school field trips, since he was not responsible enough to do so—according to his stepmother. She received these belligerent replies to the progress reports until—roughly—March 1993 when there was a meeting with her, Jessica and David Schwarz, and some representatives of HRS. Idrissi stated that during this meeting she was very positive and reinforced the fact that Andrew was happy being at home, which resulted in Jessica having a change in attitude toward her.

The teacher told the investigators that A.J. was absent from school more than was normal. He had been absent three or four days in January 1993, and when he returned to school, he had two black eyes and his nose was bruised. When she questioned him about what had occurred, A.J. told her that he had hit his nose on his bike and that he did not want his stepmother to be blamed.

Idrissi added that she often saw bruises on him, but they were in areas that would be common for a ten-year-old boy to have them.

CHAPTER 5

Jimmy was Jimmy—retired NYPD—and not afraid to voice his opinion, whether you wanted to hear it or not. He would tell you like it was.

—Detective Michael Waites

The morning after A.J.'s body was found, a woman named Connie Mason called the sheriff's office and asked to talk to a detective in reference to Jessica Schwarz. Jimmy Restivo went to her home in Lake Worth to interview her.

Mason told Restivo that on April 19 she had attended a group counseling session with Jessica, and had had a very disturbing conversation with her about A.J.

Restivo: Would you tell me some of the things you remember her saying about A.J.?

Mason: She first caught my attention because she said she had a little "Jeffrey Dahmer." After a few minutes, she said it again and I questioned her on it and she started telling me how he was abused by his original mother—and that he was uncontrollable. She talked a good twenty to thirty minutes about him.

Restivo: Just about A.J.?

Mason: Just about A.J.

Restivo: Did she ever say anything about hurting him because he dunked one of the girls [under the water]?

Mason: She stated, I believe, that he held one of the girls under and she grabbed him by the throat and pulled him out of the pool, slammed him up against the fence, and said that she would "kill him and cut him up in pieces if he ever touched one of her girls again." Jessica said that she'd call the cops and turn herself in and go to prison for the rest of her life, but he would never hurt her children again.

Restivo: Did she tell you about something she had told a judge?

Mason: She stated she told the judge that if A.J. ever— I think this might've been in reference to molesting the girls—because I did ask about that. Was she afraid that he would do that to one of the girls and she, ah—

Restivo: You mean sexually molest?

Mason: Yeah. 'Cause he had been—she said that he had been. She said that she would kill him. She said, "I even told the judge I would kill him if he hurt one of my girls—and he still gave me custody of the kids."

Restivo: When she was saying these things, did you believe her? What was your reaction? Honestly?

Mason: I wanted to help her help the child—that's how I felt. That I could probably—by talking to her—help her love the child, as he needed more love. I felt like he needed more love, 'cause he was far from getting it, with her calling him a Jeffrey Dahmer. That's the wrong way.

Restivo: But she did talk about killing this little boy?

Mason: She said she'd kill him—several times. She said—not only the incident when she told him that she'd kill him—but she said to the whole meeting that if he hurt her girls, she would kill him. She said another thing about waking up in the morning. I wish I could word this right. She said everybody just had to leave her alone until like ten o'clock in the morning, as she was mean—extremely mean—in the mornings. And that A.J. just didn't comprehend that she was mean—to leave her alone. Sometimes he just didn't get it through his head.

Restivo: Did she ever indicate that she'd hurt him in the morning?

Mason: Not that I recall.

Restivo: Did she talk about her husband?

Mason: I know his name is Bear. I know she said he was big and she did talk—I just don't know what was said right now. It might come to me later. She did talk about him—I don't know. I believe he's on her side. You know, as far as taking control of A.J.

Restivo: Did she mention about how he would treat A.J.?

Mason: No. No. Not that I—

Restivo: Anything else come to mind, Connie?

Mason: The abuse, I say, would be from her.

Restivo: Excuse me?

Mason: I'm saying the abuse—I could tell it was being done by her. So, whatever she said about her husband, it didn't hit me like he was [abusing A.J.]. I thought she had a good husband because they had their home and a pool. I figured she had someone taking care of her family.

Restivo: Anything else come to mind?

Mason: I just think she held him under there.

Restivo: You think she held him under the water?

Mason: I do.

Restivo: Why do you get that feeling?

Mason: It just hit me in the gut when I seen it on TV.

Early in the afternoon on Wednesday, May 5, Detective Waites met with Ilene Logan (A.J.'s natural mother) and Patsy (A.J.'s half sister) at their home in Fort Lauderdale. Ilene told him that her ex-husband David Schwarz had been given temporary custody of both Patsy and A.J. because of an abusive situation that had occurred with another ex-husband. She said Patsy was the victim of the abuse and claimed that A.J.

had not been abused. David had been given temporary custody, with the court intending for both A.J. and Patsy to be returned to her.

She had since regained custody of Patsy and claimed that three weeks before her son's death, she had asked a judge for an emergency hearing to get A.J. back, but the request was denied.

Patsy told the detective that while she was living with David and Jessica, A.J. was fed only bread and water and sometimes was forced to eat bread off the floor. If he didn't clean the garage "good enough," he was not allowed to eat at all.

When he cleaned the kitty litter box, if he didn't do it right, "his face would be put into the litter box." He also had to clean dog feces from the backyard using his hands, but he was allowed to wear gloves.

Patsy told him about other incidents, including ones in which Jessica struck both her and A.J. She explained that she lived with Jessica and David from November 1990 until February 1992—when HRS removed her from their home. Arrangements were later made for Patsy to give a sworn statement in front of a court reporter—with Ilene present.

Later that day, Waites served a subpoena on the custodian of records for Indian Pines Elementary School for school records pertaining to Andrew J. Schwarz. The records showed that A.J. was just below normal in IQ testing. The principal of the school advised him that A.J. did not qualify for special learning disability classes, as had been requested by his stepmother.

Chris Calloway returned to Triphammer Road that afternoon to interview more neighbors. There he talked to an older woman, Shirley Leiter, who told him that every Thursday morning for the past year she had seen A.J. collecting aluminum cans from yellow recycling bins that the residents of the Concept Homes area put out in front of their homes for collection. The last time she saw A.J. was on April 29 when he stopped by her house to pick up additional cans that she had saved for him.

A.J. told her that he had been up since 4:45 that morning and that he was hungry. He couldn't go home and eat unless he had "a whole bunch of cans," and his stepmother would "put him in jail" if he didn't bring enough of them home.

Leiter had given him three doughnuts.

She had become very concerned after talking to him and, about 8:00 that morning, called the CPT. She was referred to a 1-800 number. She spoke to a man named Dave Davis, who told her to call Palm Beach County Truancy. Instead, she called the Indian Pines Elementary School and spoke to a lady whom she believed to be the principal. The woman told Leiter that the school would be taking care of the problem.

Three days later, A.J.'s body was found floating in the aboveground swimming pool.

Detective Calloway next talked to Ronald Pincus Sr., the father of the young man who had seen A.J. walking his dog in the wee hours of the night. Pincus Sr. told the detective that he had heard Jessica Schwarz verbally abuse A.J. on many occasions. The weekend before A.J.'s death—on Saturday—he heard A.J. saying, in a loud voice, "I have a big mouth. I get people in trouble. I'll never do it again." The boy was standing in front of his own house, but Pincus Sr. could hear him inside his home.

A.J. had been repeating the phrase for two hours when Pincus Sr. left at eleven o'clock in the morning. When he returned four hours later, A.J. was still standing there, repeating the same phrase, and continued until five o'clock in the evening.

He had also heard Jessica call the boy "Jeffrey Dahmer."

Pincus Sr.'s twelve-year-old stepdaughter, Jennifer Sullivan, told the detective that she had been in the Schwarz home at least ten times since January 1993. One of the times she was over there, she had heard Jessica tell A.J. that he was to be home by 2:10, and if he didn't make it home by then, she would "tie him up with duct tape, throw him in the road, and run him over."

On two different occasions, she had seen Jessica strike

A.J. About a month earlier, she had been over there playing in Lauren's room and heard Jessica say, "Come here, young man." Jennifer walked out into the living room and saw Jessica strike A.J. on the side of the face and he went into his room and cried. When she saw him later, his eye was red.

In January of that year, she was playing in the pool in the backyard of the Schwarz home. She looked into the kitchen area of the house after she heard A.J. cry out, "Don't do this! Please don't!" She saw Jessica strike A.J. in the eye three times with her hand. When she later talked to A.J. about it, he told her not to tell anybody or he would get in trouble.

During Scott Cupp's time in Live Oak—the seat of Florida's Third Judicial Circuit—he prosecuted a case against Luz and Guillermo Hernandez, charging them with criminal responsibility in the death of their four-year-old daughter, Sonia. Sonia had suffered from birth with severe brain disorders that left her unable to sit up, nearly deaf, blind, incontinent, vegetative, and prone to fevers and infections. She died of pneumonia in 1990. The problem was that her parents hadn't taken her to see a doctor for the two years prior to her death.

The prosecution alleged that the reason they didn't was because they had joined the End Timers, a religious cult led by Charles Meade. The End Timers espoused faith healing instead of doctors. The cult, Meade, and the manslaughter/child neglect case against the Hernandezes captured the attention of the *Miami Herald,* ABC's *20/20,* and the fledgling Court TV, which covered the trial live.

The trial brought Dr. Joseph Burton to town. The chief medical examiner for several counties in metropolitan Atlanta, Georgia, he specialized in pediatric pathology.

Largely because of him, the jury compromised and found the couple guilty of the medical neglect charge—but acquitted them on the manslaughter charge. The doctor convinced everyone that the child was well cared for by the parents and, in retrospect, Cupp felt that the jurors made the right decision. Little did he realize that one year later, their paths would cross again. But this time, if everything worked out the way he planned, Cupp would be asking him direct questions—instead of cross-examining him.

What Scott Cupp remembered most about Dr. Burton—from when he took the witness stand in Live Oak—was his presence and his demeanor. It was as much how he said things as it was what he said. He had an open, warm approachable manner, and Cupp couldn't help but like him.

His credentials were outstanding and he had a reputation for testifying for defense attorneys—as well as prosecutors. That told Cupp that he was brave. If he came to an opinion in a case, he wasn't afraid to say it—regardless of whom it helped or hurt.

After the Benz fiasco, Cupp felt as if all eyes were on him. Everyone involved in the investigation of A.J.'s death knew they needed a second opinion, but whose? They began making calls to various other medical examiners in Florida. Cupp didn't say anything, but his gut told him that everyone in Florida was going to back Dr. Benz.

And Cupp didn't just want a second opinion—he wanted a second autopsy.

How were they going to do it? Could they do it? He never had. At that point in Cupp's career, he had been involved in only a few homicides, and the Hernandez case was the first one in which he had been the lead prosecutor.

He began by telling Detective Waites, and Waites's superiors, about Burton—but Burton was in Atlanta. How could this be accomplished? What would state attorney Barry Krischer say? He had been in office just long enough to get the furniture in the right place—and Cupp was going to tell him he needed to go toe-to-toe with the chief medical examiner in a purely circumstantial-evidence homicide? Not only that, but the man he wanted to do the second autopsy was in Atlanta!

Cupp started by looking at the statutes, and what he found was Florida Stature 925.09, AUTHORITY OF STATE ATTORNEY TO ORDER AUTOPSIES: "The state attorney may have an autopsy performed, before or after interment, on a dead body found in the county when he decides it is necessary in determining whether or not death was the result of a crime."

He would later refer to this law as "the state attorney trumps the medical examiner" law. It didn't say anything about the autopsy being performed within the state, so maybe they could pull it off. Cupp decided to approach Krischer.

He knew he had a fighting chance. Krischer had a true commitment to improving child abuse prosecution in Palm Beach County, and had made it an issue in his campaign. When he took office, there were only three prosecutors doing child abuse for six criminal divisions. Krischer planned to give Cupp enough positions so that they would have one per division. Additionally, his background was solid.

Prior to becoming the state attorney, Barry Krischer had been the attorney for the Child Protection Team. It was obvious that when he spoke about legal issues involving child abuse, he knew what he was talking about. But how would he react to this? One could easily envision all sorts of very bad—and very public—endings. The media hadn't done much with A.J.'s death at that point, but they would. They were watching and waiting. Scott Cupp was hearing—which meant Krischer was hearing—that HRS "had really dropped the ball" this time.

Cupp had already been present at the hastily called meeting at the PBSO, attended by a rather large number of HRS personnel. He knew that was significant—for two reasons. First, it was at the sheriff's office—and not at HRS. Second, it was attended by a man from the inspector general's office in Tallahassee—an agency whose task was to conduct internal investigations of state agencies like HRS.

Many things were going on behind the scenes and probably none of them would be primarily designed to make the prosecution of A.J.'s killer any easier. They would have to move quickly.

The morning he planned to approach Krischer with the letter he wanted him to sign, Cupp arrived for work early. From here on out, he would be arriving for work early most mornings. He was surprised to find Krischer already at work in his office. No one else was there yet, so Cupp had his undivided attention.

Krischer asked, "What are you doing here so early?"

Cupp could tell from the look on Krischer's face that he knew it had to do with A.J.'s case. It was important to him that right from the beginning he didn't pull any punches. He wanted to convey very clearly that this case had enormous potential—if not handled correctly by everyone involved— to go very, very badly.

Cupp replied, "We need to talk."

"Okay."

Barry Krischer had a way of quickly reading a person's demeanor, and when necessary, he took on an almost fatherly tone and attitude. That would make them tell him everything—sometimes more than they had wanted.

This was one time Cupp held nothing back. He, quickly but thoroughly, told Krischer about the various meetings that had already taken place. Saying it to Krischer made Cupp realize just how extraordinary the case already was. Although it was only a few days old, it was already consuming many, many hours of a lot of people's time.

Scott Cupp could tell by Krisher's reaction that he was not surprised in the least about Benz's behavior. They spoke about HRS's role and the possibility of investigating them at some point.

Finally Cupp presented the letter he had prepared for Krischer's signature. He told him about the power he felt Krischer had—under the statute—to order a second autopsy. He told him about Joe Burton and how strongly he felt that a second autopsy—if Krischer would order it—had to be done by someone with no official ties, not only to Palm Beach, but to Florida as well.

Cupp told him there wasn't a doubt in his mind that Jessica had murdered A.J. And after viewing the tape of her at the sheriff's office, he knew—if given the chance—he could make a jury feel the same way. Not just convince them—but also make them feel the same way he was feeling.

The meeting didn't last as long as Cupp thought it would, and it didn't involve as many people as he thought it would. After twenty or thirty minutes, Krischer seemed to know all that he needed to, but he was intent on making sure that Cupp was okay with his own decision.

"Are you sure this is what you want to do?"

"Yes, sir."

Cupp's formality with Krischer told him that he was firm in his resolve to go forward—not just professionally, but personally as well. He was letting him know that he would do what needed to be done and see it through to the end.

Few state attorneys would want to inform the chief medical examiner that they were taking custody of a body and ordering a second full autopsy to be done. And, chances are, none of them would have signed the letter after barely reading it and making no changes—and without having a chief assistant state's attorney or deputy lend their counsel to the situation. By putting his personal and political trust in Scott Cupp, Krischer galvanized Cupp's resolve even more.

Five days after his tragic death—and four days after the first autopsy—A.J.'s body was packed in dry ice, placed in a container specially made for such things, and flown to Lawrenceville, Georgia, a suburb of Atlanta, to have a second full autopsy performed on him.

It was on Friday, May 7, that Detective Michael Waites had the somber duty of accompanying the body—transported by the Aviation Unit of the sheriff's office—at the request of the state attorney's office.

After Dr. Joseph Burton examined the body and performed the second autopsy, which took three to four hours, he advised Waites that the victim had been abused.

As Dr. Benz had done earlier in the week, Dr. Burton listed the cause of death as drowning, but he left the manner of death undetermined, pending microscopic examinations of standards recovered from various bruises on the victim. A complete copy of the autopsy report would eventually be provided to the sheriff's office, the Palm Beach County Medical Examiner's Office, and the Palm Beach County State Attorney's Office.

Scott Cupp would never forget A.J.'s second autopsy, which he had orchestrated successfully. As Joe Burton performed his work, Cupp was at home playing with his two daughters, four-year-old Kaity and two-year-old Elizabeth. He was trying his best to enjoy the evening. It was his thirty-seventh birthday.

CHAPTER 6

*He never had the life of a child. He looked for af-
fection—and would cling to it when he found it. He
wanted to be a little boy, but never had the chance.*

—Detective Michael Waites

The same day that A.J.'s body was flown to Georgia,
Detective Calloway continued his investigation by doing a
follow-up interview with thirteen-year-old Jamie Falk at her
home. Jamie was a seventh-grade student at Christa McAuliffe
Middle School. He asked if she had ever witnessed any abuse
directed at A.J.

She told him that about a year earlier she had seen A.J.
seated at the dinner table with a plate of food in front of him,
but he had tape over his mouth. He could not eat the food but
was made to sit there with his mouth taped.

On several occasions, she heard the stepmother screaming and hitting A.J., but she had only actually seen her strike
him once.

Two months earlier, the teenager had taken it upon herself
to call the HRS abuse hot line. She told the personnel at
HRS that A.J. was "always getting hit," but since she had no
proof, they told her they couldn't do anything.

Calloway then talked to another neighbor girl, twelve-
year-old Serena Perryman, at her home. She told the detective that she had seen A.J. walking past her house on his way

home from school three months earlier. Jessica Schwarz had come outside and yelled down the street to A.J. that if he did not get down to his house on the count of five, she would make him walk down the street naked.

Serena had also heard Jessica call A.J. a "fucking bitch" and many times she had seen bruises on A.J.

Next was nine-year-old Teresa Walton, a third-grade student at Indian Pines. The child told the investigator that she believed that Jessica Schwarz had made A.J. eat a cockroach. She was standing outside A.J.'s house when Jessica came to the front door—holding a cockroach in her hand—and called A.J. into the house.

Jessica told A.J. she was going to make him eat it because she had found the cockroach in the kitchen cabinets near the dishes and that he didn't do a good enough job cleaning the dishes.

Teresa walked into the kitchen and saw A.J. standing in a corner, "chewing on something."

The little girl also told the detective that A.J. was allowed only five minutes to eat his dinner, and if he didn't finish in that time, the food was given to the dog.

Teresa had also seen A.J. sitting at the dinner table with his mouth taped shut—with a peanut butter and jelly sandwich and Kool-Aid in front of him. His hands were behind the chair, but she didn't think they were bound. She believed that he was simply told to keep his hands behind the chair.

Over a 3½-year period, Teresa claimed that she had seen A.J. with tape over his mouth at least seven or eight times, and sometimes there was writing on the tape, such as "I'm an asshole" or "I'm an idiot." About two months earlier, she had seen him outside his house with silver tape—she thought it to be duct tape—over his mouth.

Later in the afternoon, Calloway met with a woman who had previously lived across the street from the Schwarzes. Gail Ragatz was a pest exterminator who had performed her services at the Schwarz house once a month.

She believed that A.J. had been abused—mentally and emotionally— by his stepmother.

In December 1992, Ragatz had gone over to visit, and while she was there, she saw Jessica put A.J.'s bowl of food next to the kitty litter box. Jessica told A.J., "If you want to act like a dog, you're going to eat like a dog." Ragatz remembered the incident vividly: the bowl of food contained macaroni and cheese and a hot dog with ketchup.

Yet another neighbor, Diane Mostov, related two strange incidents to Calloway. About one week prior to A.J.'s death, she was coming home from work at 5:30 in the morning and saw A.J. walking down the street carrying a garbage bag over his shoulder. It was still dark outside and she wondered what a child his age was doing out so early in the morning.

A few weeks earlier, she was taking her own child for a walk and passed the Schwarz house. It was early—between noon and one o'clock—in the afternoon on a school day and A.J. was sitting on the ground outside the garage door. He had no clothes on. He did not speak to her or ask for any help.

Mostov added that she was aware of the Schwarz family and "figured it was just one more of Jessica's unusual punishments."

On Saturday morning, Detective Waites returned to the Palm Beach County Medical Examiner's Office and A.J.'s body was released later that day to the funeral home that his natural mother, Ilene, had requested. He was buried the following Monday in Fort Lauderdale.

Detective Calloway returned to Triphammer Road to talk to Louis Steinhauer and his wife, Anne. The Steinhauers had lived directly across the street from the Schwarzes for about 1½ years. Mrs. Steinhauer said that about three times a week she would meet A.J. on the corner and drive him to school. She had asked A.J. if she could take him to school because she felt sorry for him, since he had to walk every day. A.J. accepted the rides from her—but only if she would pick him up on the corner, because he didn't want his parents to see him riding in a car.

During these rides, she learned that A.J. was grounded most of the time, and when she asked him what he was doing early every Thursday morning, he told her that he had to collect aluminum cans for his stepmother because she was on probation and made him collect the cans.

A.J. was up early every morning doing chores. He had to clean the garage about five days out of seven, but the Steinhauers had never seen the girls doing any chores.

Most disturbingly, Mrs. Steinhauer told the detective that on Saturday, April 24, she saw A.J. working in the garage, and Jessica had walked up behind him and placed her hands around his neck and picked him up off the ground. A.J.'s arms were limp at his side and his feet were off the ground. While holding him by the neck, Jessica started walking around the garage, saying, "See this! Look at this!" Mrs. Steinhauer believed she was showing A.J. certain areas in the garage that he may have missed cleaning.

Mrs. Steinhauer had heard—on a daily basis for 1½ years—A.J. being called "shit for brains," "stupid," and an "idiot."

Next the detective talked to Catherine Turner, the neighbor directly behind the Schwarz residence. She also had seen A.J. with a black eye and had asked him what happened. He told her that he "fell down."

Turner had baby-sat for Jessica in the past and said that they had changed the lock on A.J.'s room so that it was on the outside, instead of the inside.

Jessica had told Turner that she would make A.J. walk around the house naked as a form of punishment.

Turner told the detective that in the wee hours of the morning on May 2, she was awakened by a child's voice crying, "I won't do it again!" About five minutes later, she heard the same voice: "I won't do it again!"

She said that she did not recognize the voice, since she

had been sleeping, but the sound came from the back of her home.

Another neighbor, Bob Clayton, told Calloway that he had seen A.J. picking up aluminum cans around the neighborhood and had heard him being verbally abused by his stepmother.

Six months earlier—in reference to his ten-year-old daughter—Jessica had screamed at Bob Clayton, "Your little bitch is throwing things in my pool!" She cursed him and they had an argument about the accusation.

Clayton claimed that he had seen Lauren and Patsy swim naked in the pool many times—but the only times he saw A.J. swimming in the pool was when he was cleaning it.

When Detective Calloway interviewed Beth Walton on Monday, May 10, she said that she had met Jessica and her children in 1990 and had baby-sat for her on several occasions. One of those times, in October 1991, when Jessica arrived at her house with A.J., he was wearing a white T-shirt with the words "I'm a worthless piece of shit—don't talk to me" written on it. When Walton asked Jessica about it, she replied that she had written the words there because he violated one of her rules.

Jessica told her not to allow A.J. to talk to anyone or to watch TV while he was there.

Later in the day, Walton had an appointment at the NutriSystem Center, so she put another shirt over the one A.J. was already wearing. That way, he wouldn't have to lie if his stepmother asked him if he had left the shirt on all day.

On another occasion, when Walton was baby-sitting A.J., she gave him a peanut butter sandwich, and after he ate, he asked her if he could "wash" her bathroom—because she was nice to him.

On yet another occasion—in May or June 1992—A.J. was sitting at her kitchen table when Jessica appeared "obviously intoxicated." Jessica grabbed A.J., shook him, and smacked him in the head. Then she told him to tell the people—apparently HRS—that the only reason she took him out of school was because of doctors' appointments. At this time, Jessica was being investigated by HRS and the PBSO for physical abuse on A.J.—and drug abuse.

According to Walton, when Jessica grabbed A.J. and shook him, she told him that she was going to "knock the fucking crap out of him."

Jessica later told Beth Walton that A.J. was pulled out of school because he was supposed to wake her up on time—and he didn't. Also, he was supposed to empty a cat litter box and Jessica didn't think he had cleaned it well enough. Therefore, she was going to make him stay home from school.

Sometime in 1992, when A.J.'s natural mother was trying to get visitation rights, Walton claimed that Jessica had told A.J. that if he told the judge he wanted see his natural mother, she "would kill him."

On Tuesday, May 11, Detective Calloway interviewed Susan Simpson, a woman who had attended three group counseling sessions with Jessica Schwarz. Simpson told him that Jessica was "outrageous and obnoxious" during the meetings. Jessica talked about A.J. at every meeting and she called him Jeffrey Dahmer. Jessica also told her that she locked A.J. in his bedroom at night because she "was afraid he was going to be standing over her bed with a knife."

At one of the meetings, Jessica walked in and said, "Well, I fed the bastard."

Over the next several months, the investigation nearly came to a standstill until, finally, in the second week of August 1993, Scott Cupp received the autopsy report from Dr. Joseph Burton. An extremely complex case, Dr. Burton had spent numerous hours on its evaluation, as well as reviewing it with other experts on his staff.

It was his determination that if A.J.'s body had been found in any situation other than in water—and the postmortem and autopsy findings being as they were—that it was unlikely that the case would have been classified as anything other than a "homicide." He based his opinion, in part, on the numerous bruises, many of which were in locations that are not routinely found in accidental occurrences.

Dr. Burton stated in his report: "In arriving at a determination of cause and manner of death, the Medical Examiner must consider every aspect of the investigation. The determination of cause and manner of death is not dependant solely on the observations found at a postmortem examination and autopsy."

He explained that the autopsy was only a piece of the puzzle and must be put into context with the entire investigation—all the information known about the case.

"That is what I have done with this case and I have treated it as I would have, had it occurred in my own jurisdiction. This case has been reviewed in its entirety with four of my most experienced forensic investigators, having approximately sixty years of homicide and death investigation experience, collectively."

His entire staff—including other pathologists—was unanimous in its opinion.

They had found it fairly simple to rule out natural causes as the manner of death. A.J. had no significant underlying medical problems.

Nor was there anything to indicate a reason why he might have drowned accidentally—let alone any explanation as to why he might have been in the pool naked in the middle of the night or early in the morning. A.J. was a good swimmer and had no history of epilepsy or blacking out. The pool was only four feet deep, so even if he (at 4'4" tall) would have had cramps, he could have walked on his tiptoes and kept his nose above the water. Or he could have even bounced off the bottom to the pool edge—due to the small size of the pool.

The design and size of the pool also made it unlikely that he dived in, hit his head, and knocked himself unconscious. And the abrasions on his face, nose, and ears were not injuries caused by scraping or hitting the plastic-lined pool.

As to the possibility of suicide, Dr. Burton found it unreasonable to conclude that A.J. had taken his life intentionally by drowning. He had investigated many adolescent suicides during his career and could not recall a single one in which a child had committed suicide by drowning. He had also contacted other medical examiners in other jurisdictions around the country and could find no case in which a child of this age was felt to have committed suicide by drowning. Indeed, it is rare for adults to take their own lives in such a manner.

Was Andrew Schwarz's death a homicide?

Dr. Burton and his colleagues took many things into consideration.

"There is without question evidence of physical abuse to this child. The patterns of bruises on the scalp could—in no way—have been caused by some type of accident. They are multiple—involving all four quadrants of the scalp—and there are no lacerations or abrasions of the skin surface.

"The bruising on the upper inner left arm and behind the knees, as well as on the inner upper thighs are consistent with where someone may have forcibly held this child. Most of these appear to be of recent origin."

Burton determined that there was ample evidence from the investigators' interviews with neighbors and others that A.J. had been physically and emotionally abused—apparently, by his stepmother primarily.

"The investigative history and the postmortem examination and autopsies of Andrew Schwarz disclose irrefutable evidence that Andrew was physically abused."

In fact, Jessica Schwarz had been seen grasping A.J. beneath the head and holding him up off the ground by the neck—at some point previous to his death. Dr. Burton stated, "The bruises beneath his chin may certainly have been accounted for by such an act. This does not constitute proper treatment of a ten-year-old child."

He noted the information in the records that A.J. had been punished in the past by being made to run down the street naked:

"If this is true, it is certainly of interest that—when his body is discovered—he is naked. Ten-year-old boys are usually very self-conscious about their body. It is very unusual to find a child of this age who would be willing to swim in the nude—even in the middle of the night.

"In addition, the stepmother finding him missing from his room at 6:00 a.m., also is suspicious since she reportedly does not rise until 10:00 in the morning or later."

When David Schwarz found A.J. floating in the pool between 6:00 and 6:30 A.M., A.J. was already in a state of rigor mortis. Taking all factors into consideration—including the temperature of the water at eighty-two degrees, the size of the child, etc.—Dr. Burton concluded that the rigor mortis at least suggested that A.J. might have been dead for several hours prior to being discovered.

"When he went to bed, reports indicate that he was okay and no family member states anything about any visible injuries on his face.

"Yet on the face to the left of the mouth is a scrape-like abrasion. On the right side of the nose is a somewhat linear abrasion. Behind the ears are abrasions—one more intense than the other. Beneath the left arm is a recent bruise. On the inner aspect of the thighs there are recent bruises.

"The above pattern of injuries are consistent with someone having held Andrew's head with the hand placed behind the head and possibly another hand across the nose and mouth and submerging him until he aspirated enough water to become unconscious and die.

"This child's past psychiatric history is certainly questionable since most of the information given to treating physicians was supplied primarily by the stepmother. There is obvious bias in the stepmother's opinion of this child and her opinion is in direct conflict with some statements taken from school officials and from other people in the health care field.

"Although this child—at least by the parents' history—had exhibited in the past unruly behavior, possibly aggressive behavior, the circumstances of this case strongly suggest that this child's death is the result of physical child abuse with the terminal mechanism of death being submersion or drowning.

"The injuries to the scalp are sufficient in and of themselves to have caused the death of a child.

"In summary, at the very least Andrew's death should have resulted in an investigation and intervention on the grounds of physical and emotional child abuse. There is overwhelming evidence to support the above.

"The diagnosis of death by drowning does not exclude the manner of this occurrence as having been due to a 'homicide.'

"The evidence in this case overwhelmingly demands that the death of Andrew Schwarz should either be classified as 'homicide' or that the involved agencies should present all of the evidence to a grand jury or similar investigative body to conclude whether such a classification is warranted.

"There is nothing wrong with Dr. Benz having classified the death as 'undetermined.' In fact, I might also list the classification as such, although I feel more strongly now than when I was first involved in the case, that had it occurred within my jurisdiction that I would have classified the death as a 'homicide.'

"My report would reflect, as it does here, that the facts of the case not only suggest, but demand, that a grand jury or other body of non biased individuals review the case in its entirety and determine whether there is evidence for the legal system to proceed.

"If the determination is that there is not enough evidence, then at least it could be said that everything had been done to be sure that the questions surrounding his death were explored in their fullest in an attempt to speak for, to protect, and obtain justice, even though he has died."

Due to the findings of the autopsy, the case remained open pending further investigation.

"Hands/fists/feet" was listed as the suspected weapons that had been used on A.J. Schwarz.

Soon after he received the autopsy report from Dr. Burton, Scott Cupp asked a young colleague of his, assistant state attorney (ASA) Joseph Marx, to join with him in the investigation of A.J.'s death and—hopefully—the prosecution of Jessica Schwarz.

On the morning of August 11, Detective Waites asked David Schwarz to meet with him at the sheriff's office to discuss the finalized autopsy report.

Detectives Waites and Calloway interviewed Bear later that morning and explained the report—and Dr. Burton's qualifications to him. They also told him about the various bruises and injuries documented at the time of the autopsy.

When the detectives asked if he had any knowledge of problems between Jessica and A.J., David told them he did not. He added that when he had been employed as a truck driver, he had called home whenever he went on an overnight trip and there was never an indication of any problems.

David asked if he needed to contact an attorney and Waites explained to him that it was entirely his decision and that if he wanted to do that, the interview would be concluded until he had the opportunity to do so. David asked if he was being charged with any crime and the detective explained that, at that point, he was still being considered a witness in the investigation.

David decided to continue with the interview.

He felt that if problems existed between Jessica and A.J., his two other children would have told him about it. He claimed that Lauren or Jackie had never told him about any such problems. Lauren and Jackie were still in the custody of Jessica's parents.

Waites again described the bruising that was observed on A.J.'s body, and David had no explanation for—and claimed that he had no knowledge of—them.

When the detectives told him about the incident that Jessica had described to them in which A.J. was supposedly in the garage, striking himself in the head with a cane, David further claimed that he was not familiar with the incident and Jessica had never told him about it.

When asked what type of rewards A.J. received for good behavior, David said that he would get toys for "extra good behavior" and an "extra helping of food at dinner for daily good behavior."

When Waites asked him about the information that they had received in reference to A.J. collecting cans in the morning before going to school, David said that he did it to assist Jessica with her community service and claimed that the other two children also helped with collecting the cans. He said that he would wake A.J.—between five and six o'clock in the morning—before he went to work so that the boy could collect the cans before going to school.

To the best of his knowledge, David said the worst punishment A.J. had ever received was going to bed without dinner for one or two nights in a row. And that—at no time—had he ever seen A.J. being physically abused. Anytime he heard what he considered to be verbal abuse, or very loud yelling, at A.J., he would put a stop to it and did not allow it to continue.

Waites asked whether or not, if A.J. was being abused or physically punished, he would offer any resistance. David said that A.J. would not, and that he became very passive when anyone raised his or her voice at him.

He repeated the same story he had told them before about the morning he found A.J.'s body in the pool. Incredibly, he claimed that there had been no conversation between Jessica and him concerning A.J.'s death since May 2, the day A.J. died.

Soon after that, Michael Waites and Jimmy Restivo decided to "take another run" at David Schwarz. They really thought—especially Restivo—that armed with Burton's report, that Bear would turn on Jessica and give them something direct that had happened between Jessica and A.J. that night, early morning, or close in time to the murder.

When he didn't, they were left in the same position—there was no direct evidence that led to A.J.'s murder.

On August 31, Detectives Waites and Calloway went to the Schwarz home on Triphammer Road and attempted to interview Jessica Schwarz. When they arrived, Jessica spoke to them from inside the house and refused to unlock the door and talk face-to-face with them. She asked if she was under arrest and they told her no.

She told them that she needed to put some clothes on and then she would speak with them. A few minutes later, she came to the door and—speaking from inside the house through the locked door—told them to "fuck off."

Waites informed her to have her attorney, Sam Marshall, contact either him or Detective Calloway so they could set up an appointment to conduct an interview with her regarding the autopsy report.

At 12:30 that afternoon, Sam Marshall, who was representing Jessica in the dependency hearing involving Lauren and Jackie, contacted Waites, and the detective explained to him that they had received the final autopsy report, listing the manner of death as homicide. Not surprisingly, Marshall stated that he was not inclined to allow his client to be interviewed.

Later in the afternoon, Detectives Waites and Calloway met with Scott Cupp to review the investigation. As a result of the meeting, the case was tentatively set to be presented to the grand jury on October 5, 1993—unless there was a conflict with Dr. Burton's schedule. The possible charges that would be presented to the grand jury were first-degree murder, aggravated child abuse, emotional and mental abuse, as well as the possibility of an unrelated charge involving A.J.'s half sister Patsy.

CHAPTER 7

I just can't help but feel that Andrew is programmed. Things just don't ring true. His affect is flat.

—Dr. Richard Zimmern

In September, Scott Cupp read—for the first time—the progress notes that Dr. Richard Zimmern had written over the period of time that he was A.J.'s guardian. It was, indeed, a poignant glimpse into the tragic life of Andrew J. Schwarz and the relationship he shared with the person who cared about him, perhaps more than anyone else—his volunteer guardian ad litem.

When Dr. Zimmern spoke to Jessica Schwarz on July 23, 1992, she told him that when she first met David, he was "on the rebound" from Ilene and that he had A.J. and Patsy every weekend.

It was obvious that Jessica had little regard for A.J.'s biological mother, Ilene, calling her "a slob and a slut. She is a game player and a manipulator." According to Jessica, Ilene appeared to be high on "speed or cocaine."

(This of course, was Jessica's opinion and the facts were not verified.)

Jessica told Dr. Zimmern that A.J. was a hyperexcitable child with a poor attention span, but that he got decent, passable grades.

His notes reflected some of her additional comments:

"He is impulsive with poor judgment and cannot be trusted alone."

Jessica claimed that A.J. tried to drown Jackie when she was two years old. She told the guardian that A.J. had had a near drowning experience when he was about two or three years old and was unconscious for several minutes, but he was not hospitalized.

After accusing Jessica of verbal and physical abuse, Patsy was removed from the Schwarz home in May 1992 and placed in foster care. The fact that Patsy had threatened suicide was instrumental in her being removed from the Schwarz home, but Jessica felt that Ilene had orchestrated the whole scenario for revenge.

Dr. Zimmern's notes from August 27, 1992, indicated that Jessica had finally set up an initial appointment for A.J. at South County Mental Health for September 10—even though he was supposed to have started counseling in March, immediately after his release from the Psychiatric Institute of Vero Beach.

Nor was he on the imipramine that had been prescribed for him. After A.J.'s discharge, Dr. Thomas Uttley, the doctor in charge of his case, had given Jessica one additional prescription for imipramine, but, according to Jessica, A.J. started to vomit the medicine.

At some point—again, according to her—she took him to a local family doctor who refused to renew the medication. The antidepressant is prescribed to relieve symptoms such as feelings of sadness, worthlessness, or guilt, loss of interest in daily activities, changes in appetite, tiredness, sleeping too much, insomnia, and thoughts of death or suicide.

A.J. was not on Medicaid at the time because HRS had suddenly dropped him from the program. Jessica claimed she was told that he was too old, yet the two girls and David continued to receive their cards. When A.J. finally received a card for August, Jessica called South County Mental Health to make the counseling appointment.

Jessica stated that she did not believe in counseling and

claimed that A.J. was never helped by imipramine. Ironically, she felt that what he needed was a strong, well-structured home where he would feel safe and wanted.

On September 18, 1992, there was a hearing before Judge Carney in the Broward County Courthouse. Through her attorney, A.J.'s biological mother, Ilene, asked that he be placed in a foster home, but the request was denied. The judge, however, was disturbed by the fact that A.J. did not start counseling until September 10—six months after his discharge from Vero Beach—and was also concerned about the variance in A.J.'s behavior in school and at home.

Dr. Zimmern's notes indicated that on October 7 he had had a long visit with David and Jessica in an attempt to become better acquainted with the family.

"Andrew was pleased to see me and readily talked about school. He quickly told me he didn't want to see his [biological] mother or sister—or even talk to them. He seems afraid that they will somehow re-enter his life. Andrew is a quiet passive child who appears to be easily dominated. I believe that he has many fears; he certainly is outwardly tense."

And, on October 29: "I just can't help but feel that Andrew is programmed. Things just don't ring true. His affect is flat."

There was another court hearing on October 30: "Andrew does not have to speak to or visit [with] Ilene Logan or Patsy Spence until he has Kathy Merritt's (his counselor) okay. Patsy is getting together with her mother and they will be united in the near future."

A few weeks later, Dr. Zimmern noted a telephone conversation he had with Jessica: "Andrew is getting into trouble in school and is not reporting his demerits to Jessica. He is hiding the teacher's notes. His schoolwork is going downhill. Jessica is angry with his teacher and the school in general.

"I have suggested he be placed on imipramine."

On November 24, he again visited the Schwarz home and discussed A.J.'s hyperactivity and talkativeness with Jessica. He urged her to take him to see his doctor and get a prescription for imipramine. They also talked about Jessica's handling of A.J.: "She is bugged by his 'lying.' She will not budge on softening her stand. I will approach his teacher and try to work from that end."

He visited Indian Pines Elementary School in December to talk to Mrs. Idrissi. Andrew was a good child in school, anxious to please, eager to help. Idrissi, aware that he was starving for affection and approval, gave him lots of both.

Dr. Zimmern suggested that there be no more notes home—that Mrs. Idrissi work out her own system of discipline within the class.

"Jessica Schwarz's character and attitude are now well known among the teachers at Indian Pines. Andrew will miss the December 10 [field] trip, which was lost because of lying and failure to bring home notes from the teacher. He knew, of course, that he would be punished and naturally hid the notes. Jessica is very resistant to changing her ways. Tough love!"

According to his notes on January 19, 1993: "Jessica and Andrew are a totally mismatched pair. Considering Andrew's current emotional developmental state, she is psychologically unable to give him the support he needs. Jessica must have significant problems herself. Her brazen, combative attitude is now well known in the neighborhood and in school. Everybody on Triphammer Road must hate her guts!

"Jessica has no concept of flexibility in her approach to Andrew. She has no concept of his emotional needs, and trying to meet those needs. Luckily, Mrs. Idrissi has the interest and capacity to mother him and give him the touching and hugging he needs. Home must be a dismal place for Andrew, including an absent father who gives him no support in any fashion.

"I think Andrew will be in reasonable shape as long as he has Mrs. Idrissi as a mother figure in school. I will try to call a conference on Andrew in June to decide whether or not he should remain with Jessica and David. They probably won't change and he will have to go to a foster home. I guess

Jessica just doesn't like him. She tolerates him, and his father just doesn't care. No one cares but Mrs. Idrissi and me."

On January 26, Richard Zimmern received a phone call from Ms. Janet Heinrich, the guidance counselor at Indian Pines Elementary School. She told him that a neighbor had reported that Andrew had a broken nose and two black eyes. Heinrich reported it to the abuse hot line and the call was referred to Barbara Black, the HRS investigator. Andrew was not at school that day or the day before.

"Ms. Black and a police officer went to the Schwarz home. They believe that Andrew's injuries were an accident, which occurred when he was on his bicycle. He has a broken nose?"

That afternoon, Dr. Zimmern visited Andrew: "He does indeed have a broken nose and two black eyes. He says that on Sunday the 24th at about two to three in the afternoon, he was walking his sister's bike into the garage when he tripped and fell against the handlebars." Nothing medically had been done for A.J. at that point, but he was scheduled to see his psychologist and family doctor the following day, on January 27.

"Andrew seemed depressed and subdued this afternoon. I told him I did not think he hurt himself falling against the bike handles. He persistently repeated the fall against the bike handle story. I just don't see how such a fall could generate enough force to break his nose."

That same day, Dr. Zimmern talked to Mrs. Idrissi on the telephone: "She cares for him a great deal. He has been absent nineteen out of the last forty-nine days."

On January 28, he noted that Andrew went to see his family doctor the day before, and, according to Ms. Black, his nose was not broken.

He talked to Mrs. Idrissi again on February 18: "Am concerned about Andrew's absenteeism in school; he has not been sick. Why would Jessica keep him home? She could be using school as a punishment since she knows Mrs. Idrissi cares for him. Andrew spends a lot of time in school getting hugs and touching from Mrs. Idrissi; he needs it badly. He is doing C work, which is remarkable considering his background. He is depressed and sad. No love or affection at home—just endless punishment."

On February 23, there was a staff meeting at the Center for Children in Crisis concerning A.J.: "The staff psychologist feels that Andrew is a very sick kid—almost at the end of his rope. Jessica Schwarz, a combative, rude, simplistic woman with no real love for Andrew, is the worst possible stepmother for him. Serious consideration is being given to removing him from the Schwarz home and placing him in a foster home. This home would have to be carefully selected; a warm loving person like Mrs. Idrissi would be fine. Barbara Black of HRS will set up a meeting in the near future."

In the column to the right of his notes, Dr. Zimmern jotted, "Need review in mid-May."

He talked to Jessica on February 24: "She is having health problems—either kidney or liver. Her auto license plates were stolen so she has no transportation. She is going to the doctor's tomorrow and plans to take Andrew with her because of a rash.

"She says Andrew is having problems in school again—behavior problems.

"Mrs. Idrissi tells me he just has his usual needs for attention and affection—plus his hyperactivity."

On March 2, he discovered that between September 14, 1992, and February 22, 1993—out of a total of fourteen appointments—there had been three cancellations and three no-shows. A.J. had not been to counseling since February 2.

The following week, Dr. Zimmern had a discussion with David and Jessica regarding their handling of A.J.: "They believe Andrew is irrevocably flawed because of his early years with his biological mother. They feel that little can be done to change this. Jessica's father has stated to her, 'His eyes are dead—he has no soul.'

"I urged them to believe that Andrew is an emotionally disturbed child who can be helped—even cured—through therapy and love and security.

"Andrew does well in school and this part of his life should be fostered and aided. Do not use school or any aspect of it as part of his home disciplinary regime. As soon as you are able he should be returned to his therapist.

"Andrew needs to know that you care, and that you believe in him. Try not to always outsize him. Find things that he can be praised for—he needs to feel good about himself.

"When Andrew's eyes go dead he is withdrawing from the world because he finds it all just too painful. His self-esteem is now so low—try to build it up any way you can.

"Andrew is a difficult person to live with because his past life was so bad. His present habits are ones he developed to cope with life as it was. When his life improves he will shed those habits because they will no longer be necessary."

On March 24, Dr. Zimmern made the following notation: "Andrew was in a fight yesterday. A local boy named Tristan mouthed Jessica—Andrew fought for his [step] mother's good name. For this he was punished—kept out of school and grounded. He is now grounded until Christmas of 1993. This means confined to the house and chores after school.

"Andrew is afraid he will be sent away to a foster home which he does not want. I believe he willfully disobeys and forgets his chores, homework, and jobs. It must be his way of fighting back, his way of being noticed, his way of asserting himself, his way of bolstering his self-esteem.

"Every Thursday, he collects cans from five to seven in the morning. I gather that on those days, he does not go to school.

"In many ways, Andrew's home is his prison.

"Jessica sees Andrew as a four-year-old emotionally who she cannot control. Andrew frustrates her—makes her angry. Jessica's method of handling this anger is a head on 'in-your-face', abrasive, verbal counter attack with threats, which totally undermine Andrew's security. He panics inside, another failure, which further undermines his fragile self-esteem. He fights back by disobedience and forgetfulness—the usual ploy of helpless creatures.

"Jessica states that Andrew has had a bad month—hitting girls—fighting with boys—not abiding by the rules—not listening to anyone."

On March 26, Dr. Zimmern attended a meeting at the HRS office; also present were Barbara Black, Dottie Daniels, who was Black's supervisor, the Schwarzes, and Mrs. Idrissi.

"Jessica came on strong at first with her profane, combative, 'in-your-face' attitude. This is wholly defensive and covers her insecurity and low self-esteem in the presence of people who could do her harm. She calmed down once she realized that this meeting was not a trial, and she had not been prejudged guilty of abuse and/or neglect.

"Mrs. Idrissi spoke well, indicating that Andrew was bright and capable. He does need a lot of support, including hugs and touching. He seems starved for affection. Mrs. Idrissi and Jessica exchanged verbal blows, finally coming to understand each other—without liking each other.

"The HRS supervisor made it plain to Jessica that they knew that unknown neighbors were calling in the abuse to harass her. She also made it plain that they have to follow the rules and investigate each call. She made it clear that HRS is not her enemy, but just an agency whose purpose here is to help Andrew. She suggested changes in Jessica's approach: less negativity, more kindness, more rewards on a day to day basis, trying to find positive things in Andrew's life to support.

"I stated that we all know that Andrew has had a horrible past which we are all trying to help him overcome. He needs support, he needs his counseling, and he needs steady school attendance. School is one place where he succeeds, where he has fun, where he finds someone to love him. He trusts [Mrs. Idrissi] and confides in her. Considering his past, Andrew is doing very well?

"Jessica has to be strict but needs to show warmth and acceptance. She needs to respect Andrew as a person, not think of him as an emotionally disturbed kid operating on a four-year-old level.

"No discussion of removing Andrew to a foster home.

"I believe real progress was made—all the parties said their piece. Jessica now knows we are not monsters out to get her, but people who want to help her keep Andrew in her home and provide for him in a useful and practical way.

"His new social worker is Sandra Warren."

On March 31, he noted: "Jessica had a fight with Ms. Russo of South County Mental Health. David was responsible for getting Andrew to the clinic. When he missed, he did not call. Ms. Russo is rightfully angry with Jessica and David. Jessica hung up on Ms. Russo, but called Sandra Warren at HRS to explain. She will attempt to mend the relationship and get Andrew started back in counseling.

"Jessica is also angry at all the little daily gifts Andrew receives from Mrs. Idrissi. She thinks he's being spoiled."

Dr. Zimmern made a quick visit to see Andrew on April 10 to give him and his sisters Easter baskets. "Everyone seems quite happy and together. Can a real family be forming at last? Andrew needs David's support and love—in a visible way."

He also visited A.J. on his birthday, April 24. "He had his usual long face and was cleaning up outside. I gave him his Battle Trolls, as he requested; he brightened up and began to show them to his sisters. Later we finished his outside chores together.

"Jessica wants to talk to me about Lauren—she has been acting up, and saying that Andrew gets all of the attention. We agreed to get together the first week in May."

And then the heartbreaking entry on May 3: "Andrew is dead. He was found in a pool yesterday. Heard the news on the eleven o'clock newscast. Schwarzes deny complicity. Jackie and Lauren removed by HRS. No details available."

And later in the day, he noted: "I spent the morning at the guardian ad litem office. I feel so badly. I should have pressed the panic button earlier, instead of waiting for the school year to end. I knew Jessica was a hard taskmaster, but I never thought of her as a sadist.

"Jessica called the office to talk to me. She said she

awoke between five and six in the morning to go to the bathroom. Going to the kitchen she noted Andrew's light on and his room empty. She checked the house and then woke up David. David found Andrew's body in the pool—already stiff. Saturday night the family had a happy time—singing and laughing.

"Jessica did not sound depressed or sad—just very angry. That seems to be her principal emotion—anger and hostility. Now her anger was aimed at HRS and the police, who took her daughters and placed them with her parents, up the coast a bit.

"When she called I thought we might cry together. She thundered—raging at the world as personified by the police and HRS. She had no soft spot in her heart for Andrew—no compassion—no feeling for his early suffering—or his current needs.

"God was unkind to Andrew. He gave him Ilene Logan and her lovers, followed by David and Jessica Schwarz. No one can hurt him anymore. In the end, we all failed him. I should have saved him; now I must live with my failure."

CHAPTER 8

Make no mistake—Richard cared deeply for A.J.

—Scott Cupp

Dr. Richard Zimmern's notes contributed much to the overall feeling of sadness, frustration, and anger that Scott Cupp was already feeling; but, most important, it strengthened his resolve to build a case against Jessica Schwarz.

At that time, Cupp had little respect for most in the child protection field. Rightly or wrongly, he perceived most as incompetent and untrustworthy, and he felt that most lacked sincerity. Richard Zimmern clearly was none of those things and Scott Cupp knew that A.J. was fortunate to have had him.

Ironically, Zimmern was the "volunteer" among all the "professionals," which perhaps spoke volumes about the system in place to protect abused children. Tragically—as even Dr. Zimmern himself acknowledged—in the end, he felt he also failed A.J.

Compounding Scott Cupp's determination was the psychosocial and psychological evaluation from the Psychiatric Institute of Vero Beach regarding A.J.'s hospitalization in February 1992. It should be noted that David and Jessica Schwarz were the sources for the information pertaining to A.J.'s behavior and history.

At the age of eight, A.J. spent six weeks in the psychiatric hospital for evaluation and treatment of underlying depression. The main concern was that he had been "irritable and unpredictable, as well as dangerous to himself and others."

Jessica and David saw him as "increasingly dangerous," claiming that he had "run into traffic recklessly, jumped off ladders, and attempted to drown his sister on various occasions."

David reported that A.J. did not talk clearly until about the age of five. He also told them that A.J. "drowned" at the age of three—he was underwater for three to five minutes.

A.J.'s natural mother abused alcohol and drugs and he was subjected to physical and emotional abuse from her during his childhood, and David claimed that Ilene had "disappeared with his children—out of state—for three years."

He also claimed that A.J. had "always been physically abusive towards pets, sisters, and smaller friends," and that he had recently "tried to drown" his younger sister.

By court order from Broward County, Ilene was not allowed to have contact with A.J., due to past abuse of A.J., and the boy claimed not to want any contact with her.

According to the report: "The patient (A.J.) has been abusive to the family members, and parents are having difficulty managing his behavior. More specific information has not been obtained due to stepmother's inability to engage in treatment, due to allegedly not being able to find transportation, as she cannot drive because she lost her license for six months. This is reported to the hospital two days after the patient's admission. The natural father cannot attend due to working as a truck driver, and being out of town for weeks at a time. We will need to further work with this resistance in order to engage the family in his treatment. This will be a very important component to this child's treatment.

"There appears to be little or no involvement at this time.

"It would appear there has been little consistency in this child's life."

During A.J.'s stay at the hospital, many psychological tests were administered, including the thematic apperception test (TAT)—a projective personality test that was designed at Harvard in the 1930s by Christiana D. Morgan and Henry A. Murray. One of the most widely used tests, it is one in which a person's patterns of thought, attitudes, observational capacity, and emotional responses are evaluated on the basis of responses to ambiguous test materials. The TAT consists of thirty-one pictures depicting a variety of social and inter-personal situations and the patient is asked to tell a story about each one.

A.J.'s TAT stories reflected his low self-esteem and poor body image, "partially rooted in his view of the world as an unpredictable place.

"There is anxiety regarding family gatherings, the mother figure and self perception, especially since he refused to make stories for these indicating, 'I can't, it is too hard. I can't even see their faces.' "

Also, he made a reference to missing one of his sisters, whom he believed to be in another state.

When A.J. was administered the Rorschach (inkblot) test, he saw alligators, fire, ghosts, lions, and dead dragons with blood on them. According to the psychological evaluation report, he was also preoccupied with angels.

The summary on the report read: "A.J. is a depressed and anxious youngster for whom hospitalization seems warranted at this time given his dangerous behaviors, and deteriora-tion. He is experiencing a great deal of anger and sadness, which is believed to be at the root of much of his unpre-dictable behavior. Group therapy may help him begin to process these feelings, but individual therapy will need to be continued in order to boost his self-esteem.

"A.J. appears to be suffering from the loss regarding not only his mother, but also his sister. He will need to mourn and grieve in supportive therapy. Family therapy will be nec-essary to help A.J. bond more appropriately with current family members."

* * *

The case against Jessica Schwarz was presented to the Palm Beach County grand jury on October 4, 1993, and as a result—on October 8—a sealed indictment was delivered, charging her with one count of second-degree murder, four counts of aggravated child abuse (second-degree felony), two counts of felony child abuse (third-degree felony), and one count of witness tampering (third-degree felony).

The four counts of aggravated child abuse presented by the grand jury were that Jessica Schwarz had maliciously punished Andrew Schwarz by forcing him to eat food from a bowl placed next to a cat's litter box, by repeatedly forcing him to remain home from school, by forcing him to wear a shirt with the writing "I'm a worthless piece of shit; don't talk to me" (or words to that effect), and by forcing him to edge the family yard with regular house scissors—all causing him unnecessary or unjustifiable pain or suffering.

One of the counts of felony child abuse presented was that Jessica willfully (or by culpable negligence) permitted A.J. to suffer mental injury, by forcing him to sit naked outside his house.

The second count of felony child abuse presented was that Jessica willfully (or by culpable negligence) permitted Jackie to suffer mental injury by forcing her not to discuss the circumstances surrounding the life and death of A.J.

The count of tampering with a witness presented that Jessica did knowingly use intimidation or physical force, or knowingly did threaten or attempt to threaten, or did offer pecuniary benefit or gain to Jackie, with intent to influence her testimony.

At 1:00 that afternoon, Jessica Schwarz was arrested at her home on Triphammer Road. Jimmy Restivo, Chris Calloway, and Michael Waites went to the front door while uniformed patrol circled around to the back—to make sure she didn't try to make a run for it. Hoping they wouldn't have to break the door down, they banged on it until Jessica finally opened it, and they were able to serve the warrant.

Jessica had been talking to her attorney on the phone and

he was still on the line when the detectives entered. While the others read her rights to her and handcuffed her, Detective Waites picked up the telephone, which was on the floor, and informed Sam Marshall that Jessica was being taken to jail and that he could meet them there.

She was transported to the Palm Beach County Stockade and was held without bond.

On Friday, October 15, 1993, thirty-eight-year-old Jessica Schwarz pleaded "not guilty" to all the charges against her.

There was a two-hour hearing on Monday, October 25, 1993, to determine whether or not Jessica Schwarz should be released on bond. Her lead attorney, Rendell Brown, tried to convince the judge that his client was a responsible woman who—even when she knew she was going to be arrested—stayed to face the charges against her.

Scott Cupp painted a much more sinister picture—one in which Jessica Schwarz had assaulted her husband and even threatened some of the children in the neighborhood.

When Brown stated that A.J. had been placed in the care of Jessica and David because his biological mother had hit him in the head with a frying pan, Ilene Logan, who was seated in the gallery of the courtroom, cried out angrily, "You son of a bitch! No!"

Quite emotional, she struggled to stand up, but her father, who was seated next to her, held her down firmly and clamped his hand over her mouth in an effort to keep her quiet.

Apparently embarrassed and perhaps not wanting to be recognized later, David Schwarz wore dark sunglasses when he took the witness stand. When questioned, he quietly admitted that he did not attend his own son's funeral.

Cupp: You don't even know the day he died.
David: It was May 8.
Cupp (disgusted): It was May 2.

After viewing the videotape of Jessica ordering Jackie not to talk to the detectives, Judge Walter Colbath released

Jessica on $150,000 bond, with the stipulation that she was not allowed to leave her house—except to attend court proceedings. She was also prohibited from having any money or car keys.

And she was forbidden to have any contact with her daughters.

Jessica Schwarz's father, Edward Woods, paid the bond and she was allowed to leave the stockade late that afternoon.

One neighbor, after she learned of Jessica's release, was so frightened that she asked the police for additional patrols in the area.

On October 29, Detective Calloway met with twelve-year-old Ariel Walton, Teresa Walton's sister, at Christa McAuliffe Middle School. Ariel told the detective that she was Lauren Cross's best friend and that she used to visit Lauren "all the time."

She stated that when Jessica and her daughters would go to the grocery store or would leave the house for any reason, they would lock A.J. outside the house in the backyard area, on numerous occasions.

Ariel had heard Jessica frequently tell A.J. that she hated him. Jessica had also told her, "I'll never love that boy." And that she was going to "kill him someday and bury him under the pool."

She had seen Jessica strike A.J. across the face and head with her hands on numerous occasions. She, too, had seen A.J. perform the strange chore of edging the grass with scissors—and added that he usually cleaned the garage out "every day." A.J. was made to do "all the chores," but the girls did "next to nothing."

On one occasion, A.J. accidentally dropped some toothbrushes in the toilet, so Jessica told him that he wasn't allowed to brush his teeth anymore.

Jessica cursed at A.J. "all the time" and Ariel had overheard Jessica call him a "fucking retarded kid" and tell him that he was "no good."

About a year earlier, Jessica made A.J. eat a cockroach. She told Ariel that she was going to make A.J. eat every one of them that she saw in the house. Apparently, it was A.J.'s "job" to make sure there were no cockroaches in the house.

A little while later, Ariel saw A.J. using the garden hose to wash his mouth out, and he told her "the cockroach tasted nasty."

CHAPTER 9

*Calloway put his heart into this case, just like he
did every case he ever worked. I have worked with a
lot of detectives and investigators over the years, and
he is one that I highly respect.*

—Detective Michael Waites

Scott Cupp went before the grand jury in November to
question the HRS workers who had been responsible for
protecting Andrew Schwarz—the same grand jurors who
had indicted Jessica Schwarz the previous month.

Early in 1992, when Patsy claimed that Jessica had given
her a bloody nose and was then returned to Broward County,
A.J. remained in the Schwarz home, under the supervision
of HRS.

Then in January 1993, Eileen Callahan made the "anonymous" phone call to HRS informing them that she believed
Jessica Schwarz had broken A.J.'s nose. After the investigation by HRS and the sheriff's office, the charge was considered to be unfounded.

A few days later, A.J.'s therapist, after questioning him
about his story that he hurt himself when he fell off a bicycle, expressed the opinion that she was not satisfied with his
explanation.

The following week, Jessica took A.J. to see a counselor
at the Center for Children in Crisis and the second counselor

found that there was "rather severe and continuing emotional abuse" and recommended that there should be a more thorough investigation by HRS.

Incredibly, it was over a month later before the HRS workers even met with the counselors and school personnel to discuss A.J.'s case. The end result of the meeting was that everyone—including Jessica—agreed to work more closely together.

Barely a month later, A.J. was dead.

Andrew Schwarz had been in protective custody for thirty-six months—twenty-seven months longer than policy recommended.

The grand jury heard testimony from fifteen witnesses and reviewed numerous records and documents produced by HRS, the Child Protection Team, the guardian ad litem program, and the Palm Beach County Sheriff's Office.

Initially, all of the HRS workers were cleared of any criminal wrongdoing.

It seemed that no one in the system that had failed A.J. so miserably—and repeatedly—would have to take the slightest responsibility for his death or the abuse that he had suffered.

However, when the grand jury returned in December, they decided to revisit the case and then returned an indictment against Barbara Black. She was arrested and charged with extortion by threat—a second-degree felony punishable by up to fifteen years in prison. She had threatened Eileen Callahan, saying that she would charge her with an abuse complaint if she continued to call in about A.J.

Also, as a result of its investigation concerning the conduct of HRS during the time A.J. was under HRS supervision, the grand jury issued the following scathing report:

"It has been determined by the grand jury, based on the evidence presented, that HRS is not performing adequately to meet the public's expectations to protect the general welfare of children.

"The investigation revealed that HRS's policies and procedures were not followed. There was a lack of diligent follow-up and communication between counties, groups within the department, and with the police investigators.

"Caseloads are placed with unreasonable time constraints. The Child Protection Team professionals' recommendations were not implemented.

"Management of records was inadequate. It is difficult to determine if records are falsified and complete when they are not adequately maintained or systematically reviewed by management. There were important files that were not completely filled out in that there were omissions of important information. Changes were made to files contrary to standard record keeping practices. White-out, overwriting, cutting pages, and taping pages over each other were observed. It is an accepted practice to use a single line to strike out a sentence so that what was originally stated could be read; it would then be initialed and dated so it could be determined who made the change and when.

"Insufficient personnel was evident. Only one Quality Assurance person assigned to South Florida, regardless of how efficient and qualified, is not enough to ensure that the state policies are being implemented properly. Throughout the investigation, HRS witnesses testified that there are insufficient resources available to do detailed investigation with adequate follow-up visits, to ensure investigation with adequate follow-up visits, to ensure the welfare of the children they are to protect. Further testimony revealed there is a large workload coupled with mandated time constraints that demand quick decisions. Tracking and follow up of recommendations from the various staffing meetings to make sure each group carries out the recommendations appear to need more time than is permitted.

"Communication appears to be inadequate, as demonstrated by the current methodology and ineffectiveness of turning over cases from county to county and coordination with the police, guardian ad litem, and the Child Protection Team. Examples presented to the grand jury were: the lack of continuity with case workers changing jobs, the police not being fully informed of the circumstances surrounding an investigation they were called in to assist, follow up on a staffing meeting with the Child Protection Team where recommendations were agreed to but were not followed through, and the case closed prematurely.

"Andrew J. Schwarz's files had enough information in them to strongly suggest removing him from the home. There appeared to be an overwhelming drive by HRS to keep Andrew J. Schwarz with his natural father even when the Child Protection Team, staff meetings, and other documented information showed this was not in his best interest.

"Based upon testimony presented to the grand jury, it appears that responsibilities are either unknown or inadequately implemented. Various departments within HRS are performing different tasks concerning the same individual. When this occurs the various departments pass requests back and forth with little or no follow up. Independent verification and day-to-day supervision to assure personnel are taking on their assigned accountability is sorely lacking. Cases have been closed before all departments have completed all assigned tasks."

After reviewing the case, the grand jury made the following recommendations to HRS and, as appropriate, to the legislature:

"The supervisors should be more responsible for adherence to policies to ensure the workers make all appropriate collateral contacts. More emphasis must be placed on the quality of work, not the speed with which the work is accomplished or the quantity of cases closed. Supervisors and Quality Assurance personnel should monitor cases to determine if collateral contacts are actually being made. This monitoring should be documented when performed.

"HRS needs to ensure that their representatives perform their duties in a professional, encouraging, and non-threatening manner resulting in community cooperation as it relates to the safety and welfare of children. Based upon testimony presented to the grand jury, there is a genuine fear of the Department of Health and Rehabilitative Services' power to remove children from anyone involved (e.g. reporters of an incident) at the discretion of HRS personnel.

"A central filing system is needed that involves having one central file on each child which would include reports of abuse and neglect (including unfounded cases), foster care, counseling, medical reports, etc. These records must be made available to the various departments within HRS, the Court, law enforcement agencies, Guardian Ad Litem, and the State Attorney's office.

"The grand jury recommends that access to files on unfounded complaints be limited to the State's Attorney, law enforcement, the Court, and HRS. The name of the perpetrator and the file in which the complaint was [deemed] unfounded should continue to be withheld from any public request as an exception to Florida Statute 119. This recommendation is based on the concern that although one complaint may be held to be unfounded, additional complaints may reveal a pattern of abuse. This could aid in identifying and prosecuting the perpetrator.

"The grand jury feels it is questionable to have HRS investigating criminal activities even with the help of the police. HRS investigators are not trained in criminal investigations and should not be required to perform in this capacity. There are police criminal units trained in the investigation of criminal acts against children and would perform adequately if they were given complete history records of each case, ongoing and previous.

"When various departments pass requests back and forth to each other there should be a structured follow up. The various action items resulting from staffing meetings should be tracked to closure. This includes action items passed on to other departments and counties in south Florida. Independent verification and day-to-day supervision should ensure personnel are taking on their assigned accountabilities. Cases should not be prematurely closed before all departments have completed their assigned tasks.

"Additional trained personnel are needed in the areas of Child Protective Services, Child Protective Investigations, and Quality Assurance. In order to meet this criteria there needs to be sufficient resources.

"There needs to be more attention to detail when reviewing the case workers' and investigators' notes for trends, and that appropriate actions are initiated.

"In summation:

"It is the grand jury's desire that this report not be ignored but be carefully considered to determine the necessary changes the Department of Health and Rehabilitative Services must make to protect the children in its care and to prevent them from being abused again once they enter HRS's system."

Barbara Black was released on bond and continued in her role as an HRS child protection investigator.

On Thursday, December 23, there was a hearing to determine whether or not Jessica would be allowed to spend Christmas with her two young daughters.

Lauren and Jackie were present in the courtroom, seated between their father and their maternal grandmother. Except in the courtroom, Jessica had not seen them since her arrest.

Rendell Brown tried to convince Judge Colbath to allow the girls to have weekend visits with their mother, claiming that they had become depressed while living with their grandparents.

When Dr. George Rahaim testified, the psychologist told the judge that he had seen Jessica wave to the girls when she came into the courtroom and then make a "crude gesture" moments later to ASA Joe Marx, co-counsel for the prosecution. Although he couldn't say for certain that the girls had seen what their mother had done, he said that it was an example of her "silent manipulation. It's very subtle. These are girls riding to school in the rain while their brother had to walk. I liken it to a trustee in a concentration camp, where you have to live with unspeakable things happening to other people."

The psychologist also claimed that Jessica had engaged her daughters in a "conspiracy of abuse."

Judge Colbath ruled that the defendant could write letters to Lauren and Jackie and would be allowed to send them presents, but she could not visit with them, stating that he was "very concerned about the subtle abuse."

On December 28, Detective Calloway interviewed Laura Perryman (Serena Perryman's mother), who also lived on Triphammer Road, across the street and several houses down from the Schwarzes. Laura was known in the neighborhood to have a special talent for growing plants and that was how she came to know Jessica Schwarz.

Sometimes Jessica would send one of her children over to ask Laura Perryman a question regarding plants, and Perryman said that many times she walked over to Jessica's house to discuss plants with her. During those visits, she realized something was wrong in the household as related to A.J. She believed that he suffered from attention deficit disorder (ADD), as she herself had children who suffered the same disorder.

On one particular occasion—approximately one year before A.J.'s death—Jessica told Perryman that "A.J. tried to drown Jackie in the pool." Laura tried to explain to her that she believed A.J. had ADD and that children with that disorder are very impulsive and lack the ability to think before acting—and that she did not feel that A.J. would do anything to Jackie intentionally.

Jessica's reply was totally emotionless and cold: "If anything bad happens again, I'm going to kill A.J." When Laura Perryman tried to tell her that she did not actually mean that, Jessica Schwarz convinced her that that was exactly what she meant.

CHAPTER 10

You bring me a confession, I'll call it a homicide.

—Dr. James Benz, to Detective Jimmy Restivo

Rendell Brown filed a motion with the court to sever the abuse charges from the murder charge, and on Thursday, March 17, 1994, there was a hearing to address the issue. He successfully argued that there was no evidence linking Jessica to A.J.'s drowning, and the allegations that she had abused him previous to that could not be used to show that she caused his death.

Until Judge Colbath granted their motion to sever, Cupp had been operating under the naive assumption that there would be one trial. When he realized they would have to try an abuse case without a victim—with no mention that the defendant was being charged with his murder—he was momentarily devastated.

In essence, it meant that the jury would be allowed to know that A.J. was deceased and that he, obviously, was unable to testify. But they would be told that the facts and circumstances of his death had absolutely no relevance to and nothing to do with the issues involved in the trial.

The state would have to caution all of their witnesses to avoid mentioning his death—not to refer to his passing in any way that would draw any attention to his death. In theory, for all the jurors would know, A.J. had been hit by a car or died of cancer prior to the case going to trial.

The conditions of Jessica's bond required that she stay inside her house on Triphammer Road and that she refrain from communicating with any potential witnesses, in any way; but she had defiantly continued to be the terror of the neighborhood.

On April 13, 1994, at yet another hearing in Judge Walter Colbath's courtroom, Anne Steinhauer and Ida Falk testified that Mrs. Schwarz had stood outside her front door on the previous Sunday and shouted sarcastic, obscene remarks at them.

Mrs. Steinhauer told the judge that Jessica had shouted at her from across the street, "There's fucking Mother of the Year! There's fucking Mother of the Year!"

Both women testified that their daughters were so afraid of Jessica that they were having trouble sleeping. Ida Falk said that her daughter, Jamie, on one occasion had even hidden in the bathroom with a wooden bat.

"She's afraid Jessica is going to come over and hurt us."

The women were extremely relieved when the judge ruled that Jessica Schwarz had violated her bond and granted Cupp's request that she be returned to jail.

Everyone involved in the case—especially her neighbors—let out a collective sigh of relief. The overall stress level went down tremendously. Some of the kids in the neighborhood had literally been hiding in their rooms while she was on pretrial house arrest. It also went a long way in letting them know the authorities were working hard to protect them. All along, Scott Cupp worried that when it came time for trial, they would wilt and backslide when pressed on the stand.

Many times, lay witnesses' testimony at trial doesn't approach what it was when they initially gave their stories to the investigators. In this case, it was all the prosecution had.

Cupp was afraid if one witness started to back off, it would spread like a disease. If Jessica stayed out, he was afraid she would become a constant visual reminder to each of the witnesses that if she was acquitted, she'd be right back among them with no one to protect them if they had testified against her.

The following month, Jessica's attorneys, Sam Marshall and Rendell Brown, took a deposition from Dr. James Benz, the medical examiner for Palm Beach County. He, of course, would not be testifying in the abuse trial, but at the murder trial—for the defense.

He was brash, loud, and sarcastic, and he was "famous" for trying to shock people—especially jurors. It wasn't unusual for him to find a way to get the word "maggots" into his testimony—even when it didn't apply. Add to that the fact that he had a reputation for hating lawyers and it made for a rather bizarre deposition.

The tall, rotund man had been the medical examiner for Palm Beach County since March 1983, and he estimated that he had performed "approximately four hundred autopsies a year for the last ten years."

Peering at Sam Marshall through thick glasses, he stated, "I went to premedical school at Indiana University. I attended medical school at the Indiana School of Medicine. I had a one-year clinical internship at Lima Memorial Hospital in Lima, Ohio. All my other training has been at the Indiana School of Medicine. That consisted of four-years residency training in the area of pathology and in forensic pathology. I'm certified by the American Board of Pathology in anatomic pathology, clinical pathology, and forensic pathology."

Marshall: During the time that you've been the medical examiner, has there ever been a time where the state attorney has asked for a second opinion regarding autopsies performed by you? Other than this case?
Benz: Not that I can remember off the top of my head.

There was one other case that they didn't like my opinion. They had another pathologist review it, but I don't think he did a second autopsy.

Marshall: So you would say he just reviewed your opinion, but to your knowledge you can't recall other situations where another doctor did an actual postmortem—a second autopsy?

Benz: Not that I can remember.

Marshall: And were you aware of a second autopsy [that was] going to be done prior to it being done? Were you aware of that?

Benz: Yes. As I recollect, the state attorney came into the office and talked to me about it. There was a discussion as to the manner of death, primarily. And I had voiced my opinion on the death circumstances that the manner of death was undetermined. The police agency involved and the state attorney, as I recollect, felt this was a homicide. And so they wanted to find somebody else that would examine the child and see if they could come to a different conclusion.

Marshall: Do you know who preformed the second autopsy on Andrew Schwarz's body?

Benz: Yes. A pathologist by the name of Dr. Burton, I believe, in Atlanta.

Dr. Benz explained how, after conducting his autopsy on A.J.'s body on May 3, 1993, he came to the conclusion that the manner of death was undetermined.

"First of all, the child had evidence of having sustained child abuse somewhere in the past. Meaning he had bruises and things about his head and back and buttocks and so forth. He had a number of bruises that couldn't be readily explained by anything other than child abuse.

"Secondly, there was a history of child abuse—an alleged history of a history of alleged child abuse—by, I think, it was both parents—the father and the stepmother.

"And thirdly, the cause of death in my opinion was drowning.

"Understand that in my opinion the majority of the injuries that were present on his body were older injuries—a day or older than a day—other than some minor things."

He stated that he couldn't detect any significant trauma that was recent or that couldn't be explained by resuscitation efforts.

"And yet there wasn't any reasonable story or explanation in my opinion as to why this child was in the swimming pool and what exactly happened to him. There were certainly a lot—not a lot—but there were some suspicious circumstances.

"So you've got several things you can do. One is just pend the case, but eventually you're going to have to sign a death certificate.

"It was my opinion the child drowned and I couldn't come to any acceptable conclusion in my mind as to whether this was an accident or a homicide or even a suicide, although I thought that was a very remote possibility."

He explained that in order to complete a death certificate—"for the purpose of estates could be closed and things of that nature"—he completed the death certificate with the manner of death listed as "undetermined."

It was Dr. Benz's opinion—within a reasonable degree of medical certainty—that none of the bruises or injuries that he observed on the body of Andrew Schwarz were sufficient in and of themselves to cause his death.

"I didn't feel I had enough information to explain what exactly had happened to this child."

Marshall: And did you feel justified, based on having done the autopsy of Andrew Schwarz's body, to call his death a homicide?
Benz: No. If I would have, I would have so certified.
Marshall: Did you find any indication that Andrew Schwarz was gagged or tied up when he drowned?
Benz: No, I didn't find anything that suggested that.
Marshall: Did you find anything suggesting that Andrew Schwarz was physically held in the pool?

Benz: Not to my satisfaction—no.

Marshall: What would you have looked for?

Benz: You're talking about a ten-year-old boy. If somebody is going to take a ten-year-old boy and hold him submerged in the pool, you're going to have a struggle. You're going to have a fight on your hand[s]. You expect to see more damage. Then you track the more obvious things. He's in the backyard, there are neighbors, and this is one-thirty at night. You would expect to hear a struggle and I'm told nobody heard anything unusual.

Marshall: The information [that you received] is basically what was attached to your autopsy report, as it related to the investigation of facts that were supplied to you by the sheriff's office? That's the only information that was ever supplied to you?

Benz: I read the newspaper. I got newspaper clippings. There were suspicions about the case and so forth.

Marshall: Were there any taped statements of any witnesses provided to you—any police reports provided to you with statements of witnesses included?

Benz: All I got here is a report from South County Mental Health Center.

Marshall: What do you see your duty as being—[as] a medical examiner?

Benz: To investigate the death and, in those cases where an autopsy is required, do an autopsy, record, and document the findings, issue a death certificate.

Marshall: And as it relates to Andrew Schwarz—it's your opinion that this was not a homicide in the case of Andrew Schwarz?

Benz: No—I said it's undetermined. I didn't know whether it was or not.

Marshall: Your position is still that it's undetermined?

Benz: Right.

Marshall: So are you saying—just based on the medical

evidence—within the reasonable degree of medical probability, you didn't feel justified in calling this a homicide?

Benz: Not from the information that I have—no.

Marshall: And do you know whether or not there was any other information contained in Dr. Burton's report that's different from your report—in terms of actual medical findings?

Benz: Well, initially he received a lot more information than I had.

Marshall: Were you asked to look over any of this additional information by the state attorney to make a determination as to whether or not your position would change?

Benz: It's my position [that] the purpose of the medical examiner's office is to—by the laws of this state—determine the cause of death. Whether or not there's a crime involved or not is under the purview of the law enforcement agency—not this office. This office is not in the [business] of "playing Quincy" and go out and do our own individual investigation to see if a crime has been committed. That's in the purview of the law enforcement. So we try to stay out of that purposefully, so we don't conflict with the law enforcement agency that's conducting the investigation.

Now, in his report, Dr. Burton tended to advise the opinion that it was the duty of the medical examiner to see that justice was done—or some statement like that—which sounds great in the press and in the media. But I see nothing in the Florida statute concerning the medical examiner's office that relate to that issue.

Marshall: You don't see that as your duty—to see to it that justice is done?

Benz: No. I think it's more the duty of this office to do a careful and complete examination, tend to documentations, and to come to the best conclusions you can. But you work in conjunction with law enforcement agencies or various other agencies to gain information that will help you come to a logical conclusion, which you hope is the correct conclusion.

On cross-examination, Cupp asked the medical examiner if he had any problem with the concept—or the idea—that a second autopsy is done in a case.

Benz: Oh, there are a lot of cases that we'll do second autopsies.

Cupp: Do you mean by a separate pathologist?

Benz: Yes.

Cupp: This is something that's accepted in the medical examiner's field?

Benz: Yes.

Cupp: Happens quite a bit?

Benz: When I write a report [or when] you dictate a report, you know it's going to be reviewed and questioned. And in the same way in this state, the prosecutor has the ability if he wants somebody to do a particular autopsy—he can supersede the medical examiner to have it done someplace else. It was discussed with me.

Cupp: You had no problem with it up front?

Benz (arrogantly): No problem with it having been done obviously. I don't know how to put it, Mr. Cupp, other than: If you prepared a case for trial and you were all set to go and I said, "Well, I want somebody else to do it because I think somebody else can do a better job, so I'll have somebody else do this." I don't know how you'd feel about that.

Cupp: Did you feel that was said to you here?

Benz: Yes.

Cupp: Who said that?

Benz: Oh, the police.

Cupp: The sheriff's office?

Benz: Yes, oh, sure.

Cupp: Who said that?

Benz: I think there was a conversation. I don't know whether you were in the room or not, but yeah.

Cupp: You're not saying that the state attorney's office—

Benz—his voice rising—interrupted and claimed angrily that the "police" had looked at him and said, "Come on, God-damn it, you know this woman killed the kid. Goddamn it, you know that. What the hell's wrong with you? You know that!"

Cupp—struggling to maintain his composure as sprays of little "spitballs" flew from Benz's mouth and actually landed on him—feigned sincerity and asked mockingly, "Who said that?"

Benz admitted that he didn't know exactly who had said it—only that it was "one of the cops" who had said it "in a similar manner."

Cupp inquired, "I was present for that?"

Cupp said it as though he wasn't sure himself if he was at the meeting or not, and his tone implied, "Hmmm, I must have missed that."

As the doctor launched into a lengthy answer to the simple question, Scott Cupp stayed calm and tried not to react, in the hope that Benz would bury himself deeper.

"I don't know who was there. There was several police, a couple of my examiner assistants. My investigators are here—they remember. And my point is, it's not the purpose of this office to arrive at conclusions for the purposes of convicting someone of a crime. That's not the purpose of this office.

"I find that rather abrasive for a police officer to make that type of a statement in the first place. My reply to him was, yes, there was no doubt there was a lot of information alleging that these people had been abusive to that child.

"There were indeed a lot of physical findings on the body that tended to support that this child had been abused. But I found nothing that would allow me to think that this child had been murdered, and therefore I still to date have a number of unanswered questions.

"Here's a ten-year-old child. Why is he outside walking his dog at one-thirty—unsupervised? Does he do that often? Why is he in the pool? How'd he get in the pool? The father said he had to get the ladder to put it up against the pool and so forth.

"So there's a lot of unanswered questions. The whole thing just sounds hokey—or whatever word you want to use to try and describe it. There are too many unanswered questions. [There] just is not a clear-cut explanation as to how and why this ten-year-old boy came to his death by drowning in a pool. And there you have it.

"His findings are consistent with drowning, coupled with the information that he is found at the bottom of a swimming pool, your conclusion is that he drowned.

"Now, there are many things that could have happened to this child that might be different than what is laid out in front of me at this time. But as I say, that requires police investigation, not medical examiner investigation. Was there a crime committed? Who did it? And so forth.

"And then [there is] my opinion that this is not in the purview of this office and that indeed if this office provided that course, then we're treading into an area where it's a law enforcement agency and you're going to cross wires and there's going to be a lot of difficulties. It's going to create more difficulties than it's going to solve problems.

"Obviously we have to work with police and they get information, which they provide us. We get information, which we provide them. But most of the time—approximately ninety-five to ninety-eight percent of the time—the facts that are derived tend to support a conclusion [that] is acceptable to both people.

"In this case, obviously my conclusion [is] that I don't know how this child came to drown somewhere between one-thirty and six-thirty in the morning.

"You have a lot of unanswered questions for me and somebody may have the answers to all these questions. I assume they have sufficient answers to the question[s] because they're taking somebody up on a murder charge, and I presume for that they have a lot of facts to provide answers to the questions.

"But again that isn't in my purview, that's the state attorney's office purview. So I don't ask what they are—that's fine. The information that's been provided to me—these are my conclusions on them—and I have no reason to change them now."

Cupp: And I'm not asking you to. Could I get back to my original question? I just want to make sure that I'm clear. At the beginning of your last answer, you stated that you felt like you were—that the law enforcement officer was telling you he didn't like your results, so we're going to get a second autopsy?

Benz: Well, you're either saying that or they're saying we're going to find somebody who will be willing to state this is a homicide—and apparently you did.

Cupp: As you sit here today, do you feel that the state attorney's office was responsible for that or law enforcement?

Benz: Well, it's hard to say because you both came together to discuss it.

Cupp: Getting back to the contact you referred to with one of the law enforcement folks, but you don't recall which one it was. Did you feel threatened by that?

Benz: Not threatened—a little surprised.

Cupp: Did you take it that he was trying to influence you to—

Benz: Oh, yeah. I took it that he was trying to influence me.

Cupp: Did you report that to any of his supervisors?

Benz: No, he's rendering his opinion—fine.

Cupp: There's a difference. That was pretty strong. Wouldn't you agree there's a difference between rendering an opinion and threatening someone?

Benz: I didn't take it as a threat to me. He wasn't threatening me. I think what he was stating was a strong opinion as to how he felt about it and he may have had more information that I did. He may have interviewed these people and had formulated some feelings.

He obviously had forgotten that Scott Cupp had been present at the entire meeting, so Cupp knew Benz was lying about the yelling and intimidation—which made him even angrier at the medical examiner's behavior. Cupp had endured being roared at—and spit at—about an event that had never occurred. He wanted to stand up and yell back and push him out of his face. It made him go from fearing Benz's appearance at the murder trial to patiently planning for it—and eagerly anticipating it. Cupp wanted not just to neutralize him, but to show him to be a liar.

Cupp: Do you feel like you've been withheld information on this case by law enforcement or any other source?
Benz: Not necessarily, no.
Cupp: The reason I ask is your answer to one of Mr. Marshall's questions. You refer to Dr. Burton's report—that it appeared he had additional information that you didn't have. I might have misheard that. Did you feel he had additional information that you did not have?
Benz: Oh, yeah.
Cupp: Can you cite any of that?
Benz: He seemed to have the details as to what happened that night or some story in more detail than what I had—that I recollect.
Cupp: So you felt like you were given—I don't want to say inadequate, but . . . incomplete information?
Benz: No, I think they gave me what information they knew at the time. But this situation with Burton, this went on for—his report's in August. I mean, you're talking about he had phone calls, he had other stuff people were providing him with, other information all the way up

through August before he finally got around to getting a report to you.

Cupp: Yeah, I guess that's what I'm trying to get at. What additional information, regardless of what time he got it, do you feel that he received that you—for whatever reason—weren't provided?

Benz: I don't have any other comment on that.

On redirect, when Marshall asked the medical examiner if he could give a physical description of the police officer whom he had referred to—the one who had tried to influence his opinion. Benz replied, "No, I don't think so."

As Cupp walked to his car after the deposition, he thought, *Remember this—don't ever forget.* He was no longer even a little intimidated by Benz and his "expertise." He knew now that—for whatever reason—the medical examiner was willing to do whatever he could to beat him and defeat the case.

On Friday, May 27, 1994, tragedy and heartbreak shattered ASA Joe Marx's family as only violent and sudden death can. Joe's wife, Karen Starr Marx, also an attorney, was shot to death while filling in for a colleague at a pretrial deposition in a courtroom in Fort Lauderdale.

Their law firm represented the American Association of Retired Persons (AARP) in a lawsuit filed by sixty-eight-year-old Julio Mora against AARP and Clarence Rudolph, the director of the Broward County AARP.

Mora, a former employee of the AARP and representing himself, was sure that he had been illegally fired from his job. When the deposition was almost finished, he pulled a 9mm semiautomatic pistol from his briefcase, shot and killed fifty-six-year-old Clarence Rudolph, his former boss. He then turned the gun on Rudolph's attorney, forty-six-year-old Maurice Hall, and thirty-year-old Karen Starr Marx.

Hall was wounded in the abdomen and shoulder and survived the attack.

Karen Starr Marx died of her injuries a short while later. She was four months pregnant with the couple's first child.

Joe Marx was preparing to walk out the door of his office, on his way to a baseball game with his best friend, when he received the phone call that devastated his life.

After her death, Joe wasn't sure he would be able to continue with his participation in Jessica Schwarz's prosecution. When his friends gave him some excellent advice—not to quit his job or sell his house or make any other major decisions right away—he took some time off.

"It was the suddenness. You wake up one day—and you're preparing to get your extra room ready for a new baby—and the next thing you know, you're alone. I just felt like my whole world was collapsing—it really rocked my foundation. My family was great. The funeral was huge. I had a lot of friends and a lot of people behind me, but it was really difficult to think about doing anything important at that time—any important work."

After about two months—as the trial date loomed on the horizon—Joe "pulled himself together" and returned to work. He had invested so much time over the previous year leading up to the trial—arguing many of the motions, taking most of the depositions, and developing relationships with the witnesses—that he felt a very real commitment.

When all was said and done, he knew in his heart that his beloved wife, who often worked on behalf of children as a volunteer for the guardian ad litem's office, would want him to complete the task that he had started—to help with, and carry through with, the prosecution of Jessica Schwarz.

CHAPTER 11

I owe it to every kid who has ever been afraid to close his eyes at night or who has ever had to crawl beneath the tightening grip of weak men and women who would cause them harm. I owe it to every parent who would rather die for their kids than inflict the physical and mental scars of wicked words and degrading gestures—of closed fists and closed minds. I owe it to the public at large because they are demanding accountability for A.J.'s death. I owe it to my family and friends. And I owe it to A.J. May this trial earn him a grain of peace.

—Scott Cupp

The case against Jessica Schwarz was a testament to teamwork, persistence, and dedication. The man-hours alone were daunting—thousands of them, to be sure. The number of people unleashed by the state attorney's office and sheriff's office on a case as critical to the judicial process as this one—the witnesses that were questioned and the miles that were walked—was impressive. Scott Cupp was proud to be a part of it.

Yet—in the end—the strategy and the tactical plan upon which the case was founded was the responsibility of just one man—and Scott Cupp was that man. There had to be a decision maker—the very nature of the business dictated it. Make or break—that was where they were headed.

Cupp liked the pressure and thrived on the intensity. He took pride in seeing beyond the mountains of paperwork to the heart of the matter. He enjoyed dissecting the various—and often conflicting—viewpoints of the team, and piecing together the fabric of what he saw as most relevant. He absorbed energy and enthusiasm from the mounting scrutiny of the press and the ever-present political machine.

The case against Jessica Schwarz was not based on physical abuse. He would not seize upon every abrasion or laceration—nor every unsightly bruise.

He would focus on the mental abuse that led to the physical abuse. He would let the jury see the kind of woman who would force a nine-year-old boy to wear a T-shirt with the words "I'm a worthless piece of shit, don't talk to me" written across the front of it. He would paint a picture of a woman who would berate her stepson in public, screaming at the top of her lungs and calling him hateful, despicable names. And—with each word—she ate away at a mind so perilously fragile that the boy would spend hours just staring into space.

The only question was how the civilian witnesses would do on the stand—especially the kids. There's never any guarantee of how a witness will come across to the jurors. This is especially true of children. One of the worst feelings for a prosecutor was sitting in the courtroom watching a child slowly—during cross-examination—recant everything they just said on direct.

But Scott Cupp was ready. He loved big trials, and this would be a big one. The eyes of South Florida would be focused on the proceedings, knowing that the outcome would cause judicial and legal ripples in every city and town where child abuse occurred.

He knew he owed his best to the men and women who had "busted their tails" for nearly sixteen months—bringing it all together.

Jessica Schwarz's trial on the abuse charges was scheduled to start on Monday, August 22, 1994. Rendell Brown had filed a motion for a change of venue and, that morning, argued that Jessica could not get a fair trial because of the pretrial publicity.

Palm Beach County circuit judge Walter Colbath temporarily denied the motion until it could be shown whether or not an unbiased jury could be seated.

As it turned out, at the end of the day on Tuesday, a panel of six impartial jurors—three women and three men—had been selected to decide her fate.

It was dawn on Wednesday, August 24, 1994, when Cupp left home. According to pretrial ritual that had evolved over the years, the office was deserted when he arrived. He made coffee, put in a tape and turned up the volume, and concentrated on his opening statement. He never relied on notes but had scribbled some random thoughts on a half sheet of paper that wouldn't even make it out of his briefcase. The general thrust of the statement had been written in his head for days.

When his colleagues at CAC started to arrive, he closed his door. With the exception of Joe Marx, there was an unwritten "Do Not Disturb" sign on the door. It wasn't anything personal—he just couldn't afford to engage in idle chatter.

There's an edge that comes with the art of prosecution—and he knew he couldn't afford to go anywhere near a courtroom minus that edge. But the truth was—nothing could have stolen Cupp's edge that day. Not with this case.

Marx and Cupp arrived at the courthouse early. It was an old building—all wood and marble with high ceilings. The reporters were waiting, but most of them were savvy enough not to ask questions the prosecutors would have to sidestep or straight-out ignore. Cupp heard a "good luck" or two and nodded in reply.

They made their way to courtroom 445. The room was packed—spectators, reporters, family members, friends, and enemies. This was a big-time media trial and heightened security had been implemented—two extra guards, which meant two more guns, and two extra sets of eyes. Cupp hoped, as he touched base with the bailiff, the clerk, and the court reporter, that they wouldn't be needed.

Marx took a seat behind the table closest to the jury box and opposite the table reserved for the defense, and when Cupp finished making his rounds, he joined him.

Cupp ignored the gallery and the swell of whispers as Jessica Schwarz was escorted to her place at the defense table. Her lawyers had her wearing a bright-colored, flower-printed dress that looked out of place and contrived. Cupp couldn't decide whether they were going for the *Little House on the Prairie* look or Andy Griffith's Aunt Bea, but he hoped the jury would see through the deception. It was too bad that they wouldn't get to see her wearing her "Cops Are Pigs" T-shirt.

There was no question that Rendell Brown would be a worthy adversary; Scott Cupp had learned that well—first-hand. When Cupp was a new felony prosecutor, he and Brown had been opponents in a heroin possession and sale case, and he had actually been relieved when the judge put him out of his misery by dismissing the case.

Brown's long, scraggly gray-and-white beard—plus the fact that a couple of his front teeth were missing—made him look ten years older than his fifty years.

His overall appearance was one of a wise old owl, and he had a way of speaking that was unique. For example, he always pronounced the word "says" with a long *a,* instead of "sez." Anyone else doing that would—no doubt—sound stupid, but with Rendell it sounded learned.

He was also skilled in making up words. Early in the trial, he accused Judge Colbath of "vamping" him in front of the jury. Colbath's response was an incredulous and somewhat annoyed "What?" Never one to be nonplussed, Rendell repeated it like they were all idiots. They guessed he meant "disrespected," but a later check in the dictionary found no meaning for "vamp" that would have come close to fitting the occasion. With Rendell, they never knew what they were going to get.

Scott Cupp didn't know Sam Marshall very well, but his handling of the witness depositions hadn't impressed him; but he was Rendell's partner, and that spoke volumes.

A moment later, the bailiff stood and issued the customary "All rise!" The judge who entered the courtroom was the Honorable Walter Colbath. At fifty-eight, he was a physically imposing ex-marine who—by all accounts—had seen his share of combat in Korea.

There was a shift in the atmosphere of the courtroom with the appearance of the judge, and then the jury.

Cupp knew everything about the jurors—where they worked, what they did for fun, their families, their backgrounds, their likes and dislikes, their prejudices, and their proclivities. He studied their expressions, their dress, and their postures.

He believed if there was one thing a jury deserved, it's respect. Lose them on that account and he risked losing his case on that singular failing alone.

The jury was sworn in. Cupp's eyes moved across their faces: solemn, sincere, and uncertain. Who wouldn't be? His worry was not that the prosecution wouldn't be able to prove the charges against Jessica Schwarz—the evidence was overwhelming. Eyewitness testimony would validate all seven counts in such graphic terms that there would be no doubt. His fear was that the jury would not grasp the devastating effect the degrading, debilitating abuse had perpetrated—over a period of three years—upon the psyche of a child.

But Cupp would not allow himself to think that society had become that hardened. He had to believe that breaking the spirit of a ten-year-old boy—that twisting his mind—that battering his body—was deserving of quick and sure justice and the punishment that went with it.

Cupp could feel the blood pumping as the clerk announced the case: the *State of Florida* vs. *Jessica Schwarz*. The charges were read: Two counts of felony child abuse and five counts of aggravated child abuse. Jessica's trial on the charges of second degree murder and witness tampering hadn't yet been scheduled, but Cupp knew full well that the outcome of that trial would hinge in great measure on the outcome of this one.

Not surprisingly, Because of the unusual circumstances of the case, Judge Walter Colbath read the following instruction to the jury:

"The constitution of the state of Florida requires the state to prove its accusations against the defendant beyond a reasonable doubt. In doing so, it is not necessary for the state to present any testimony of the alleged victim, Andrew Schwarz.

"In this case, the alleged victim has become deceased and therefore, of course, is not available to offer testimony.

"The state and the defense attorneys have stipulated that the alleged victim, Andrew Schwarz, did not give his consent to the defendant to commit any criminal offenses against him and, therefore, you must not view failure to present testimony of the alleged victim as any consent on his part.

"You should further know that none of the circumstances or events which ultimately led to his death have anything to do [with] and are totally immaterial and irrelevant to the issues in this case.

"Do you-all understand that?"

The jurors indicated that they did, in fact, understand.

In his opening remarks, Judge Colbath made it clear that this was his courtroom, where his rules applied, and he wasn't about to tolerate any demonstrations or outbursts of any kind, and anyone who wanted to tempt those rules would be unceremoniously shown to the door.

When the judge had created the mood he was looking for, he gave Scott Cupp the floor.

As he stepped to the lectern, Cupp knew he would keep his opening remarks short and precise—twenty minutes. He was not going to waste the jury's time telling them what Jessica did. He would show them what she did with the evidence presented over the course of the trial.

He began with the customary "May it please the court. Mr. Brown. Mr. Marshall." Then he faced the jury and said, "Good morning, ladies and gentlemen."

The show of courtesy was a matter of protocol and good manners.

As he spoke, he looked each and every juror in the eye; and the genuine sincerity that he felt—after living this case for over a year—was reflected there.

His plan was to introduce an authority figure that the jurors, given their collective backgrounds, could identify with: someone of impeccable character, and—not coincidentally—the prosecution's first witness.

He promised them that they would hear A.J.'s third-grade teacher, Mary Idrissi, testify about her first meeting with Jessica Schwarz, at an open house for her students and their parents.

"Mrs. Idrissi will tell you that that meeting left an indelible impression on her.

"She will tell you that Mrs. Schwarz insisted that Andrew not be given any schoolbooks. You'll learn that Mrs. Schwarz would not sign the book verification sheet given to all parents that night. Why? Because Andrew had lost his books once before, and Mrs. Schwarz had refused to pay for them, and she wasn't about to sign this year. She told Mrs. Idrissi that if she were a good teacher, she would be wise to Andrew. That he was a liar. That he was dishonest. That she didn't trust him and he was sneaky.

"She said that he was not getting any school supplies because he didn't know how to take care of them. That he would never know how to take care of them. She reiterated to Mrs. Idrissi that Andrew was a very bad boy."

Cupp's eyes moved from one juror to the next.

"At that time, ladies and gentlemen of the jury, Andrew was all of nine years old."

He paused, letting that sink in.

"And where was Andrew while the defendant was calling him a liar? Calling him dishonest? Calling him a very bad boy?

"Well, you see, Andrew was standing right next to her—hearing every word—his eyes averted, saying nothing.

"This was his introduction to his new teacher."

Cupp spoke evenly. The calm had a purpose. He wanted to let the story create the emotion—to let the words reinforce the indictment.

"Andrew J. Schwarz was born to Ilene and David Schwarz in April of 1983. After his parents separated, Andrew stayed with his mother and his half sister Patsy.

"There were domestic problems. When the problems escalated, fate took a hand and Patsy and Andrew were removed from the house and placed with Andrew's biological father, David, and the defendant, Jessica Schwarz."

Cupp allowed the jurors a moment to glance in Jessica's direction—to get a look at the smugness on her face—to view the contempt that lay just below the surface.

"The defendant and David Schwarz had a younger daughter named Jackie. Mrs. Schwarz had a daughter from a previous marriage named Lauren Cross. Lauren was older than Andrew by two years—and the same age as Patsy.

"Andrew and Patsy arrived at the defendant's home in October of 1990."

Cupp informed the jury that the case that would be presented to them dealt with the time period between October 1990 and May 1993. He took a deep breath and then introduced them to A.J.

"So, who was this child that the defendant called a liar and a sneak? Well, as the school year progressed, Mrs. Idrissi will tell you that she noticed several things and she noticed them rather quickly. Right from the beginning, she noticed that Andrew was starved for attention. That he was constantly seeking her out for hugs and reassurance. In fact, she will tell you that the rest of the class eventually became so used to the steady progression of Andrew parading to and from his desk that they took it for granted. His attention span, she'll tell you, may have been short, but he was one of the most affectionate kids in her class.

"The other thing that became clear to Mrs. Idrissi—as the year progressed—was that Andrew was missing an inordinate amount of school. How many days? Forty-two out of one hundred."

Cupp allowed these numbers to sink in. Even he had trouble comprehending the astonishing number of days that A.J. was absent from school.

"You will come to find out that Mrs. Schwarz felt that Mrs. Idrissi was spoiling Andrew with all of this attention—with all of this support—with all of these hugs—with all of this encouragement. That what he needed—according to the defendant—was more punishment. That he needed more things taken away.

"In fact, the evidence will show that Mrs. Schwarz was withholding Andrew from school as a means of punishment. School was fast becoming Andrew's one safe place and she began to take that away from him."

Cupp opened his hand in the direction of the defendant and silently invited the jury to view the woman who would do such a thing.

"Things degenerated to the point that—during a face-to-face meeting between Mrs. Idrissi and the defendant—the defendant referred to Mrs. Idrissi as a maggot and a trouble-maker and a cause for much of the problems with Andrew."

Cupp turned and looked at Jessica and the jurors followed suit.

"What Mrs. Idrissi didn't know was that she was seeing only the tip of the iceberg. She didn't know of the litany of malicious and sadistic punishments that A.J.—as his friends would call him—was forced to endure at the mouth and hands of Jessica Schwarz."

The prosecutor turned his attention back to the jurors as he told them that several neighbors would take the witness stand and testify to the atrocities they had seen and heard at the Schwarz household.

As he recited some of the profanities they had heard, Cupp circled the courtroom for a moment. He didn't want the obscene words to cause the jurors embarrassment. The reaction he wanted was disgust. And outrage.

"James Ebenhack, a Palm Beach County fire rescue worker, lived in such close proximity to the defendant that he will come in here and tell you that he distinctly remembers hearing the defendant scream at A.J., 'I hate your fucking guts! You're a useless piece of shit!'"

There was a hum in the air as Cupp continued, "Patsy Spence—Andrew's half sister—lived in the defendant's home with A.J. from October of 1990 until February of 1992. In the beginning, Patsy will tell you, she shared a room with the defendant's older daughter, Lauren. She will tell you that things went along pretty well for a while, but eventually she was ordered out of Lauren's room and into A.J.'s room. She was forced to share a room with her younger brother.

"You will hear descriptions of the absolute barrenness of that room. But perhaps most chilling, you will hear a view from inside the asylum that only Patsy had—that only Patsy witnessed.

"This is what she saw the defendant do to A.J. . . ."

Cupp paused and took in the jury—one member after another.

". . . Because, you see, by now this little boy—Patsy's brother—had developed a bed-wetting problem. Imagine that."

Scott Cupp did not even attempt to keep the sarcasm out of his voice as he continued.

"And, of course, the natural reaction one would have to this—the way one would think to cure this—would be to take the child's face and nose and rub it into those urine-soaked sheets. That is what Patsy observed. The defendant rubbing A.J.'s face in sheets soaked with urine. . . ."

Cupp could feel the heat rolling up the back of his neck, and he took a moment to fill his lungs. He realized—listening to the room—that he wasn't the only one. He turned his eyes toward the front of the courtroom, and there was Colbath—with a look as hard as granite on his face—surely recognizing that this trial would cause ripples that would stretch far beyond the Fifteenth Judicial Circuit of Palm Beach County.

Cupp turned his attention back to the jury.

"The prosecution will also call Dr. George Rahaim, a local psychologist for the state's Child Protection Team. Dr. Rahaim will be allowed to render opinions as to the psychological effects of child abuse. He will also explain to you— in terms that we can all understand—the type of mental injury that these events caused Andrew."

Cupp looked at the jurors and knew that he had timed it just about right.

He concluded, "After all the evidence in this case has been presented to you, I'll have a chance—as well as Mr. Marx—to address you. At that time, we will talk to you about returning a proper and just verdict in this case, a verdict we believe you will find—beyond all reasonable doubt—to be guilty as charged.

"At this time, I thank you for your courtesy and your attention and your patience with all of us and ask you to pay the same courtesy to Mr. Brown."

Scott Cupp held their eyes for a moment; then he retreated to the prosecution table. It was a good start. He could feel it.

Judge Colbath then called upon Rendell Brown to make his opening statement.

"As His Honor most aptly explained to you, this is Mr. Cupp's and my version of what we expect the evidence will show in this case, and while we're trying to give you a road map, this—what we say to you—is not to be accepted as fact. The facts will come from the witness stand.

"Of course, if what our notions of what the evidence would divulge were the same, you'd not be here. We would not be here.

"But this is what we expect and know the evidence will show in this case:

"Jessica Schwarz was born and reared in Long Island,

New York, with a sister. Her father was an executive with a shipping company. Jessica was educated in New York.

"Sometime in her childhood, she was struck by the bug of driving a truck and made it clear to her father that that was her station in life. She wanted to be a truck driver.

"She bought a rig—in the language—and began to drive the rig to earn a living [right] out of high school. She married a trucker. They had a daughter, a daughter from whom you will hear. The marriage didn't work out.

"In the meantime, a person unknown to Jessica, David Schwarz, was married to a lady named Ilene and living in the Fort Lauderdale area. They, too, had a child—a second child for Ilene Schwarz, as she had a daughter, Patsy Spence, about whom you've heard and I'll tell you a little more about that.

"Patsy became the stepdaughter of David Schwarz in the marriage with Ilene. Together they had a child—Andrew Schwarz.

"As with Jessica Schwarz's [first] marriage, Ilene and David Schwarz's marriage did not work. They, too, were divorced. Ilene retained custody of Patsy, David Schwarz's stepdaughter, and Andrew Schwarz, their common son.

"David Schwarz later married Jessica.

"At a point, it became known to HRS and the authorities that some terrible things were going on in Ilene's household. Andrew Schwarz and Patsy Spence were taken from Ilene and given into the custody of a maternal aunt, a sister of Ilene.

"The maternal aunt kept these children for a short time, [then] called HRS and said, 'Hey, you've got to come get these kids out of my home.'

"David was contacted and asked if he would take custody of the children and, of course, he spoke with his wife and asked her how she felt about that. And Jessica Schwarz—there are two things she loves dearly, children and animals. And so her response was 'Sure, we'll keep both of them.'

"Now, Patsy Spence, mind you, is not the child of either David or Jessica.

"No one from HRS told Mrs. Schwarz—or David, for that matter—the depth of the problems of these children and particularly Andrew Schwarz. All they knew was that both kids were in counseling and Jessica had to take these children to counseling on a weekly basis.

"She did this, but no one told her what was really going on with Andrew, what had really happened to Andrew, and the depth of his problem."

Brown explained to the jurors that Jessica's mother had been keeping her granddaughter Lauren; but after the Schwarzes were settled in their home, Lauren came to live with her mother and stepfather. He also mistakenly told them that Jessica was pregnant with Jackie when A.J. and Patsy came to live with them. In actuality, Jackie was two years old at the time.

"Jackie was to live there. Andrew was to live there. And, of course, Patsy Spence was to live there—because Jessica's idea was that you shouldn't separate these children.

"They brought all of these children into the home. She and David went out, purchased a pool for the children, put it in the backyard so that Jackie and Lauren and Andrew and Patsy could enjoy the swimming pool and yet be in the yard where she could observe them.

"The neighborhood children—the ones that will come in here and tell you all of these horrible things—practically camped out at Jessica Schwarz's home.

"Now, you will—from time to time—learn that there were problems where the kids got upset with Jessica, because Jessica—and we make no bones about that—Jessica is a mother of tough love and tender mercies. She's a disciplinarian. 'When you're in my home, in my yard, you do it my way. You act as a child should act or you've got to go.'

"And that created some little problems—and you'll hear about the problems and the results of the problems from the children—as well as from their parents—as they come in here with their concocted stories, under oath, having to tell the truth and the whole truth, as Mr. Cupp said.

"And we talked to you on voir dire about a trucker's language. Jessica doesn't talk like a Sunday-school teacher—she doesn't. That's Jessica. When it is on her mind, she says it. It's over—we're on with it. Maybe it's not the way you would react or I would react—but it's Jessica.

"You're going to have another witness come in and say he heard Jessica Schwarz say, 'I hate his (A.J.'s) fucking guts.' So she's going to keep him at home to punish him? You'll have to decide whether that fits.

"Some of Jessica's neighbors—their response was to send HRS to Jessica's house. But, thank God, they did, because HRS has to keep records. And when HRS went to the home, they had to write the date, what they observed, and they also did it without—for the most part—without alerting her. In other words, just all of a sudden, they are at the door. And what did they find? Unfounded.

"And they didn't go by themselves. They went with a trained police officer. And they didn't talk to the kids in front of Jessica. They took them off [by] themselves—took walks with the children. No evidence. No evidence of any abuse. This is unfounded—unfounded. It wasn't happening. It did not happen. It did not happen."

Rendell Brown concluded, "Ladies and gentlemen, I think you have a broad overview of what the facts are going to be. Let me stop boring you and let you hear for yourself. I think once you've heard the facts, you'll do the right thing. And the only right thing will be to return a verdict of not guilty in this case.

"Thank you very much."

CHAPTER 12

Jessica is a mother of tough love and tender mercies.

—Rendell Brown

A.J. Schwarz's third-grade teacher, Mary Idrissi, was the first witness for the prosecution. The dark-haired, bespectacled woman was the mother of two teenage children and had been a teacher for over twenty years.

Looking very much the schoolmarm in her flower-printed dress, she reminded Scott Cupp of several of his own teachers from a generation earlier.

Sitting very straight in the witness chair, Mrs. Idrissi explained to the jurors that she first met Andrew at open house at the beginning of the 1992 school year. His stepmother, Jessica Schwarz, accompanied him.

"She came over to me with Andrew. The beginning remarks were that he was a lot of trouble—that if I was a good teacher—a wise teacher—I would recognize that he is a liar. That he's sneaky and don't let him buffalo me; be wise to his tactics and his head games; that he's not to be signed out any textbooks because he loses them and she will not be responsible for them. She continued to tell me what a problem he was, and the whole time this was going on, Andrew was standing right beside us.

"Andrew said nothing. His little eyes never left the floor. He was humiliated."

Cupp: Did she mention anything about school supplies?

Idrissi: Yes, she said that she would not be giving him any—that he loses them or destroys them—and that he would not have anything for school.

Cupp: What did he do for supplies?

Idrissi: I gave him his supplies.

Cupp: You spent money out of your own pocket?

Idrissi: Not really out of my own pocket, Mr. Cupp. A teacher is given a certain amount of money for supplies every year: crayons, pencils, notebook paper, pencil boxes. Basically, it's things that all teachers have and when Andrew came to my classroom on Monday, I took care of everything he needed.

Cupp: Did you think about it over the weekend?

Idrissi: Yes, extensively. I was very bothered by it—to have an encounter like that the first time I meet a parent. But more than anything, to do that in front of this little child that was so humiliated by it. It was unbelievable that the parent would do that in front of a child.

Cupp: And what happened on Monday—if anything—between you and Andrew?

Idrissi: Well, I was very eager to see Andrew on Monday because I wanted to assure him that I was very happy to have him in my room—that it was going to be a good year and a positive year. And if there was anything he needed, as far as supplies, textbooks, whatever—that I would take care of that. I told him, "You look like a good little boy to me—you don't look like you're any problem. I know we will be good friends."

Mary Idrissi told the jurors that as the year progressed she found Andrew to be very warm and friendly with a sense of humor—but that he was starved for attention and affection.

"Andrew would come to my desk an awful lot. In fact, so

much so that the other children in my classroom just kind of accepted that anytime at all—all through the day—Andrew would be coming to my desk. And the reason I allowed that was that Andrew could not stay on task. He would start a little bit of work and he'd be looking around and just fiddling—not bothering anyone—but just fiddling, not getting the work done.

"So when a teacher sees this off-task behavior going on, she shortens her lesson and checks them constantly. So if we were running spelling words six times each, I would have Andrew write them three times and let him come to my desk and let me see what he'd done well. This was the manner in my classroom. Andrew came to my desk; he would show me his words. I would give him many, many loves, hugs, and squeezes, and he responded to that and he completed his work. He was a very bright boy."

She stated there were about three parties in her classroom between August and December, but that—at the open house—Mrs. Schwarz had instructed her that Andrew was not to go on any field trips or attend any parties.

"He attended none. He attended no field trips or parties. He was absent on those days."

Cupp: Do you know his date of birth?
Idrissi: Yes, it is April 24, 1983.
Cupp: And, if I remember correctly, [in 1993] that was a Saturday. . . . Would that child's special day—so to speak—be the day before?
Idrissi: Yes, it was an honoring day.
Cupp: Was Andrew in school that day?
Idrissi: No, he was not.
Cupp: Let me ask you about the time period of school prior to the Christmas holidays. Did your class participate in any special school activity? What was that called?
Idrissi (crying): That was called "Holiday Shop."

Cupp: Mrs. Idrissi, are you okay?
Idrissi: I'm fine, thank you. I'm all right.

The jurors were asked to step into the jury room for a few minutes.

Mr. Brown (to Judge Colbath): The problem the witness is having—and we are having the problem with the spectators as well. . . . I just ask that you have the spectators—if they are overcome by crying—that they would leave the courtroom, please.
Judge Colbath (addressing the courtroom): I think you all heard what Mr. Brown just said. But, basically, if any of this testimony or any of the other testimony in this case affects you emotionally—to the point where you're visibly or emotionally distressed—please stand up and very quietly leave the courtroom.

After the jury was brought back into the courtroom, Cupp continued his questioning of Idrissi.

"I believe we were beginning to discuss the Holiday Shop?" Cupp resumed.

She explained that the Holiday Shop was an event that took place at her school, in the library, for a two-week period every December. The PTA sponsored it and it was an opportunity for the children to purchase Christmas gifts, Hanukkah gifts, and birthday gifts, at very inexpensive prices.

The teachers would escort their classes to the Holiday Shop and the children would go around with their lists and pick out their gifts and then bring them back to the classrooms. The teachers and the students would then gift wrap the presents before they were taken home.

"And it's a very, very exciting time for the children."

Cupp: Did all of your students participate in Holiday Shop?

Idrissi: Yes, they did—all of them, except Andrew. Andrew was not allowed to go. His stepmother would not allow him to go. He could not go—he did not have any money to go.

Cupp: But at some point, Andrew did participate; is that correct?

Idrissi: Yes, he did. The children don't go just once down to the Holiday Shop; they can go several times. If they keep bringing money in, they are permitted to go. Well, the two weeks was coming toward an end. Andrew had not been—as yet—and so I gave him two dollars to go down. And I told him that he could go and purchase anything he wanted for himself—didn't have to be a gift for home. Just with two dollars, you can buy a lot of nice little things. And what he bought was all for me. It was nothing for himself and I always treasured that—this was characteristic of Andrew.

(What the jury didn't get to hear was that A.J. had confided to his teacher that Jessica had told him, "If you buy anything for me, I would burn it.")

Mrs. Idrissi testified that Andrew walked to school and that he was frequently late.

Idrissi: We do report cards every nine weeks and about midway in that nine-week period, teachers send a progress report. But a lot of teachers send a weekly progress report. I send one every Friday and I, more or less, tell the parent how the child did that week.

Cupp: And did you, on occasion, receive these progress reports back from Andrew with writing on them from the defendant?

Idrissi: Yes, I would.

Cupp: What would be the tone of those responses?

Idrissi: They were usually rude—sarcastic.

Cupp: Could you give us an example?

Idrissi: My report was signaling that Andrew did not
have a snack and asked her to please send something in.
Cupp: What was her response, if any?
Idrissi (referring to a page in a folder): Okay, this is from
Mrs. Schwarz: "A.J. gets a daily snack, but he eats it
on the way to school. Somehow you are so smart and I
am wrong. You fix the snack and the problem; in other
words, known as eating a snack on the way to school.
Your problem—not mine. Oh, well." That was a frequent comment made to me: "Oh, well, your problem—
not mine."

Scott Cupp was certain that the reason A.J. ate his snack
on the way to school—if he even had one—was because he
hadn't had any breakfast.

Cupp: Is it fair to say that the tone of the responses
that you received were consistently negative?
Idrissi: Yes, sir, they were.
Cupp: Was there ever any positive or upbeat response
that you received from the defendant on one of these
progress reports or notes?
Idrissi: Yes, there was. This would have been after the
HRS meeting. The meeting was March the 26th. I'd
say it would probably be the first week after that. If it's
all right, I'd just like to read. It says, "Mrs. I., I love
you taking things away. It really brings the point home
that no one is kidding as far as him being late. He had
twenty-five minutes to get to school, so him being
late—it took him fifty minutes to get to school? No
way. And he's grounded for the weekend and if he is
late again, well, let's just say he's going to cry a lot. He
had 3½, 4 hours last night and still didn't finish his
homework. Like being late, he just doesn't care and
does what he wants. I look forward to him doing his
handwriting over. I've tried. He hasn't done one thing

about it. Boy, this is really working out and I'm sorry I didn't get along with you sooner. Sorry. Thanks. Oh, yes, we've gotten to the point with A.J., since he keeps doing the same things wrong over and over—we're talking years—he gets no breaks, no rewards when he knows better. He loves to play games with people's heads. He's never gotten one over on me; dared his dad once or twice—me, never—and I won't let that change. Beware of lies. Today he left the house at seven-thirty. Unless he's bleeding, no reason on earth he should be late—none."

Cupp: And that's the only response that you could possibly characterize as being positive or upbeat?

Idrissi: I began to, through the request of HRS, go through a series of behavior modifications of a reward system for Andrew. When I sent something home that was negative, the response was "I love you, now you're (in essence) responding to this and because you're now seeing that he lies. I wish I would have cooperated with you from the beginning." Now that a negative comment came home, the first response was, "Mrs. Idrissi, now we really see eye to eye."

Cupp: Did you ever receive—either in writing, over the phone, or face-to-face—any contact with Mrs. Schwarz that indicated, in any way, that she was happy or pleased with anything that Andrew had done?

Idrissi: None.

Cupp: Did she ever praise him?

Idrissi: Not that I ever heard. I never saw a physical touch. I never saw a squeeze or a hug, no.

Cupp: Did she ever support him in any way that you could tell?

Idrissi: She did say in a note back to me that "I'm very glad that Andrew is doing well in school, but he's not at home. He's not doing his chores at home. Therefore, Mrs. Idrissi, you can reward him, but I'm not."

Cupp: When was it that you had a face-to-face meeting with the defendant and there were others present?
Idrissi: My first meeting with other people was at the
HRS meeting on March 26.
Cupp: Did Mrs. Schwarz say anything to you—or about
you—upon entering the room?
Idrissi: Yes, she did. I walked in and she and Mr. Schwarz
were in the room. There was no one in there but the
three of us, and when I walked in, I heard her say to
her husband, loud enough that I could hear it, "Here's
the maggot. This is the woman that causes all the trouble." And her husband laughed at what she said.

Scott Cupp took the witness—month by month—through
A.J.'s attendance record. He established that he was absent
every Thursday, many Mondays, and all party days: he had
missed 42 out of a possible 100. Idrissi stated that there were
very few—if any—notes from home explaining his absences.

She also testified that she had never had a problem with
A.J. vomiting in class.

Cupp (holding up a photograph): Was this Andrew?
Idrissi: Yes, it is.
Cupp: Was that his school picture?
Idrissi: Yes, it is.
Cupp: How old was he when he was in your class?
Idrissi: He was nine.
Cupp: This person that we've been speaking about
throughout the course of your testimony, Jessica Schwarz,
do you see her in the courtroom here today?
Idrissi: Yes, I do.
Cupp: Could you please point to her?

Rendell Brown spoke up quickly and stated, "We'll stipu-
late that the only female at the defense table is Jessica Schwarz."
Brown then rose from his chair to cross-examine the witness.

Brown: Now, ma'am, you testified that you never had any problems with Andrew vomiting—I think was the term Mr. Cupp used—or regurgitating at school. Is that correct?

Idrissi: Yes.

Brown: And isn't it also true, ma'am, that you never administered the drug imipramine to Andrew Schwarz?

Idrissi: I'm not allowed to administer any drug, sir.

Brown: Do you know what imipramine is?

Idrissi: No, I do not.

When Mr. Brown prodded the schoolteacher to "admit to the court and the jury" that there were behavioral problems with Andrew in school, she firmly replied, "Not in my classroom."

The defense attorney then challenged her with an exhibit from her files.

Brown: Did you write at the bottom of that page, "Andrew needs to learn responsibility"? Did you write that?

Idrissi: Yes, I did.

Brown: Okay. Showing you a weekly behavioral report, I'll ask you if you wrote in red ink at the bottom of that? Would you read that—if you wrote it?

Idrissi: Yes, I did. It says, "Excessive talking and playing." I mentioned previously that Andrew was not on task. Not on task is not bad behavior. Andrew was not on task because I felt he was preoccupied with home life.

Brown: You really didn't have to think about the problem because you knew for a fact that Andrew had been in Vero Beach Hospital for six weeks based—just because he had problems. . . . Didn't you know that?

Idrissi: Somewhat.

Brown: Either you knew or you didn't.

Idrissi: I knew about it, but I didn't know the extent of it—but it certainly wasn't bad behavior.

Brown: But you'll agree, Mrs. Idrissi, that you received

a full report from the hospital reference Andrew's stay at the hospital, his problems, and ways to correct them; you'll agree with that, wouldn't you?

Idrissi: I did not receive that.

Brown (handing her a copy of the report): Now, Mrs. Idrissi, if you had seen that, if you had read that, it certainly would have given you some guidance as to how to deal with Andrew Schwarz; isn't that true?

Idrissi: Probably, but I've never seen that.

Brown: And there were step-by-step pronouncements as to what that child needed; do you agree with that?

Idrissi: Just reading it for the first time, I see something going on there. Again, I have not seen that. I have a degree in specific learning disabilities. Children in my school that are not qualified for a program—for whatever reason they didn't meet the criteria—oftentimes the administration puts these children in my classroom because they know I have a degree. I saw no signs of a child with learning disabilities—or [from] what I'm reading on that paper.

Brown: How long did you study to obtain your specialist degree in learning disability?

Idrissi: A year and a half.

Brown: And nothing in your studies prepared you for dealing with a child who had an imbalance of imipramine, did it?

Idrissi: No, it did not.

Brown: And you know from Mrs. Schwarz—among others—that when Andrew left the hospital, he was placed on a heavy dosage of imipramine, don't you?

Idrissi: I do not know that, sir, no. I did not know that he was on it.

Brown: The truth is, Mrs. Idrissi—as relates to you and Mrs. Schwarz—from the very first day, you had a personality conflict, didn't you?

Idrissi: She did not make a very good impression on me.

Brown: You didn't like her, did you?

Idrissi: I won't say I didn't like her. I did not like the way she demeaned and belittled this child standing in front of her. If you were going to talk about your child, whether you're a teacher or a parent—for heaven's sakes, would you do it when the child is in front of you?

Brown (ignoring Idrissi's comments): Isn't it a fact that on more than one occasion—when you sent Andrew's report card home—he signed it himself and brought it back to you? Isn't that true?

Idrissi: Only once he did that, sir, only once.

Brown: When a person does that, what do you call that?

Idrissi: Sir, you're not going to make me make this boy out to be a liar—a bad boy. Not at all.

Brown: I'm only asking you to tell the truth and answer my questions truthfully. I'm not trying to make you make anybody anything. My question is: what do you call it when someone signs their mother's name to their report card and brings it back to school?

Idrissi: I would call it he's afraid to show it to his mom.

Brown: Oh, I see. And there is no question that Andrew did that?

Idrissi: Yes, he did that, once.

Brown: You described Andrew as being warm and friendly?

Idrissi: Yes.

Brown: Isn't it a fact that Andrew had few—if any—friends in that entire school; isn't that true?

Idrissi: Totally false—totally false. He was loved by everyone. He was very well liked—very, very well liked. He had a sense of humor; he played all the games outside that my children played. He was never off by himself. He was very well liked, sir.

Brown: And I think you said earlier, there's no way I'm going to make you say anything negative about Andrew; that's basically what we're dealing with, isn't it?

Scott Cupp objected, "That's a misstatement of the answer and it's an unfair question."

Judge Colbath replied, "Well, I think it's a little argumentative. I'll sustain the objection."

With that, the cross-examination was completed, and Scott Cupp started the redirect examination:

Cupp: Did you get the impression—from your dealings with Andrew—that he was afraid of something or someone at his home?

Idrissi: Yes, I did.

Cupp: And is it fair to say the problems that Andrew had, they didn't create any kind of barrier with you and he and his learning?

Idrissi: No.

Cupp: You were able to have him learn?

Idrissi: Yes, he did learn.

Cupp: But he had a short attention span?

Idrissi: Yes, he did. He did short assignments. When he did that little assignment, he brought it to my desk, [and] I checked it over. I praised him; I complimented him; I hugged him; I gave him stickers.

Cupp: You touched him a lot?

Idrissi: Oh, yes, a lot.

Cupp: Did you kiss him on the cheek and on the forehead?

Idrissi: Many times.

Cupp: Did he ever return in kind?

Idrissi: Oh, yes. He was very affectionate, very warm.

Cupp: Could you describe Andrew's outward appearance when he would arrive at school?

Idrissi: He was very thin. I saw many bruises on him—a lot of bruising on elbows and knees and across the forehead. I found him to be extremely thin. He was wearing a lot of clothes that were too big for him, oversize clothes.

Cupp: What about his emotional state or his outward demeanor?

Idrissi: Well, other than the daydreaming, being off task, he was happy to be in school. He loved to be in school. He loved to be with the children. The minute he would come in the room, he would come right to my desk. He was very, very happy being in school.

Cupp: It's fair to say you liked Andrew?

Idrissi: Very much.

In his recross-examination of the witness, Rendell Brown tried to get Mary Idrissi to admit that the bruises that she had seen on Andrew's knees and elbows were typical of the bruises one might see on "most little third-grade boys" from playing.

Idrissi: Not two black eyes and a broken nose. No.

Mr. Brown (to Judge Colbath): Your Honor, may we excuse the jury?

After the jurors left the courtroom, Judge Colbath addressed the witness, "Mrs. Idrissi, I know this is difficult, but you're not here as an advocate. You're here to just answer questions. And just answer the questions that are asked of you without volunteering anything.

"I'm going to ask the prosecutors to please talk with their other witnesses. I know this is a very emotional subject for everyone and to please get them to not fall prey to becoming an advocate and just simply answer the questions."

Brown: I'm going to move for mistrial, Judge. This witness has sat here . . . it's obvious from the beginning, the game she's playing.

Colbath: I'm going to ask you not to make judgmental statements, "The game she's playing." That's judgmental. I get your point anyway.

Brown: I specifically asked about knees and elbows. Specifically, there's no way you can argue I invited that comment. Judge, for her to throw that out there—there's no way I'm going to be able to eradicate the prejudice that goes to my client in this case—based on those comments. I'm going to move for mistrial based upon those statements.

Colbath: I'm going to deny it, but I'm going to admonish the jury to disregard it. (Then Colbath spoke to the witness.) Mrs. Idrissi, we've had a very difficult time picking a jury. If your answers cause me to declare a mistrial, I'm going to be very upset.

The jury was brought back in and Brown continued his questioning of the witness.

Brown: Did you know, ma'am, that Andrew Schwarz had been in counseling since he was three or four years old?

Idrissi: Yes, I did.

Brown: And that Andrew Schwarz was approximately four years old before he was ever able to talk?

Idrissi: I did not know that, no.

That afternoon—after Mrs. Idrissi's testimony and the lunch break—Judge Colbath made a statement to the jury regarding Andrew's "broken nose."

He explained the following: "The state and the defense have reduced their earlier stipulation to writing and it definitely goes a little bit beyond what I've already instructed and I think it's very appropriate that I read it to you precisely as they have agreed to it because it's a little more far-reaching and sweeping than what I instructed you to and it is as follows: 'There's no medical evidence known to the state or to the defense that Andrew Schwarz ever had a broken nose.'"

CHAPTER 13

*She would get screaming to the point that, frankly,
you couldn't even understand what she was yelling at
him.*

—Gail Ragatz, neighbor

Joseph Marx called eleven-year-old Teresa Walton—clad
in a bright, flowered dress with a very large lace collar—to
the stand as the next witness for the prosecution. A friend of
Lauren's, she estimated that she had been in the Schwarz
home more than twenty times in the three years prior to
A.J.'s death. She was only nine years old when A.J.'s body
was found floating facedown in the family swimming pool.

She testified that she only had a chance to play with A.J.
once or twice "because he was always cleaning" the kitchen,
the living room, the girls' bedroom, bathroom; he was always mopping the floor and "things like that." She had also
seen him cleaning the garage and witnessed him working in
the yard, cutting the weeds with "haircutting scissors."

Teresa heard Jessica yell at A.J. "practically every time I
went over"—many times cursing at him.

Marx (reassuring the little girl): Today is your day—
you can say these things. Tell the jury what you heard
the defendant say to A.J.

Teresa: Her calling him a "fucking asshole" and junk like that.

Marx: What did A.J. do when she called him a "fucking asshole"?

Teresa: Started crying.

Marx: Would she say that in front of people?

Teresa: Yes.

The little girl had been in the Schwarz residence at dinnertime and she stated that A.J. had special rules that he had to obey regarding how he ate his meal. Jessica would set the timer on the stove and he would have five or ten minutes to eat his dinner, and if he didn't finish eating in the given time, he had to put the rest of his food in the dog's bowl.

Marx established that Lauren and Jackie did not have to eat their meals in an allotted time.

Marx: Did there ever come a point in time that you saw an incident involving a cockroach?

Teresa: Yes. We were out washing Bear's truck and Jessica came out and said she found a cockroach on one of the plates and A.J. had to eat it.

Marx: Did you go inside? Did you see that?

Teresa: Yes. He was chewing when I walked in and then there was another half that he had in his hand.

Marx: Was he laughing? Did he think this was funny?

Teresa: No.

Marx: What was he doing?

Teresa: Crying.

Marx: Did you tell anybody about this?

Teresa: My mom.

She told the jurors that sometimes Jessica would punish A.J. by making him write, "I'm a liar. I should have never been born." She had seen him crying while he was forced to write the miserable words about himself and when he finished, Jessica hung the papers on the wall in his room.

She had also seen A.J. crying when Jessica had put "clear" masking tape on his mouth with the words "big mouth" written on the tape.

Teresa stated that "practically every time" she went over to their house, she saw Jessica strike A.J. across the face with an open hand.

> Marx: What did A.J. do after that happened?
> Teresa: He cried.
> Marx: Did you ever see Jessica Schwarz hug A.J.?
> Teresa: No.
> Marx: Did you ever see Jessica Schwarz kiss A.J.?
> Teresa: No.
> Marx: Did you ever hear Jessica Schwarz say one kind thing to A.J.?
> Teresa: No.

When she was asked to identify the defendant, Teresa was visibly shaking.

Rendell Brown started his cross-examination of the little girl by confirming that she had told her mother about the cockroach incident, and that her mother was Beth Walton.

> Brown: And she and Jessica just don't get along, do they?
> Teresa: No.
> Brown: They don't like each other, do they?
> Teresa (crying): Well, my mom liked her until what I told her about what happened in her (Jessica's) house.

Sobbing, she covered her face with her hands.

After a break to allow Teresa to regain her composure, Imogene Kelleher, the guardian ad litem who had been assigned to help the child witnesses during the trial, was allowed to sit by the young girl in the witness-box to reassure her. The judge instructed Teresa that she could not look to the woman for answers, and the defense attorney resumed his cross-examination.

> Brown: You told Mr. Marx a minute ago that you actually saw Andrew eating a cockroach?
> Teresa: Yes.
> Brown: Now, was this a little cockroach or a big cockroach?
> Teresa: I don't know. I didn't see the size.
> Brown: But you definitely testified that you saw him put the cockroach in his mouth?
> Teresa: Yes.
> Brown: Now, do you remember ever telling this story any differently, Teresa?
> Teresa: No.

She remembered talking to Detective Calloway, but insisted that she did not remember telling him anything different from what she was telling the jurors.

> Brown: Did you tell him in that statement that you did not see the cockroach, but you saw him chewing it? Do you remember telling Detective Calloway that?
> Teresa: No.
> Brown: Now, you testified earlier that Bear was there?
> Teresa: Yes.
> Brown: And you're telling this court and this jury that you were in Jessica Schwarz's home and saw David Schwarz—Andrew's father—allow her to make him eat a cockroach?
> Teresa: Yes.

A few minutes later, there was a conference at the bench when Marx objected to the fact that Jessica Schwarz was sitting at the defense table shaking her head and making facial expressions, "especially when there's a little girl up here."

After Judge Colbath asked Sam Marshall to "please admonish her," he addressed Rendell Brown. "I have a suggestion, if you don't object to it. If you just move yourself a little to the left, I think it would be—"

"You mean in front of the defendant?" Brown completed.

"You would put yourself between the two of them," the judge reasoned.

"That would be conspicuous, but I can do that."

Complying with the unusual—but understandable—request, Brown positioned himself between the witness and the defendant and continued his cross-examination.

Brown: You also testified, I think, Teresa, that Mr. Schwarz was home and Mrs. Schwarz taped Andrew's mouth shut?
Teresa: Yes.
Brown: Where did the tape come from?
Teresa: The drawer.
Brown: Who got it out of the drawer?
Teresa: Bear.
Brown: Mr. Schwarz? Andrew's father? Got the tape out of the drawer?
Teresa: Yes.
Brown: And sat there while Mrs. Schwarz taped Andrew Schwarz's mouth?
Teresa: Yes.
Brown: And you sat there and watched this?
Teresa: Yes.
Brown: Teresa, let me ask you this: do you remember A.J. having a lot of fights with kids coming home from school?
Teresa: Yes.

On the second day of the trial, the prosecution called Gail Ragatz as their next witness. During the time in question, she lived directly across the street from David and Jessica Schwarz. She worked for a pest control service and testified that that was how she became acquainted with the defendant. After Ragatz passed out flyers in the neighborhood, the Schwarzes started using the pest control service.

She met A.J. when he was about nine years old and saw the Schwarzes at least once a month—because of the pest control service—and occasionally throughout the month, as she had become friends with both David and Jessica and visited with them socially.

On one occasion, when she was at their home while they were having dinner, Jessica had fixed macaroni and cheese and hot dogs. Jessica put the plates on the table for the children, then turned around and said to A.J., "If you're going to act like an animal, you're going to eat like an animal."

Ragatz: The boy never did anything. She picked up his plate, took it over by the kitty litter pan—which was in his bedroom—and set it on the floor and grabbed him [by] the shirt, took him over, and made him sit on the floor. And as he was crying hysterically, she told him he was going to eat it, so he proceeded to eat. I left. I was mad.

Marx: Did you see Andrew Schwarz do anything improper before he was made to eat off the floor?

Ragatz: He didn't do anything.

(The jury would never hear that after A.J.'s death, Jessica Schwarz had called Gail Ragatz and told her, "Don't you ever tell anybody about that incident.")

Marx: Was that behavior anything unusual—for Jessica?

Ragatz: She was always verbally abusive with him. He was a "crackhead." He was a "bastard." He was a "bastard's baby." He was a "fuck face." She would get screaming to the point that, frankly, you couldn't even understand what she was yelling at him.

Marx: How did Andrew react when she did this?

Ragatz: Usually just close his eyes and go on.

Marx: Did it ever appear to you that he was afraid of her?

Ragatz: Absolutely.

Marx: Did she ever speak to you about how she felt about having Andrew there?

Ragatz: Yes, she did. She wanted him out of the house. She didn't like him.

(According to Ragatz, she had probably—over a period of time—seen Jessica and A.J. together approximately 150 times.)

Marx: Did you ever see Jessica Schwarz hug Andrew Schwarz?

Ragatz: Oh, no. No.

Marx: Did you ever see Jessica Schwarz kiss Andrew Schwarz?

Ragatz: No.

Marx: Did you ever hear her say one kind word to that boy?

Ragatz: No.

Marx (handing the witness a picture): One last thing. Do you recognize that?

Ragatz (crying): Yes. That's A.J.

Brown then cross-examined the distraught witness.

Brown: Mrs. Ragatz, isn't it a fact that you and Jessica were not friends; isn't that true?

Ragatz: We started out friends—yes.

Brown: Isn't it a fact, ma'am, that you and Jessica didn't get along at all; that you, in fact, did not like Jessica? Isn't that true, ma'am?

Ragatz: At the end—no, I did not.

Brown: Now, the day that you've testified about, the incident with the food . . . You and Jessica aren't getting along—you don't like her—at this point, right?

Ragatz: No, we were getting along, at that point.

Brown: How long did you stay there?

Ragatz: Two or three minutes and I got mad and I left.

He was sitting at the table, just as the other two children were, and didn't do anything.

Brown: If you were only there for two or three minutes, you [would] have no idea what transpired prior to those two or three minutes, would you—if anything transpired—would you?

Ragatz: No, I wouldn't.

Brown: And the truth of the matter is that Jessica has a tone of voice when she talks to everybody; isn't that true? I mean she's just a rough talking lady, isn't she?

Ragatz: She has an attitude, yes.

Brown: That's Jessica, isn't it? She talks to you that way, doesn't she?

Ragatz: Yes.

Brown: She talks to everybody that way, doesn't she? That's just the way she talks, isn't it?

Ragatz: I never heard her talk that way to her own children.

The next witness for the prosecution was fifteen-year-old Jamie Falk. She wasn't quite fourteen at the time of A.J.'s death, when she had approached Detective Restivo and asked to speak to him. Before Jessica Schwarz's bond had been revoked for shouting obscenities at her neighbors, Jamie had had trouble sleeping at night because of her fear of the defendant.

Aware that the teenager was nervous, Joseph Marx started by gently asking her to "sit up straight, get close to the microphone, and talk loud enough so the people in the back row can hear you, okay?"

Jamie had been friends with Patsy and Lauren and would go to their house "to talk and watch TV and watch movies and stuff." She said that "once in a while" A.J. would come into the room where they were.

"Usually he was, like, sweeping or something in the kitchen. He just always used to mop and clean the garage and pick up after the cats and dogs and stuff."

"Did you ever see Lauren and Jackie do these kinds of chores?" Marx asked.

"No."

The young witness testified that A.J. walked to school, while Lauren was allowed to ride her bike.

Marx: Did there ever come a day when it was raining out and you were late for class?

Jamie: Yeah. I missed the bus and my dad was taking me to school. It was raining and we drove by and A.J. was walking to school. We were driving up the road and we saw him, so my dad was going to stop and pick him up and drop him off at school, but we saw Jessica behind us, so we just—

Marx: Did your father keep driving?

Jamie: Yes, because he thought that she would pick him up, so we kept on driving.

But Jessica did not pick him up and A.J. continued walking to school in the rain.

Jamie also had seen A.J. sitting at the kitchen table with food in front of him, with tape on his mouth.

"He just looked embarrassed and scared and stuff. He was just sitting there. I felt bad. There was nothing I could do. I just—you know, I didn't—I felt weird. I just walked away."

Marx: Did you ever have an opportunity to hear Jessica talk to Andrew?

Jamie: Yeah.

Marx: Did she ever call him derogatory names—bad names?

Jamie: Yeah. She just used to call him stupid and worthless and stuff.

Marx: Did you ever see Jessica hug Andrew Schwarz?

Jamie: No.

Andrew Joseph Schwarz, also known as A.J.
(Courtesy of Palm Beach County Sheriff's Office)

Aerial view of the Schwarz home with the pool in back.
(Courtesy of Palm Beach County Sheriff's Office crime scene photo)

The front exterior of the house.
(Courtesy of Palm Beach County Sheriff's Office crime scene photo)

Passageway leads to the fenced-in backyard with the pool around the corner.
(Courtesy of Palm Beach County Sheriff's Office crime scene photo)

The pool with the recovered body of A.J. in the foreground.
(Courtesy of Palm Beach County Sheriff's Office crime scene photo)

The Schwarz living room.
(Courtesy of Palm Beach County Sheriff's Office crime scene photo)

The family's kitchen.
(Courtesy of Palm Beach County Sheriff's Office crime scene photo)

Jessica Schwarz's daughters' well-kept bedroom.
(Courtesy of Palm Beach County Sheriff's Office crime scene photo)

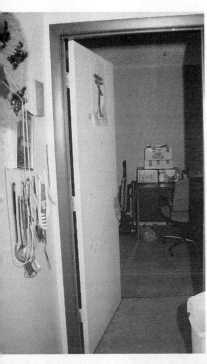

In contrast, the nearly closet-sized room where A.J. slept. *(Courtesy of Palm Beach County Sheriff's Office crime scene photo)*

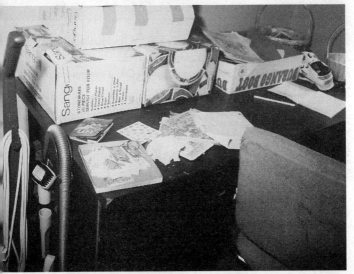

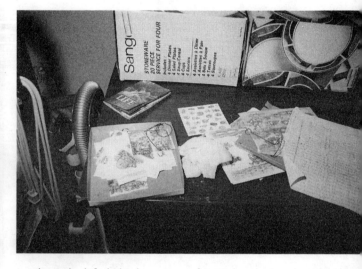

The makeshift desk where some of A.J.'s handwritten punishment assignments remained.
(Courtesy of Palm Beach County Sheriff's Office crime scene photo)

The clothes A.J. was wearing the night he died were found on the floor of his room.
(Courtesy of Palm Beach County Sheriff's Office crime scene photo)

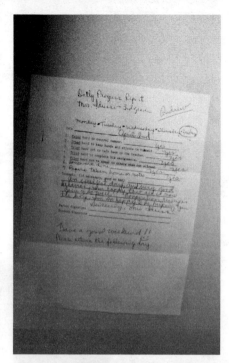

A favorable behavior report from A.J.'s teacher, Mrs. Idrissi. *(Courtesy of Palm Beach County Sheriff's Office crime scene photo)*

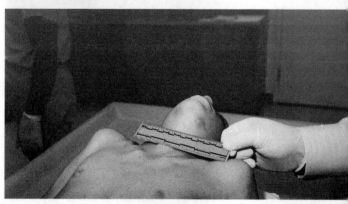

The second autopsy on A.J.'s body revealed bruising patterns consistent with abuse.
(Courtesy of Palm Beach County Sheriff's Office crime scene photo)

Joseph Marx, assistant state attorney at the time of the investigation and prosecution of Jessica Schwarz, is now a judge in Palm Beach County. *(Courtesy of Judge Joseph Marx)*

Judge Walter Colbath, who presided at Jessica Schwarz's trial. *(Courtesy of Judge Walter Colbath)*

Jessica Schwarz on the stand, being questioned by
her attorney Rendell Brown.
(Photo by Lannis Waters, The Palm Beach Post)

Scott H. Cupp in court. *(Courtesy of Scott H. Cupp)*

At A.J.'s school, a memorial plaque. (Note that his middle name is incorrect.) *(Courtesy of Scott H. Cupp)*

OUR LOVING FRIEND
...AND A GOOD STUDENT
"A.J."
ANDREW JAMES SCHWARZ
APR. 24, 1983 – MAY 2, 1993

Marx: Did you ever see Jessica kiss Andrew Schwarz?
Jamie: No.
Marx: During the entire time that you knew Jessica and Andrew Schwarz, did you ever hear her say one kind word to him?
Jamie: No.

Blond-haired, blue-eyed Troy Falk, Jamie's twelve-year-old brother, was surprisingly calm as he testified next—about an incident that had taken place one day after school.

"I had gotten home from school and I was showing my friend something . . . and I seen A.J. running down the street naked. He was across the street. He was, like, jogging, and kept on looking behind him."

"What was he doing with his hands?" Marx asked.

"He was, like, covering his privates. It was like he had his hands in front of his privates."

Marx asked the young boy to stand up and demonstrate for the jurors how A.J. had covered himself with his hands as he was running down the street naked.

"Did he look embarrassed?"

"Yes," Troy replied.

The witness said that Jessica was standing in the doorway while A.J. ran to the corner, and then "in a mean voice," she told him to "come back."

Marx: Did it look like—in your opinion—Andrew wanted to be running down the street naked?
Troy: No.
(Troy then testified that he, too, had seen A.J. with tape on his mouth.)
Troy: I went to the door to see if he could play. And when they answered, I seen tape on his mouth.
Marx: How close did you get to him?

Troy: Couple of feet away—about three feet away. [It was] like packaging tape—brown tape. They wrote "mouth" on it. He was just standing there.
Marx: Did he look like he was happy?
Troy: No.

And it continued—a long procession of neighbors and their children to the witness stand. After testifying to the verbal, psychological, and demeaning abuses they had seen and heard A.J. suffer at the hands of his stepmother, each one was asked the same series of questions:

"Did you ever see Jessica hug Andrew Schwarz?"

"Did you ever see Jessica kiss Andrew Schwarz?"

"During the entire time that you knew Jessica and Andrew Schwarz, did you ever hear her say one kind word to him?"

And time after heartbreaking time, the answer was always the same. Not one kiss. Not one hug. Not one kind word—ever.

CHAPTER 14

My children's chores took maybe ten or fifteen min-
utes out of the day. A.J.'s took all day. I used to hear
her yell at him. I never really heard her talk to him.

—Ida Falk, neighbor

After the lunch break, as rain poured down outside the
courthouse, Ida Falk knew that she would be the next witness for the prosecution. She was the mother of the two previous witnesses, Jamie and Troy.

She sighed as Joe Marx called her to the witness stand,
knowing she would have to repeat the hateful things she had
heard Jessica say to A.J.

Ida Falk had met the Schwarzes and become friendly with
them because her children played with their children; but the
friendship had ended when she saw some of the things that
were happening at her neighbors' home.

At first, she saw A.J. doing a few chores, like picking
things up in the yard or taking a bag of garbage out to the
curb, but then the chores escalated.

"Probably about a year after we lived there. He was always in the yard doing yard work. Any time I seen him outside he was working; he was doing yard work or cleaning the
garage or washing the cat litter box. My children's chores
took maybe ten or fifteen minutes out of the day. A.J.'s took

all day. I used to hear her yell at him. I never really heard her talk to him. She would cuss at him, tell him . . . she would tell him he was a stupid little f'er."

Marx: Tell us what you mean by f'er?
Falk (obviously embarrassed): Fucker.
Marx: What else would you hear her say?
Falk: That he was an asshole. She used to tell him all the time he was stupid or dumb.
Marx: What would he do when she would yell he was a stupid little fucker?
Falk: He would put his head down and keep doing whatever he was doing. She would tell him he was moving too slow; he was not doing things right—he was stupid.
Marx: Did you ever hear her talk to Lauren or Jackie the same way she talked to Andrew?
Falk: No.

She testified that while outside one day, she had seen A.J. working in his yard with tape over his mouth. He looked embarrassed and wouldn't make eye contact with her. On two different occasions, she had also seen him edging the lawn with "regular sewing scissors."

Falk: I saw him quite a few times—when he should have been in school—working in the yard. All day.
Marx: Did you ever see her—in the three years that you lived on Triphammer Road—come out of the house and give him a hug?
Falk: No.
Marx: Did you ever see her come out of the house and give him a kiss?
Falk: No.
Marx: During that time when he was doing all those chores, did you ever hear her say, "You did a good job"?

Falk: No.

Marx: Did you ever hear her say one nice thing to him?

Falk: No.

Marx: Did you ever see him vomiting on those days he was home from school working in the yard?

Falk: No.

Marx: Was there anything about him that appeared that he was ill?

Falk: No.

On cross-examination by Brown, Ida Falk admitted that she had had, over the period of time leading up to the trial, conversations with her children, Jamie and Troy, about the things she was telling the jurors. And that she had talked with some of her neighbors as well.

"In fact, that's been the hotbed of conversation in that neighborhood for over a year, hasn't it?" Brown asked.

"The hotbed of conversation? We try to not even think about it," Falk replied.

Her voice broke as she reluctantly admitted that even though she had seen A.J. out in the yard with tape across his mouth, and working in the yard when he should have been in school, she had never called anyone to report the situation.

"Are you all right? Do you need a break?" Brown queried.

Falk answered that she was okay.

Rendell Brown finished with his own series of questions. He asked her if she had ever seen Jessica Schwarz come outside her home and kiss Lauren. Or Jackie. Or David.

Mrs. Falk replied to each one that she had not.

Brown: She's just not a huggie-kissie kind of person, is she? Is she, ma'am?

Falk: I don't know.

On redirect Marx asked Mrs. Falk what her impression was of A.J.

Falk: He was a nice little boy when he was at my house. He was always very polite. Every time when I would see him outside, he always waved and asked how I was, called me by name, always very polite.

Marx: When he was at your house, did you ever have a behavioral problem with Andrew Schwarz?

Falk: Never.

Marx: Mrs. Falk, when you saw what was happening at the Schwarz residence, did you call any authorities or did you tell anybody what was happening?

Falk: No.

Marx: Why not?

Falk: Because I was afraid.

Marx: Of whom?

Falk: Jessica.

It was the state's position that Ida Falk felt intimated by Jessica Schwarz because she had seen the defendant being arrested for "punching" her husband. Even though she hadn't actually seen the assault, she had seen Jessica being hand-cuffed and put in a police car, but the jurors would not be al-lowed to hear about the incident.

Brown (on recross): Why, Mrs. Falk, were you afraid of Jessica?

Falk: Because she was always screaming and yelling and I was just afraid of what she might do.

Brown: Now, Mrs. Falk, you know—do you not?— that several different departments have hot lines which are confidential for just that purpose, don't you? I mean, you know that, don't you?

Falk: I know there are several different hot lines. I didn't know they were confidential.

Scott Cupp called the next witness for the prosecution. Beth Walton, dressed in a short-sleeved, pleated white blouse and a dark skirt, tried to stay calm as she took the witness stand. The mother of four children, she had been in the nursing field for twenty years.

While she had been waiting to come into the courtroom, she had thought back to one of the days she had baby-sat for A.J. She liked A.J. and she was smiling when she opened the door, but when she saw the T-shirt he was wearing and the words written across the front, the color drained from her face and she gasped. Then she saw the look on his face: humiliation, defeat, despair.

"He's not to take it off," Jessica had told her in no uncertain terms. "He's violated the rules and now he has to pay the price. No television and no talking—not to anyone."

When the door slammed and Jessica disappeared down the walk, Beth Walton had looked down at the shirt again. The words read: "I'm a worthless piece of shit. Don't talk to me."

Now she would have the chance to tell a jury of Jessica Schwarz's peers.

Her long blond hair falling lightly over her shoulders, Mrs. Walton listened carefully to the young prosecutor's questions. She explained to the jurors that she and Jessica had been friends for a time, but then "the relationship between us got really bizarre." She had seen Jessica strike A.J. on two separate occasions.

"He had misbehaved. I was in her kitchen and she grabbed him. She just kind of shook him and kind of smacked him in the back of the head. He was cleaning out the track in the sliding glass door at the time. A second occasion, in my kitchen, she came—I was watching Andrew at the time—and she grabbed him."

She couldn't remember exactly how long A.J. had been at her house before Jessica came in, but she stated that it was "an hour or two."

Mrs. Walton recalled how "Jessica came in through the sliding glass door at the back of my house and grabbed

Andrew in the kitchen—by the shoulders—and shook him and was yelling at him that the sheriff's department was at the house. And that the only reason that he was being kept home from school was because he had doctors' appointments and he had better stick to that story and that if he was to deviate from that, there would be problems. She was extremely upset. She was kind of in a frenzy."

Mrs. Walton frowned as she demonstrated with her hands. "She was taking him and shaking him like this. His head was whacking back and forth. She shook him like a rag doll all over my kitchen. She was screaming at him.

"Andrew was standing there with his mouth hanging open. He wasn't saying anything."

Cupp: Leaving that time period for a moment, were there any other times or occasions where you would speak with the defendant and she would tell you about punishments that she would give Andrew?

Walton: There was one occasion when she told me that she went and took him out of school because she hadn't been woke up that morning and he hadn't emptied the kitty litter box and she went and took him out of school and brought him home.

Cupp: To punish him?

Walton: She was going to keep him home for the rest of the week and he was going to do chores for the rest of the week to punish him for not doing what she told him to do.

Cupp: Did there ever come a time when A.J. was in your home and he was wearing a T-shirt with some writing on it?

Walton: Yes, there was. On one morning I told Jessica I would watch A.J. for her. He showed up at my house with a T-shirt that said, "I'm nothing but a worthless piece of shit—do not talk to me." I then called Jessica. I said, "I have things I have to do and have to take A.J.

with me and I can't take him out in public in something like that." She insisted that he had to wear it all day long and he would be questioned as to whether he wore it or not.

Cupp: What did you do?

Walton: I put a button-up shirt over it and I told Andrew, I said, "Look, if Jessica asks if you wore the shirt, tell her yes and that way you can't be punished for lying or for taking your shirt off."

Cupp: Did you ever observe Mrs. Schwarz hug Andrew?

Walton: No. Not that I can recall, at this moment in time.

Cupp: Kiss him?

Walton: No.

Cupp: Be affectionate with him in any way?

Walton: No.

Cupp: Praise him?

Walton: No.

Cupp: Encourage him?

Walton: No.

Cupp: Do you ever recall an occasion where Mrs. Schwarz said anything positive or said anything that put Andrew in a good light?

Walton: It was around his birthday that she said she thought maybe she did love him. She wasn't really sure.

On that sad note, Scott Cupp ended his direct questioning of the witness.

Rendell Brown started his cross-examination.

Brown: As a nurse, obviously you're aware of the HRS hot line and those sorts of things?

Walton: Yes.

Brown: And did you report this incident when it happened?

Walton: What incident is that?

Brown: That you told this jury and court about with the T-shirt?

Walton: No, I spoke to Jessica about it.

Brown: Did you talk with any of the appropriate authorities about it?

Walton: No, I did not. I spoke to Jessica about it.

Brown: You didn't happen to have a camera on hand to take a picture?

Walton: No.

Brown: Now, you testified that on the one hand Mrs. Schwarz is saying to you that she can't stand him; she wants to get rid of him, meaning Andrew?

Walton: Yes.

Brown: And then she tells you—on the other—she's going to keep him home for a week to punish him?

Walton: Yes.

Brown: Do you see a contradiction in that?

Walton: Not really.

Beth Walton's nineteen-year-old daughter, Elissa, took the witness stand—very briefly—to confirm the story about A.J. wearing the T-shirt with the derogatory writing on it.

The last witness of the day was Catherine Turner, the neighbor who lived directly behind the Schwarzes. She had lived there for approximately five years and was the mother of a nineteen-year-old daughter and a twenty-three-year-old son.

Mrs. Turner had been in Jessica's home on several occasions, baby-sitting for her children, and she had never had any problems with A.J.

The jurors, however, would never get to hear that she had since become terrified of Jessica Schwarz—or that Jessica had threatened to kill her dog.

She told the jury about a time when she was baby-sitting

and A.J. was not allowed to be in the home like the rest of the children.

"He was told to stay in his room, by Jessica and her husband, David. It was in a room behind the garage. I assume it was his bedroom. All the locks [on the doors] were turned around so they were locked on the outside—all the children's bedrooms and the bathroom."

Cupp: So he could be locked in?
Turner: Right.
Cupp: Was he locked in when they left?
Turner: No.
Cupp: At some point, did he come out?
Turner: A couple of times he came out and I talked to him.
Cupp: How did he appear to you, at that time, and what was [his] demeanor, his mood?
Turner: He was a little sad.
Cupp: Did it seem that A.J. was punished more than the other children?
Turner: Yes. Just seemed that the girls were always running around outside and—most of the time—when I was baby-sitting, he had to stay in his room.
Cupp: So it wasn't just this one occasion?
Turner: Right.
Cupp: Were you ever told why?
Turner: Not really, no. She just said he was a bad boy and he had to stay in his room.
Cupp: But you never had any problems with him?
Turner: No, I never had any problems.

On another occasion, Jessica told her that she had made A.J. parade around the house with no clothes on.

"She said he had exposed himself in school and he had to learn his lesson and she made him walk around with no pants on. I didn't see it, but she told me about it."

Cupp: Did you ever have a conversation with Mrs. Schwarz where she told you anything about A.J. having a bed-wetting problem and what she was doing about it?

Turner: Yes. She wasn't really sure how to handle it, as far as I saw. I think one time she told me she felt like rubbing his nose into his bedsheets.

Cupp: Did she say she actually did it?

Turner: No.

Cupp: But she felt like it.

Turner: Right.

Cupp: When she spoke with you about these things, what kind of demeanor or tone of voice was she speaking to you in?

Turner: She was a little upset.

Cupp: Did you ever have occasion to see Mrs. Schwarz be affectionate with A.J.?

Turner: No.

Cupp: Did you ever see her hug him?

Turner: No.

Cupp: Did you ever see her kiss him?

Turner: No.

Cupp: Did you ever see her praise him?

Turner: No.

Turner had backed up somewhat from her deposition, where she had stated that she was afraid of Jessica—very afraid—and the reason was that Jessica had called her and told her if she didn't 'do something,' she was going to kill her Great Dane.

When Cupp asked Mrs. Turner if she recalled the deposition she had given on December 1, 1993, she said that she did. He asked her to read a portion of it to herself.

Cupp: Having read that, does that refresh your recollection as to what Mrs. Schwarz told you at that time?

Turner: Yes. She said that she felt like rubbing his nose

in the bedsheets like when a dog wets and you punish a dog.

Cupp: Well, didn't she, in fact, say that she did it?

Turner: I don't . . . She might have. It's been a while. It's a long time.

Cupp: Do you recall the following question and giving the following answer: Question: "Did she discuss with you the bed-wetting problem?" And your answer: "Yes, she said she was going to make him lie in it. I think one time she even tried—she tried to rub his nose in the sheets like a dog."

Turner: I might have said that.

Cupp: Do you recall being asked the following: Question: "Did she say she made him sleep on the floor because he wet the bed?" Answer: "No, she used to make him sleep in the bed with the sheets wet." Do you remember that question and that answer?

Turner: Yes, I do.

Rendell Brown then confronted the witness.

Brown: Now, ma'am, during the time you've known Mrs. Schwarz, the fact is that Mrs. Schwarz is just not a huggie-kissie person, period, is she?

Turner: No, I don't think she was to any of her children.

Brown: That was just Jessica?

Turner: Yes.

Brown: You didn't question whether or not she loved her children because of that, did you?

Turner: No.

Brown: Now, you saw the kids' rooms with the locks turned to the outside?

Turner: Yes.

Brown: Was it your interpretation of Mr. Cupp's question that that was to lock the children in?

Turner: I would think it would be to lock the children in myself.

Brown: That's just your assumption?

Turner: Well, that's what it seemed like to me, at the time.

Brown: But you never saw any of those kids locked in?

Turner: I never saw them locked in. I saw that the locks were turned around.

Brown: Now, Mrs. Turner, when you raised your hand and swore to tell the truth—the whole truth—you took that oath seriously, didn't you?

Turner: Yes, I did.

Brown: And in fact, that's why—when Mr. Cupp was asking you about Jessica having told you, or you remembered her telling you, that she rubbed his nose in the urine-soaked bed—the truth is, you don't really remember her telling you that?

Turner: I remember her telling me that, but I don't remember the precise words, per se.

Brown: Mr. Cupp asked you two or three times if Jessica told you that she had, in fact, done that?

Turner: Yes.

Brown: And your answer was?

Turner: Yes, she had told me that.

Brown: When you were giving your sworn statement, and this is back in December of '93, what you said was "And I think one time she even told me she tried to rub his nose in it—in the sheets."

Turner: Yes, I said that, yes.

Brown: But now you're telling the jury that you distinctly remember her saying that?

Turner: That's not what I'm saying. I said I thought. It's been a long time. I don't remember.

Brown: It's been a longer time than it was since 1993 when you made the statement?

Turner: Yes.

Brown: You don't really remember her telling you she did anything like that, do you?

Turner: Not that—she might have said it, you know. She did say something to that effect, but I don't know if she actually did it, if she really did rub his nose in it. It was conversation. It was just back-and-forth conversation.

Brown: And during that conversation, she just might have said that?

Turner: Yes. Well, she said she had thought about it or was going to do it, but I never saw her do it. I never—you know.

Brown: My question is, and I want to be clear in my question so you can be clear in your response to this jury: are you telling this court and this jury that you have an independent recollection of Mrs. Schwarz ever telling you that she, in fact, put that child's nose in any urine-soaked bed?

Turner: She mentioned it, but—it's been so long, I don't remember. I don't remember.

On redirect examination, Scott Cupp had only a few questions.

Cupp: When Mrs. Schwarz told you these things about speaking about the bed-wetting, how did that make you feel? Do you recall how you felt?

Turner: Well, I didn't think it was right.

Cupp: Was she laughing when she said it? Was she saying it in jest or was she serious?

Turner: No, she wasn't laughing; she wasn't laughing.

Cupp: And did you do anything about what she told you or any of the things that you observed? Did you tell anybody; did you do anything?

Turner: No, I didn't.

At that point, Cupp told the judge that he needed to approach the bench. He told him that he intended his next question to be, "Why not?" He explained that it was in the record—she had stated it in her deposition—how "very afraid" she was of the defendant—and why.

Brown objected, saying it was "far beyond the scope of my cross."

Judge Colbath ruled in favor of the defense.

CHAPTER 15

He said he couldn't go to school because he had to collect aluminum cans for his [step]mother.

—Candace Ahern

On Friday, fourteen-year-old Serena Perryman was the prosecution's first witness of the day. She lived with her family four houses down from the Schwarzes on the opposite side of Triphammer Road.

Home-schooled and extremely intelligent—literally a genius—she was very direct and slightly stilted in her speech and delivery.

Serena testified that she had never been inside the Schwarz house, but had played in the yard with Lauren and Patsy; and in the three to four years that she had known the family, she had never had the opportunity to play with A.J. because he was "never allowed to play." He was made to do chores on a daily basis, including watching Jackie, picking up "junk" in the yard and driveway, and sweeping the sidewalk.

Until Patsy was removed from the Schwarz home and placed in foster care, she was also required to do chores on a daily basis, but not Lauren or Jackie.

Serena had seen many bruises on A.J.—too many to count—and had witnessed the defendant strike A.J.

"I was standing on the sidewalk in front of their house. Jessica opened the door, yelled obscenities at A.J., and

yanked him and struck him as they were entering the house.
She said—I don't remember exactly, but she said 'fuck,' and
something."

> Marx: Was that the only time you ever heard the de-
> fendant use the word "fuck" towards Andrew?
> Serena: No, lots and lots of times she used it.
> Marx: Would she use other derogatory names at Andrew?
> Serena: Yes.
> Marx: Would he be standing there when she'd be say-
> ing those things?
> Serena: Many times, yes. He generally wouldn't do
> anything. He wouldn't say anything, either. He just
> sort of looked down.

One day Serena had been outside "on the easement" in
front of her house and saw A.J. walking home from school
by himself. She looked down the street and saw Jessica at
the front door of her house, "sticking her head out." Then
she heard her yell "ferociously" at A.J., "If you're not home
right this instant, I'm going to make you run down the
street naked." A.J. started walking faster and looked frightened.

> Marx: Was there anything blocking your view or keep-
> ing you from hearing what the defendant said that day?
> Serena: There was nothing keeping me from hearing
> what the defendant said.
> Marx: Would A.J. always walk home and walk to
> school?
> Serena: Every time I saw him, yes.
> Marx: Did Andrew seem strange or abnormal to you?
> Serena: No, not at all. He was polite and respectful,
> sort of quiet.
> Marx: Serena, how would you describe Jessica Schwarz's
> attitude toward Andrew?
> Serena: Oh, it was very hateful—because the way she

looked and what she said to him, there was no warmth at all, just like cold.

Marx: Did you ever see this woman hug Andrew Schwarz?

Serena: No.

Marx: Did you ever see this woman kiss Andrew Schwarz?

Serena: No.

Marx: Did you ever see this woman say a kind word to Andrew Schwarz?

Serena: Never.

Brown, on cross-examination, tried—unsuccessfully—to convince the young witness that instead of A.J. "watching Jackie," what she actually saw was A.J. and Jackie playing together.

Brown: Now, do you know what kinds of things Andrew liked to do as far as playing is concerned?

Serena: No, because I never saw him play.

Brown: When you saw Andrew in the yard with toys, you chose to believe that he was picking up Jackie's toys; is that correct?

Serena: I didn't choose that—I saw that.

Brown: And, Serena, you say that you saw bruises all over his body?

Serena: All the parts that I could see that weren't covered with clothes. As long as I knew him, every time I came within a distance, I could see bruises on him.

Brown: Were these big bruises?

Serena: Some of them were, but others were medium-sized.

Brown: Would you agree if somebody were looking for those bruises, they should have seen them?

Serena: Certainly.

Brown: And I think you told Mr. Marx that the bruises we're talking about here were too many to count?

Serena: That's right.
Brown: Did you ever see Jessica hug or kiss Lauren?
Serena: I don't remember.
Brown: Have you ever seen Jessica hug or kiss anybody?
Serena: I don't remember.
Brown: How did you say you met Jessica Schwarz?
Serena: I met Jessica when they moved in. She was staggering down the sidewalk in front of her house and my mom asked her a question. I think she asked, "How are you doing?" And she said, "How should I be? I have four kids." And she continued staggering down [the sidewalk]. And later in the day, I saw her passed out under the neighbor's bush.

Her answer brought a degree of levity into the courtroom—for everyone, of course, except Rendell Brown. She just rattled off her answer before Judge Colbath—or anyone—could stop her. It was obvious by the way she said it that it was absolutely, 100 percent true. That was as close as anyone would have even thought about laughing out loud during the trial. For a very brief period of time, it reduced the tension.

Not surprisingly, Brown asked to approach the bench.

Brown: Your Honor, I'm going to ask the court to take the responsibility to direct these witnesses as to what is and not coming in, in this trial. Now, I mean you're going to tell me, "You asked her." The idea is to keep this stuff out. I asked how she met her and she goes into [a] diatribe, but the court has already said this is not coming in, in this trial.
Judge Colbath: I know we've touched on this subject and I understand your dilemma, Mr. Brown, but, as I said before, short of listening to the testimony out of the presence of the jury, I don't know how anyone could ever have anticipated this kind of an answer. It is a very truthful answer.

Brown: I don't know if it's truthful.

Judge Colbath: Let me say this: it's certainly a responsive answer, whether or not it's truthful, at least from the viewpoint of a fourteen-year-old girl. Can you switch gears?

Brown: I'm going to have to.

Judge Colbath: Let's move on.

Brown (to the witness): Serena, do you recall the last time you spoke with Patsy?

Serena: No, I don't.

Brown: Can you get us in the ballpark?

Serena: I don't remember.

Brown: Now, you never saw Andrew Schwarz naked, did you?

Serena: No.

Eleven-year-old Brittany Ahern was the next witness for the prosecution. Scott Cupp informed the judge that her mother would be the next witness, so she was not present in the courtroom. Imogene Kelleher, the guardian ad litem, sat next to her while she was on the witness stand.

Outside the presence of the jury, the judge addressed the little girl. "Brittany, some of the questions that either Mr. Cupp or Mr. Brown may ask you could possibly deal with when certain events took place, when did you do this or when did you see this or something like that. Try not to refer to A.J.'s death as a point in time to reference your answer. Do you understand what I'm saying?"

The girl answered, "No, I don't."

Judge Colbath patiently tried to make it clearer to the child. "Well, in other words, if Mr. Cupp or Mr. Brown say, 'Well, Brittany, when did this take place?' Instead of saying, 'Oh, it was right after A.J. died or it was just before A.J. died,' try to give a month and a year, if you can do that. Do you understand what I'm saying?"

Brittany answered, "Yes."

The jury was brought in and Cupp elicited the information from the girl that she and Lauren Cross, Jessica's daughter, had been classmates and friends. And that the first time she had been in the Schwarz home was to attend Lauren's party for her tenth birthday.

Having been a "latchkey kid," her mother made arrangements with Jessica for Brittany to go there every day after school until about 6:00 or 6:30 in the evening so she would have someone to play with, and her mother also dropped Brittany off in the mornings on her way to work so she could go to school with Lauren.

Brittany testified that she had seen Jessica hit A.J. "kind of hard" with her hands "a lot of times" on his face, his head, and his butt.

Cupp: Did you ever see Jessica punch A.J.? Do you know what I mean by punch?

Brittany: Yes.

Cupp: How do you punch somebody? Show me. Hold up your fist.

(The witness balled up her fist and showed it to the prosecutor.)

Cupp: Did you ever see Jessica punch A.J.?

Brittany: Yes.

Cupp: On what part of A.J.'s body would Jessica punch him?

Brittany (hesitantly): I—I don't remember.

Cupp: Were you ever over at Lauren and A.J.'s house at one time when A.J. got home from school late?

Brittany: Yes.

Cupp (gently): Could you tell us what happened? Take your time.

Brittany: One day, he came home from school and he was late—because he was supposed to be home by a certain time and he wasn't—and she yelled at him and made him take off his clothes and run down the street naked. I didn't see it, but then later on in the day, kids were saying, "Why was A.J. running around the street naked?"

Cupp: Did you hear Jessica tell A.J. to take his clothes off?

Brittany: We were in the kitchen and the kitchen was kind of connected to his room and she was telling him.

Cupp: What made him come back?

Brittany: She called him back.

Cupp: What did A.J. do after he got back?

Brittany: He was crying—in his bedroom.

Cupp: Did you ever hear Jessica curse at A.J.?

Brittany: Yes.

Cupp: Now, I think it would be okay with your mother—just for today, just this one time—that you say what you heard. Is that okay?

Brittany: Yes. She would call him "asshole" and "shit for brains."

Cupp: Did you hear it just one time or more than one time?

Brittany: More than one time.

Cupp: All the times that you went over there, did you ever see Jessica hug A.J.?

Brittany: No.

Cupp: Did you ever see her kiss him?

Brittany: No.

Cupp: Did you ever see her help him do anything or encourage him?

Brittany: No.

Cupp: Was she ever nice to him—at all?

Brittany: I don't think so.

On cross-examination, Brittany reiterated for Rendell Brown that she never personally saw A.J. running down the street naked—that she heard it from Troy Falk.

Brown: Now, during the times that you remember seeing Jessica hitting Andrew, you said she hit him hard?

Brittany: Yes.

Brown: Was it hard enough to cause bruising?

Brittany: Yes.

Brown: Did you see bruises yourself?
Brittany: Sometimes I would see bruises.

Scott Cupp's redirect questioning was brief and to the point:

Cupp: Brittany, when you were over there when A.J. came home late and Jessica told him to take his clothes off and run down the street—what did Jessica say to you and Lauren?
Brittany: She told us—she told me, "Now don't go telling your mom about this."
Cupp: You heard her tell A.J. to do this, right?
Brittany: Yes.
Cupp: But you didn't walk outside and watch him do it?
Brittany: No.
Cupp: You never talked to those kids about this, did you?
Brittany: No. I heard what Troy said on television.

Candace Ahern, Brittany's mother, took the witness stand next. She testified that on one of the afternoons when she went to pick Brittany up at Jessica's house, A.J. was outside and she noticed that his eyes and his nose were swollen and black and blue.

"It was so noticeable that his nose didn't look like a nose; it was almost disfigured-looking."

A.J. followed her into the house and, when they were inside, she asked A.J. what happened to his face—and Jessica laughed at him.

"She laughed hysterically, laughed at A.J. and his face, and called him 'shit for brains,' which I thought was abusive."

"What was A.J. doing?" Cupp asked.

"Crying. He started to cry," Ahern replied.

One morning, when it was raining, she was taking Brittany to school and went by to pick up Lauren. She saw A.J. and offered him a ride to school too.

"He said he couldn't go to school because he had to collect aluminum cans for his [step]mother."

On another occasion, Jessica called her and was complaining about A.J., telling her that he was "giving her a very hard time and he was very hard to handle." Mrs. Ahern told her that if he was that difficult maybe she should give him back to his mother.

"What was her response?" Cupp asked.

"That she did not want to pay child support."

Jessica Schwarz shook her head from time to time and scribbled on a notepad at the defense table as she listened to the accusations. Her defense attorney then began his cross-examination of the witness.

Brown: Now, Mr. Cupp asked you about a swollen nose and black eyes?

Ahern: Yes.

Brown: And you were going to tell this court what Andrew said to you about that and he stopped you. Did you ask him what happened? Did you ask how he got the swollen nose and black eyes?

Ahern: Yes, I did. He said he ran into something in the garage.

Brown: Okay. He told you he was riding the bicycle in the garage, didn't he?

Ahern: I think that's what he said.

Brown: His little sister's bicycle?

Ahern: It was a little bicycle.

Brown: Somehow he ran into the wall with the bicycle; isn't that what he told you?

Ahern: That's what he told me.

Brown: Andrew never told you that "my [step]mother makes me collect cans," did he?

Ahern: He said, "I'm collecting cans for my [step] mother."

Brown: Okay. He never told you that she made him collect cans?

Ahern repeated: He said, "I'm collecting cans for my [step]mother."

Brown: You never talked to HRS about any of this stuff that you told us?

Ahern: No, sir.

Brown: Did Mrs. Schwarz ever tell you about the effort she was making to get HRS to do something about the problems with Andrew?

Ahern: An effort? No.

The next witness was Anne Steinhauer, the neighbor who lived directly across the street from the Schwarzes. An attractive young mother, with very long hair and impeccable makeup, she knew A.J. because occasionally he came over to her house to see if her little girl could play with Jackie, and she also "took him to school once in a while."

Steinhauer: I always thought he was very thin, but he was always very polite. When I took him to school in the morning, he always said, "Thank you, I appreciate the rides." He was a nice boy.

Marx: When you picked him up to go to school, did you see him with lunch?

Steinhauer: One time I took him to school, he had a banana and an apple.

Marx: How many times did you take him to school?

Steinhauer: I took him pretty regularly. Whenever I would pass him, if he were on the road, I'd ask him if he wanted a ride.

Marx: More than twenty times?

Steinhauer: Oh, yes.

The young boy would get in the car, look from side to side, then "scrunch down" underneath the window so no one would see him. He told her he wasn't allowed to have rides to school.

Many, many times, she had seen A.J. doing chores.

"He cleaned the garage, seemed like every day. He would pull everything out of the garage, put it into the driveway, sweep out the inside of the garage, and then he'd haul everything back inside. He did this almost every single day. I can't understand how a garage can get that dirty.

"He used to mow the lawn with an electric lawn mower. He fed the cat; he'd clean the litter box.

"He was—all day he was outside doing chores from when he got up until it got dark at night. He was out there all day. When I got up, he was already out there when I got to the front of my house. I usually get up about seven A.M. and he was probably out there until the sun started to go down."

She had seen A.J. sweep the driveway and the sidewalk—with a paintbrush.

"It seemed like he was trying to be very particular; he was trying to get every piece of grass, and the whole time he was out here, he was screaming, 'I [am] bad, do bad things and I do bad things and I get people in trouble and I won't do it again.' He said it all day.

"Jessica would come to the window in the front and she'd say, 'I can't hear you.' And then David was in and out all day, saying, 'I can't hear you. Say it louder.' And then A.J. would say it and then she'd say, 'I can't hear you. Say it louder.' It was just all day long."

Marx: Did you ever see A.J. playing?
Steinhauer: Playing? No, I never saw him have any friends over or anything.
Marx: Did you ever see Lauren and Jackie doing chores?
Steinhauer: Doing chores? No, they were always playing in the driveway or on the sidewalk out front with their friends.
Marx: Did you ever hear the defendant call A.J. derogatory names?
Steinhauer: Yes. It was quite often; she'd say that he was worthless, he was no good, he would never make

anything of himself, he had shit for brains, and he was a worthless piece of shit that would never go anywhere or do anything with his life.

Marx: Did there ever come a point in time when you saw the defendant strike or accost Andrew Schwarz?

Steinhauer: I never saw her hit him, but one time—when he was out cutting the grass—she came up behind him and she put her hands around his neck. She had like a chokehold around his neck and she picked him up and his feet were like six inches to a foot off the ground and she was swinging him around showing him things in the garage. The only thing I could hear her saying was "Look at this and look at this." And then when she let him down, she dropped him. She didn't let him down—she just dropped him. (While she was testifying about what she had seen, Steinhauer placed her hands around her neck to demonstrate how Jessica was holding A.J.)

Marx: Did he fight back?

Steinhauer: No, he just let his hands swing from side to side. He didn't grab onto her arms to try and release the hold or anything.

Marx: Approximately how big was this little boy?

Steinhauer: He was probably fifty pounds—if that. He was very thin. He wasn't a very big boy at all.

Marx: What did you do after you saw these things take place?

Steinhauer: Well, in January, I called Child Protection Services, but when I felt that they didn't do anything, I didn't call anymore. I felt nothing was being done and I had done my part.

Marx: Did you ever see the defendant hug Andrew Schwarz?

Steinhauer: No.

Marx: Did you ever see the defendant kiss Andrew Schwarz?

Steinhauer: No.

Marx: Did you ever hear the defendant say a kind
word to Andrew Schwarz?
Steinhauer: No.

On cross-examination, Rendell Brown asked Mrs. Steinhauer if she had ever seen A.J. with any bruises; the witness
replied that she had seen him with two black eyes. Other
than that, she had not.

Brown: And you saw him practically every day, didn't you?
Steinhauer: Not every day, but I saw him regularly, yes.
Brown: And you saw him up close because you had
him in your van. You drive a van, right?
Steinhauer: Yes.
Brown: So you had a pretty good look at him?
Steinhauer: Well, I wasn't looking at him while I was
driving. He'd get in—I wouldn't inspect his body
when he got in my car to see if he had bruises.
Brown: Did you ever see David kiss Andrew?
Steinhauer: No.
Brown: Did you ever see David hug Andrew?
Steinhauer: No.

After the lunch break, Eileen Callahan was the next witness to take the stand. The young mother of three young children had, at one time, been a neighbor of the Schwarzes—and
was the victim of Barbara Black's threats.

Even though A.J. had only been to her house twice to play
with her children, her impression was that he was "a very
nice little boy."

In May 1992, she had seen A.J. working in the yard in the
rain—on his hands and knees—edging the sidewalk with a
pair of household scissors.

Marx: Is this the only time you saw Andrew doing chores?
Callahan: No.

Marx: Did it escalate during the time you were living there at Triphammer Road?

Callahan: Yes. I saw Andrew cleaning the car, washing the car, cleaning out the garage on weekends, mowing the yard with an electric lawn mower, raking up pine needles—or leaves, if you will. I saw him cleaning out the cat litter box. One weekend I saw him cleaning the cab of a big tractor-trailer truck.

Marx: Would this go on all day?

Callahan: Yes.

On another occasion when she saw A.J. edging the lawn with scissors, her husband went over to help him with some of the yard work. When she saw A.J. the next day, his eyes were black and blue.

Marx established the fact that during the period of time in question, Mrs. Callahan was a stay-at-home mom who had been pregnant and "couch ridden."

Marx: Did there ever come a point in time that you made a phone call in regards to what you saw? Was that after you saw him with the black eyes?

Callahan: Yes. I called the state attorney's office, the hot line number to get some information, ask questions, and then I called Child Protective Services.

Marx: Do you know if somebody came out to the Schwarz residence in regards to that phone call?

Callahan: Yes.

And then the same series of poignant questions with the same series of heartbreaking answers, establishing that the witness had never seen Jessica Schwarz hug A.J., or kiss A.J., or even say one kind word to him.

The next witness was Margaret Pincus. She and her family had lived next door to the Schwarzes and she, too, had seen A.J. down on his knees, trimming the lawn "around the edges" with a pair of household scissors.

"When I walked out, it was maybe late morning and he was out there—seemed like it was all day long because it was getting dark when he went in the house. I heard noises coming out of the house and to the effect of 'Say it louder— I can't hear you!' It sounded like Jessica, but I couldn't swear to it."

Cupp: Did it sound like an adult female?
Pincus: Yes.
Cupp: And what was A.J. saying, if anything, that he had to yell louder?
Pincus: "My name is A.J. I lie on people to get them in trouble and I'll never do it again."
Cupp: Did you hear him saying this throughout the day?
Pincus: Repeatedly. All day long.

CHAPTER 16

There is much I could say about Richard and his devotion, work, and love for A.J. He needs no one to apologize for him—or to make excuses for him. Certainly no one has the right to question whether Richard could have or should have done more to help A.J. No one has that right. No one cared more during those last months. No one.

—Scott Cupp

Scott Cupp's next witness was the gentleman that he had grown, over the months since A.J.'s death, to care deeply about—and even feel protective of: Dr. Richard Zimmern, Andrew Schwarz's guardian ad litem. Although he was an average-looking man, with neatly combed salt-and-pepper hair, his kindness and his humanity were anything but ordinary. A.J.'s death had broken his heart.

Well-dressed—but casual—in his blue button-down collar shirt, gray dress pants, and sport coat, Dr. Zimmern entered the courtroom and walked slowly to the witness stand.

In his soft voice, the retired pediatrician from Connecticut explained to the jurors that a guardian ad litem is a volunteer who is appointed by judges in various courts to aid and assist any child who is going through the legal process. He had been a guardian for almost four years and had been A.J.'s from July 1992 until May 1993.

"At that time, in July of '92, A.J. was scheduled for a hearing before Judge Birken in Broward County."

> Cupp: So this case, A.J.'s case, was not a Palm Beach County case, but it was a Broward County case? But A.J. was physically living in Palm Beach County; is that correct?
> Zimmern: Correct.
> Cupp: Would it be a fair statement that your role as a guardian in Palm Beach County was kind of a courtesy to the program in Broward so that that guardian wouldn't have to come all the way up to Lantana or Lake Worth?
> Zimmern: Correct.

When he first got the case, Dr. Zimmern went to meet with Jessica and David Schwarz, which was the normal routine, so that he could gather enough background information so that he would be able to present a reasonable and coherent report to the judge. He had a heavy caseload at the time and was told by his supervisor that he would just be covering for Broward County and that it was routine—a court hearing that had to be covered.

He had no idea how complex the case was, how much background there was, or "all the ins and outs of what was going on."

"And, of course, you get paid the same thing for this case that you get paid for all of your cases—and that's what?" Cupp asked.

"We're all volunteers."

At some point, Dr. Zimmern became aware that A.J. had been hospitalized in 1992 for six weeks in the Psychiatric Institute of Vero Beach. As part of his role as a guardian, he requested copies of the discharge summary, the admitting history, and the physical evaluation.

Cupp: And there were several rather specific things that were to happen—according to the hospital?

Zimmern: Yes, there were.

Cupp: You being a pediatrician and physician, you would be familiar with drugs, certain types of prescription drugs that are dispensed and prescribed by physicians? Are you familiar with imipramine?

Zimmern: Imipramine is a drug that has been discovered to have certain calming effects in hyperexcitable children.

Cupp: Anxious children?

Zimmern: Anxious children, learning-disabled children. When it works, it has a very dramatic effect.

Cupp: And one of the recommendations from Vero Beach was that A.J. be placed on imipramine; is that correct?

Zimmern: Yes.

Cupp: When you picked up the case, did you become aware that Andrew was not on imipramine? How did you become aware of that?

Zimmern: In my discussions with Jessica Schwarz, I kept asking her about the drug and two things came out: Number one—he had vomited the drug.

Cupp: According to—

Zimmern: According to Mrs. Schwarz.

Cupp: During the time that you were his guardian, through his third-grade year, he wasn't on imipramine at all?

Zimmern: As far as I know, he was never placed on imipramine. (The guardian had visited Andrew approximately seventeen times, had taken copious notes, and dated them.)

Cupp: I believe you visited Andrew on January 26 of '93. Do you recall that? Did you observe anything unusual about his appearance?

Zimmern: Yes, I observed that he had two black eyes and a swollen nose.

Cupp: Were these . . . I mean, there are black eyes—
and then there are black eyes. Was this just a little red-
dening under the eyes?

Zimmern: No, these were good black eyes.

Cupp: Did you notice anything about his demeanor or
his affect?

Zimmern: Well, he was depressed. He seemed to me to
be depressed, subdued, looking down. He frequently—
when he was upset—would sort of look down, sort of
hunch.

Cupp: Another one of the discharge recommendations
from the Vero Beach hospitalization was that he, as well
as family—including Mrs. Schwarz—needed desperately to get into counseling; is that right?

Zimmern: They recommended counseling.

Cupp: Individually and family?

Zimmern: Yes.

Cupp: How long of a delay was there from the time
that he was discharged to when any counseling ever
took place for Andrew?

Zimmern: He was discharged on March 20, [1992],
and I believe his first appointment was September 10.
A little less than six months. Andrew had fourteen
appointments; three were canceled, three were no-
shows.

Cupp: Did you ever have a conversation with Mrs.
Schwarz in which she relayed how she felt about
Andrew? Was there one conversation in particular that
disturbed you? And what phrase or what terms did she
relay to you to describe him?

Zimmern: The phrase that scared me was "His eyes
are dead. He has no soul."

Dr. Zimmern then told the jury about his visit to see
Andrew on April 24, 1993—his tenth birthday. When he
pulled up in front of the house, the young boy was edging
the lawn with a pair of household scissors. During the time

he was there, there was no talk of a birthday party or of any other birthday gifts.

> Cupp: And you brought him a birthday present?
> Zimmern: Yes, he had wanted some Battle Trolls.
> Cupp: How did he feel about that?
> Zimmern: Well, he was kind of sad that day, but the trolls cheered him up.
> Cupp: Did you ever see Jessica embrace or have any physical contact or affectionate connection with Andrew?
> Zimmern: No.

On cross-examination by Rendell Brown, Dr. Zimmern admitted that the only time he had seen Andrew with any bruises was the one occasion when the child's face was injured.

> Brown: And your visits were actually drop-in kinds of visits, weren't they?
> Zimmern: My visits—all of them were appointments.
> Brown: You had an appointment on the day of his birthday?
> Zimmern: I would usually call to make an appointment. The only time that I didn't was his birthday, I guess, and Easter. But Mrs. Schwarz knew I was coming the day of his birthday because she was the one who told me to get Battle Trolls.
> Brown: Was that in response to asking her what he would like for his birthday?
> Zimmern: Correct.
> Brown: And did she say to you, "No, he can't have anything for his birthday"? She didn't tell you that, did she? In fact, she said, in response to your question, "He would like some Battle Trolls"?
> Zimmern: Correct.
> Brown: And she allowed you to bring those Battle Trolls and give them to him, didn't she?
> Zimmern: Yes.

Brown: Let me ask you, sir, if you'll look at that report and tell me if you recognize that report?

Zimmern: Yes, I do recognize it. This is my report to Judge Birken at the first hearing in September of '92.

Brown: As a guardian ad litem, reports of minors—which are otherwise confidential and not reviewable by the public—are reviewable by you; is that correct?

Zimmern: Yes.

Brown: You can get into the reports and read the reports? And, in fact, that becomes sometimes necessary for a guardian ad litem to do his job properly; isn't that true?

Zimmern: Yes.

Brown: And did there come a time when you began to get into the reports regarding Andrew Schwarz? His files, the proceedings that were going on in Broward and what those proceedings were about? You read all of that stuff?

Zimmern: I read the stuff that I was given.

Brown: Now, Jessica and David Schwarz lived in Palm Beach County at all times that you were aware of them; isn't that correct?

Zimmern: Yes.

Brown: And yet there was a court proceeding going on in Broward County; isn't that correct? And there was a reason for that, wasn't there?

Zimmern: Yes, I presume that it was because the case originated there.

Brown: And who lived in Broward County, where the case originated?

Zimmern: Ilene Logan, his natural mother, and—at that time—Patsy, his sister.

Brown: You've indicated that you have some knowledge about a drug called imipramine?

Zimmern: Yes.

Brown: It's intended to alter certain behaviors; wouldn't you agree?

Zimmern: It is a mood-ameliorating drug.

Brown: And the behaviors that it's intended to correct are those organic behaviors that usually have set in on a person by the formative years—which is four to five years of age; isn't that correct, Doctor?

Zimmern: Partially. Imipramine can be used for learning disabilities, for children who have hyperexcitability syndromes and it also can be used in certain situations as a plain old tranquilizer. If something is congenital and it is an inborn condition, then it will become apparent. However, it becomes apparent at different times in different situations. Learning disabilities generally don't become apparent until kindergarten or first grade when a child is put under the stress—the actual stress of learning.

Brown: The cause, however, is generally set in the formative years; wouldn't you agree with that?

Zimmern: It's hard to give that a precise yes or no, black and white, because—actually, I'm not an expert witness on this.

Brown: You were a little bit out of your area when you started with Mr. Cupp with those answers, weren't you?

Zimmern: I would disagree. Any practicing pediatrician, using imipramine all the time, learns to use it, to adjust dosages, knows the side effects.

Brown: You will agree that at some point you concluded, from your involvement with Andrew Schwarz, that not only should Andrew continue his counseling, but there should be intensive counseling offered to the family as well; isn't that correct?

Zimmern: The recommendation for the family counseling came from Dr. Uttley in his discharge recommendations. I really pushed mostly for Andrew's counseling.

Brown: And the truth of the matter is, Doctor, that not only did you push mostly for Andrew's counseling, but so did the entire Child Protection Team; isn't that correct?

Zimmern: Well, they were pushing for counseling, of course.

Brown: For Andrew, I mean?

Zimmern: For Andrew, yes.

Brown: And during your involvement with the Child Protection Team and with HRS, never once, never once did anybody push for counseling for the family—as the law requires, did they? Did they, Doctor? Did HRS ever make any recommendation or push for counseling for the rest of the family other than A.J., to your knowledge?

Zimmern: Not in my presence.

Brown: Now, there is no question that Dr. Uttley, who treated this child for six weeks, who determined what his problem was, and who put him on the medication to try to help him, made the recommendation that there be intensive counseling for the rest of this family as a part of this discharge summary, didn't he?

Zimmern: Correct.

Brown: Now, Doctor, the truth of the matter is that from the very beginning, when you first met Jessica Schwarz, she was telling you then that Andrew needs help, emotional help, wasn't she? Isn't that true?

Zimmern: No, it's not true. As a matter of fact, sir, quite the reverse. Mrs. Jessica Schwarz was quite clear that she didn't believe in counseling and she didn't believe in drug therapy.

CHAPTER 17

The overwhelming thing I remember about Richard was his kindness—his humanity. Easily loved. When he broke down on the stand—briefly—I wanted to leave the courtroom. It was horrible! It broke my heart. I wanted to scream. He loved A.J.

—Scott Cupp

Rendell Brown then requested that the doctor read his entire guardian ad litem report to the jurors, and Dr. Zimmern was eager to comply. "Certainly. Sorry, I'm meticulous." The transcript was as follows:

"History: Andrew Schwarz comes from a highly dysfunctional family setting. He was abused and neglected by his drug abuse natural mother and suffered verbal and physical abuse from her paramours.

"Andrew has been living with his father and stepmother, David and Jessica Schwarz, since he was adjudicated dependant in mid-1990. Mr. Schwarz was given custody of his son November 19, 1990.

"Andrew received outpatient counseling at the Youth Services Bureau in Palm Beach County in 1991. On February 6, 1992, he was admitted to the Psychiatric Institute of Vero Beach under the care of Thomas E. Uttley to remain there for six weeks. Reasons for admission were withdrawn behavior, depression, thought-processing problems, suicidal behavior and violence towards his younger sister.

"His discharge diagnoses were depressive disorder, post traumatic stress disorder with extreme anxiety, specific learning disability, parent/child problems, extreme and enduring psychosocial stress factors.

"Discharge recommendations were six months of anti-depressant medication, imipramine, 125 milligrams per day and in divided doses, intense and extensive individual and family psychotherapy to work through issues of loss and abandonment.

"He had classes at [Indian River Memorial Hospital] and laboratory monitoring of his drug levels. Andrew was discharged on March 20.

"On May 1, 1992, Judge Birken decreed that the natural mother and sister of Andrew Schwarz were enjoined and restrained from contacting him, either directly or indirectly; also, that no adult was to disparage any other involved adult in his presence.

"On the same date, David Schwarz signed a protective services plan in which the following problems were identified: Medical needs, social stimulation and non compliance with HRS.

"Sources contacted: Andrew Schwarz, child; Jessica Schwarz, stepmother; David Schwarz, father; Ms. Heinrich, guidance counselor at the Indian Pines school; Linda Hunter, second grade teacher, Indian Pines school.

"Source unable to contact: Thomas Uttley, psychiatrist at the Psychiatric Institute of Vero Beach.

"Updated findings: Jessica Schwarz, Andrew's stepmother, reports as follows: In 1990 HRS placed Andrew and his sister, Patsy Spence, with the Schwarzes. Andrew has made great progress while in their care. When Mrs. Schwarz first met him six months ago, he was a frightened waif who would hide his face and was totally inarticulate, malnourished, dirty, and ate ravenously with his fingers.

"While in Palm Beach, Patsy received counseling at the

Center for Children in Crisis. Patsy, who will be thirteen years old next month, accused Mrs. Schwarz of verbal and physical abuse. She also threatened suicide, which apparently triggered the hearings that placed her in foster care.

"Mrs. Schwarz feels that the children's natural mother, Ilene Logan, whom she regards as a slob, a slut, a game player and a manipulator, orchestrated these actions for revenge.

"Mr. and Mrs. Schwarz attended court ordered parenting classes in 1990. She used the principles learned in those classes as a basis for handling Andrew, keeping her wall chart, recording of his bad deeds and rule infractions.

"Andrew kept breaking rules repeatedly and therefore never won praise for good behavior. He was always behind and consequently grounded far into the future.

"Mrs. Schwarz would arrange deals in which a large number of bad deeds would be exchanged for a few good ones, but this did not work very well.

"Mr. and Mrs. Schwarz attended two of the sessions held for parents at the Vero Beach hospital. It was hard for them to get there, considering their routine. They did attend the discharge meeting and received advice and instructions, according to Mrs. Schwarz.

"Andrew remained on imipramine for a short while but he was vomiting the pills. When the hospital prescription ran out, a local family doctor refused to renew the medication.

"Due to errors in administration, Andrew did not receive a medical card until August, 1992. Mrs. Schwarz then called South County Mental Health Unit and arranged for an appointment on September 10. Her husband and two other daughters did receive their cards. HRS reportedly told Mrs. Schwarz that Andrew was dropped because he was too old.

"Mrs. Schwarz feels that Andrew is an extremely excitable child with a poor attention span; that he's impulsive, has poor judgment and cannot be trusted alone. She's upset by Andrew's lying, sneaking about, and his refusal to talk. She feels he knows what he is doing and uses rule infractions as a way to get attention; that he's 'a bad boy with a grin on his face.'

"Mrs. Schwarz acknowledges that she's a tough, combative person, not a warm or touchy-feely person. She believes in tough love and thinks that psychological counseling is of little value. She also feels that Andrew was never helped by imipramine and that he needs a strong, structured home with firm rules and prompt punishment for all deviations. Here he would feel safe and wanted.

"David Schwarz is a long distance truck driver who's rarely home. He's had a difficult life but recalls Andrew's birth in 1983 affectionately. Even though Patsy was not his child, he loved her, and was happy to take her into his home, as well.

"Ilene Logan told Patsy that Mr. Schwarz was her father and that he did not want to accept Patsy and Andrew. Mr. Schwarz has been baffled by Andrew's increasing depression and withdrawal over the past fifteen months, accompanied by sleep disturbance, insomnia and bed-wetting. His son's impulsiveness, unpredictability has frightened him. Mr. Schwarz really doesn't know how to handle Andrew so he tries to keep order and keep his child safe.

"The guardian ad litem walked with Andrew about his neighborhood for about an hour. He was quiet, non-spontaneous, and did not engage in any conversation but would answer innocent questions. He did not permit prying into his thoughts by a stranger.

"Andrew did say that he does not want to see or speak to his natural mother and stepsister.

"Mrs. Schwarz told me that Patsy told Andrew she hated him and that she had physically abused him.

"Linda Hunter, Andrew's second grade teacher, said she loved Andrew and described him as a very bright child who was never a behavior problem, never acted strange or irrational, and never did anything in school to hurt himself or other children. She thought that Andrew was scared to death of something or someone. He was very loving toward her and she felt he needed love in return.

"Ms. Hunter said she often sent good behavior notes home and would receive strange letters filled with negative things about Andrew. He was forbidden by his stepmother to receive any snacks or goodies in school, attend any school parties, or go on any field trips. Mrs. Schwarz explained to Ms. Hunter that these prohibitions were necessary to balance the long list of bad things he had done at home and that he was deeply indebted—behavior wise.

"Ms. J. Heinrich, guidance counsel [or] at Indian Pines school, could tell the guardian ad litem very little about Andrew because she had been forbidden by Mrs. Schwarz from speaking to him or to his sister, Patsy, when Patsy was in school. She said that when Patsy was in school there, she acted like a little mother to Andrew and was very concerned about him. Andrew seems immature to Ms. Heinrich. She also said he's frightened, doesn't smile, although he always says everything is fine. She feels he's afraid to speak out.

"At the request of the Schwarzes, Andrew has been before the Child Study Team three times. On each occasion they concluded he was not a candidate for classes for the emotionally disturbed. They felt that Andrew was not a behavior problem, but did have trouble concentrating. They also found a conductive loss in the child's left ear and requested the parents follow through with their family doctor.

"In 1991, Andrew did receive counseling at school from Ed Carpenter of the Youth Services Bureau. In general, Ms. Heinrich feels that Mrs. Schwarz has been hostile to her, and the teachers in this school, in their efforts to help Andrew. She has written negative notes to the school and has not been at all friendly.

"Dr. Thomas Uttley, attending psychiatrist at the Psychiatric Institute of Vero Beach, did not return the guardian ad litem's calls.

"Summary: Andrew is a depressed, anxious child with severe and long standing parent problems. Last spring he became suicidal, withdrawn, and was unable to assess reality. He may have come close to a psychiatric breakdown. If Andrew cannot live in our world, he will withdraw into his own.

"Andrew seems to do well academically in school so far. Intellectual observations are not onerous in this early grace period. This may change as the material studied becomes more difficult and requires increased concentration and effort. Andrew's behavior in school has been fine, as well. He has not been a problem to his teacher, his peers, or himself.

"However, Andrew does not function well at home. He cannot follow the family rules, resists doing his assigned chores and is just generally uncooperative. Something is wrong here. Changes must be made. Why is Andrew so cooperative in school and so rotten at home?

"Andrew loves and needs Mr. and Mrs. Schwarz. When they did not visit during the visiting in Vero Beach he was overwhelmed and de-compensated completely. Perhaps Jessica Schwarz should alter her patterns to fit the patterns of his illness. Certainly the family, Andrew, Jessica, and David—if possible—would benefit greatly from individual counseling and imipramine for the six months suggested by Dr. Uttley in his discharge recommendations.

"Andrew suffers from poor self-esteem and a sense of rejection. He perceives himself as worthless, with a lack of identity. Andrew needs to be built up and given this identity. His self-esteem should be enhanced and he can no longer be rejected as a bad boy, unworthy of love or respect.

"The guardian ad litem strongly recommends that Andrew continue in individual counseling and Jessica Schwarz and Andrew participate in family therapy; David Schwarz, too, if possible."

Zimmern: And that's it.
Brown: You do not have the signature page?
Zimmern: Sorry. "Andrew must be treated again with imipramine, as suggested by Dr. Uttley, and HRS con-

tinue supervising this family, the court review this case in six months, the guardian ad litem continue to monitor the case."

Brown: Now, Doctor, it's exceedingly clear that this entire family needed help to deal with this situation; isn't that true?

Zimmern: I would say yes.

Brown: Now, you're not a part of the Child Protection Team, per se?

Zimmern: No.

Brown: So getting the family counseling and that sort of thing is not really your bag, is it? That's what the Child Protection Team does?

Zimmern: It's not my job to arrange for counseling.

Brown: But when a father comes to you and says, "I really don't know how to handle my child, so I just try to keep order and keep him safe," doesn't that sort of set off red flags that he's asking for help? That the family needs help?

Zimmern: The family needs help in handling Andrew and Andrew needs help in handling himself.

Brown: And you're not a trained psychologist?

Zimmern: No.

Brown: But you were able to see the need here?

Zimmern: I was able to see the need that Andrew had for help.

Brown: Okay. What about Mr. Schwarz and Mrs. Schwarz?

Zimmern: Yes, I would say that both Mr. and Mrs. Schwarz needed help.

Brown: Now, you also said that there were no problems with Andrew as far as behavior at Indian Pines is concerned, correct?

Zimmern: No, there were no problems according to the two teachers, Ms. Hunter and Mrs. Idrissi.

Brown: Did that have anything to do with any requests on your part to the school regarding his behavior, sir?

Zimmern: Yes.

Brown: Did you personally ask Mrs. Idrissi to set a different standard of rules and regulations for Andrew than the rest of the children? Did you?

Zimmern: I certainly did.

Brown: My question is: if his behavior is on par, there's no need to do that, is there?

Zimmern: I really can't answer that yes or no because there are . . . All right, yes, if his behavior is on par, there's no need to do that.

With that, Rendell Brown ended his cross-examination. Scott Cupp then began the redirect questioning.

Cupp: You've already testified that you couldn't get anything out of Andrew Schwarz? He wouldn't talk about what was going on inside the home?

Zimmern: Absolutely not.

Cupp: Ms. Heinrich, the guidance counselor? Usually a pretty good source of information for you—for kids in your cases? Now, reading briefly from your report, "Ms. J. Heinrich, guidance counselor at Indian Pines, could tell the guardian very little because she had been forbidden by Mrs. Schwarz from speaking to him or his sister, Patsy." So, she couldn't give you any information?

Zimmern: No.

Cupp: And the other source you had—other than the other two I'll get back to—was Linda Hunter? The second-grade teacher?

Zimmern: Yes.

Cupp: And Linda Hunter basically said, in a nutshell, "When I have the kid, he's fine, there's no behavior problems, he's a good kid, sweet kid. . . ." All the rest of the adjectives, correct?

Zimmern: Correct.

Cupp: So that leaves two people who—

Zimmern: David and Jessica.

Cupp: So at that point, all the information that you had, all the history was coming from the defendant? And her husband?

Zimmern: Yes.

Cupp: And they painted a pretty bleak picture of Andrew, didn't they?

Zimmern: Yes.

Cupp: Isn't that the same basically, with the intake at Vero Beach, the history source for A.J. for the hospital was the very same two people?

Zimmern: Yes.

Cupp: So all you really had to go on, at that point, was what she said?

Zimmern: Yes.

Cupp: Did you later come to find out that practically everything that she had told you about Andrew was false?

Zimmern: Yes.

Cupp: During the six weeks that Andrew was in Vero Beach . . . it's a little ways from here? At least two hours?

Zimmern: Two hours.

Cupp: Andrew gets delivered up there and he's there for forty-two days and his loving stepmother and biological father see him twice; is that right?

Zimmern: Well, that's the information I had.

Cupp: And it's in the records?

Zimmern: Yes.

Cupp: Isn't it also in the records that that was a major source of problems for him while he was there, that he would—the term, I think, is "decompensate," when they would not come to see him?

Zimmern: Yes.

Cupp: You can't have group therapy when you're by yourself? You can't have family therapy when you don't have a family?

(Dr. Zimmern sadly agreed.)

Cupp: When did A.J. arrive to live with the Schwarzes?

Zimmern: I think it was November of 1990.

Cupp: When you have this conversation that you've read to the jury about David Schwarz being baffled by Andrew's depression and withdrawal over the past fifteen months . . . Now, he told you that—sometime after Andrew arrived—these things happened; is that right?

Zimmern: Yes.

Cupp: After Andrew arrived in the Schwarz home—he was there for many months—and then for the past fifteen months, when David was talking to you, we've got problems of sleep disturbances, insomnia, bed-wetting, increasing depression, withdrawal?

Zimmern: Yes.

Cupp: So they started when he was in the Schwarz home, right?

Zimmern: These symptoms started in the Schwarz home.

Cupp: According to David?

Zimmern: According to David.

Cupp: And the point is that Mr. Schwarz specifically told you that these conditions started occurring some fifteen months prior to the time he talked to you?

Zimmern: There was an acute onset fifteen months prior to our conversation.

Cupp: That would have been during the time period that he was in the home and in the primary care of the defendant; is that correct?

Zimmern: Correct.

CHAPTER 18

The most important thing in this little boy's life was
that he do his work and get it all done.

—Dr. George Rahaim

In an earlier hearing, Judge Colbath had ruled that—because of her fear of the defendant—it would not be necessary for Patsy Spence to come into the courtroom and take the witness stand; but, instead, she would be allowed to testify via closed-circuit TV, from his chambers.

A therapist who had counseled the young girl had testified at the hearing that Patsy had nightmares about Jessica and not being able to save A.J.

From the adjoining room, Scott Cupp established that Patsy Spence was almost fifteen years old, her natural mother was Ilene Logan, and that there had come a time when she and her half brother, A.J., had had to leave their mother's home. They lived with an aunt for a short period of time and then were placed with Jessica and David Schwarz, even though Patsy was not a blood relative of either one of them.

When they first went to live with the Schwarzes, the only other child in the home was David and Jessica's natural daughter, Jackie, who was two years old at the time.

At first, Patsy and A.J. were treated well.

At some point, Lauren, Jessica's natural daughter from a

previous marriage, came to live with them. She was a few years younger than Patsy and they shared a bedroom for a while. According to Patsy, the girls got along "all right" at first.

Cupp: Did there come a time when you could no longer stay in the same room with Lauren?

Patsy: Yes.

Cupp: Tell me what happened that caused that?

Patsy: When I let one of my friends come in to use the phone and Jessica came home and she caught him leaving the house, so she put me in my brother's room.

Cupp: Was that during the day or at nighttime?

Patsy: Around like five.

Cupp: About how old was the boy?

Patsy: About thirteen or fourteen.

Cupp: And about how old were you?

Patsy: About twelve or thirteen.

Cupp: Who else was home when the boy came in?

Patsy: Just me and Lauren.

Cupp: What happened when Jessica came home?

Patsy: She started hitting me.

Cupp: Was her hand open or closed?

Patsy: Open and closed.

Cupp: So she slapped you?

Patsy: And punched me.

Cupp: What part of your body did she punch?

Patsy: My face. My nose started bleeding.

Cupp: Did she say anything to you?

Patsy: She was calling me names, like "bitch," "cunt," "slut," "whore."

Cupp: After that, what was your punishment?

Patsy: To sleep in my brother's room for a year.

Cupp: Did you ever get to sleep in the room with Lauren again after that?

Patsy: No.

According to Patsy, there were many times—when A.J. didn't do his chores right—that Jessica punished him by making him eat bread and water while sitting on the floor in his room.

Patsy could not remember A.J. ever having a problem with wetting the bed when they were living with their natural mother, or at their aunt Dodi's house, or while they were in foster care. And he did not have a problem with it when they first came to live with Jessica and David.

But at some point after Patsy was staying in the same room with him, A.J. started wetting the bed.

Cupp: Would Jessica do anything?
Patsy: She would rub his nose into it.
Cupp: Did you see this happen?
Patsy: Yes.
Cupp: What would A.J. do when this would happen?
Patsy: Cry.
Cupp: Did you ever see Bear do that?
Patsy: No.
Cupp: Did Bear even know that it was happening?
Patsy: Yes.

Patsy was so afraid of Jessica that even after she was removed from the Schwarz home and placed in foster care—leaving A.J. behind—she didn't tell anyone about the abuses she had seen.

The state offered Dr. George Rahaim, the next witness, as an expert in the field of psychology in connection with child abuse. He was the team psychologist for the Child Protection Team.

As a result of his involvement in the case of Andrew Schwarz, he had reviewed a huge amount of material: records of the Child Protection Team, a complete set of records of A.J.'s six-week hospitalization, school records, and "an enormous pile of HRS records," records from the South County Mental Health Center, the Atlantic Counseling Center in

Delray Beach, the records of the guardian ad litem, and the medical records of Dr. Sheju Ukuedojor.

He reviewed the police reports documenting interviews with the Schwarz family and most—if not all—of their neighbors and many of the depositions. In addition, the psychologist interviewed Mary Idrissi, A.J.'s third-grade teacher, and viewed the videotape of Jessica, Lauren, and Jackie.

Upon A.J.'s admission to the Psychiatric Institute of Vero Beach, he was immediately placed on suicide precaution—someone looked in on him every fifteen minutes—day and night.

The psychologist testified that Dr. Uttley, the attending psychiatrist, prescribed imipramine (an antidepressant) and Ativan (a tranquilizer) for A.J. The child underwent psychological testing and evaluation and a physical. Dr. Uttley also ordered that he have individual counseling, group counseling, and family psychotherapy.

"He participated there in a great many therapeutic activities: counseling with staff, group therapy with other patients and staff, play activities. He went to school there. He was prescribed medication, took the medication."

Jessica and David had given a history that he suffered brain damage by virtue of being a cocaine baby, suffering fetal alcohol syndrome, having been struck in the head with a frying pan, and, ironically, a near-drowning experience very early in his life.

A.J. had a CAT scan, at least two electroencephalograms, blood tests, thyroid profile, and a battery of psychological tests.

Even though the psychological records indicated that some of his behavior was abnormal, Dr. Rahaim had found no evidence that Andrew Schwarz, who had been investigated quite thoroughly, had any organic problem or abnormality with the functioning of his brain—no brain damage.

"The medical records ruled it out quite conclusively."

Dr. Rahaim testified that when Andrew Schwarz's intelligence capacity had been tested in school in March 1990, his

IQ had been 101—average. He was tested again in October 1991 and his IQ was 91—low average. A.J. was tested a third time in February 1992—during his stay in the psychiatric hospital—and, astonishingly, his IQ was 86—very low average. In less than two years, there had been a 15-point drop in A.J.'s IQ.

"That's a serious drop in intelligence ability."

At one point, during A.J.'s hospitalization, he was given a list of twenty goals and asked to check off the ones that were important to him. He checked all twenty items. Then he numbered the three most important ones: Get my chores and schoolwork done. Do better in school. Understand my feelings better.

"The most important thing in this little boy's life was that he do his work and get it all done."

He was not quite nine years old at the time.

"He asked the staff if he could please not leave the hospital, that he wanted to stay there because he was allowed to do things there."

A.J. suffered from depression and also experienced many of the symptoms of post-traumatic stress disorder: nightmares, insomnia, very frequent agitation, and constant fear.

"He was a remarkably passive person, exhibited a passive withdrawn approach to almost everything. He also was very agitated and he exhibited behaviors that you think of when you think of somebody who can't stand to be in their own skin—they're constantly fearful and anxious. All during the hospitalization, they noted that over and over."

A.J. had become a bed wetter, but the problem disappeared while he was in the hospital.

"The bed-wetting appears to have started very early in 1991, a few months after Andrew arrived at the Schwarz home. It continued until the day that he was admitted into the psychiatric hospital. I think the bed-wetting was one of many, many symptoms of being abused and harmed."

A.J. found himself sobbing in front of other people in school and other places—"just broken-down sobbing." He exhibited regressed behavior—fingers in the mouth, baby talk—one of the hallmarks of an abused child.

"Andrew experienced just an overwhelming anxiety and agitation, what I think is best described as kind of a constant sense of dread and fear."

A.J. became close to psychotic in the hospital when there were no visits and when visits were promised, but they did not occur.

"My understanding [is], except for the time that he was actually brought to the hospital, that Jessica Schwarz visited him once and that David Schwarz visited him once, even though there were apparently many telephone calls and one letter literally begging for them to be involved with the child, letting them know that the child was decompensating, was deteriorating because of no access to the parents—that they expected that the child would do very, very badly because of no involvement of the parents in treatment."

Overwhelming insecurity and need to be made secure and safe. Constantly needed to be hugged and touched and made to feel safe. Grabbed the staff and tried to hug them. Always wanted to be hugged and comforted. Withdrawn. Preoccupied. Passive. No spontaneity except for needing security. No spontaneous information.

"He was described as having problems that he was keeping deep inside; that he was so withdrawn that he couldn't tell you much about his life. His thoughts were disorganized. He couldn't think straight, if you will. His affect was flat. You didn't see emotion, you know, laughter and things like that. He was just zombielike.

"He had no trust in anyone. He wouldn't complain. If you asked him what was wrong, he'd tell you 'he' was wrong. His identity was just very badly shattered. In my opinion, he felt like he was worthless—that all bad things were due to him."

He was unable to have relationships, to personally have friends, to share stories, or to trust anyone.

"And there was a deep overwhelming learned humiliation about the boy."

The continued use of derogatory words by the defendant ground down his spirit. He was so frequently and consistently degraded that "he knew that it was true."

"Children up to around the age of eleven or twelve are learning who they are and what they are, if you will. They are learning their identity. The effect of this constant cursing, being put down, belittled, degraded, was that he learned that he was garbage—not even that he felt like it or thought it—but that was him and that's overwhelmingly destructive."

Dr. Rahaim testified that the date of Dr. Richard Zimmern's report—September 9, 1992—was significant in isolating a time period. David Schwarz had told the guardian ad litem that he was baffled by A.J.'s increased depression and withdrawal over the previous fifteen months, accompanied by sleep disturbance, insomnia, and bed-wetting. His son's impulsive, unpredictable behavior frightened him.

"What he indicates is that the date of onset of all of these symptoms of abuse was a few months after A.J. came to live in the Schwarz home."

At the time of A.J.'s discharge from the psychiatric hospital, there was a very angry telephone conversation between the social worker and Jessica Schwarz. In this exchange, Jessica indicated that she was not going to come up there, and if they wanted to discharge him, they could discharge him. However, they'd have to bring him back home because she wasn't going to come and get him.

"It's hard to have family therapy without a family?" Cupp proffered.

Dr. Rahaim agreed.

"I certainly thought that the child needed to be removed from that home. It was my opinion that the child was a targeted child, he was being abused, and that the best thing we could do to protect him was to get him out of there.

"I felt that this child was at terrible risk. I thought he was at the end of his rope. I thought we had to get him out of there quick."

CHAPTER 19

He told me that he didn't want to talk to his natural mother because she and her men friends had been mean to him in the past. He said they had beaten him with belts and belt buckles. He said he wants to remain with his dad.

—Janie Sutherland

The prosecution rested its case and Rendell Brown called Janie Sutherland to the witness stand as the first witness for the defense. She was employed by the Juvenile Justice Department, but in 1991, she worked for HRS in Child Protective Services.

"I was given a caseload and it was my responsibility to monitor that particular case. My duties included home visits, court, and basically just supervising the child."

She was neither present at the dependency hearing on August 17, 1990, when Andrew Schwarz was adjudicated dependent and placed under protective supervision, nor at a review hearing on November 19, 1990, when A.J. and Patsy were placed in the custody of David and Jessica Schwarz. She was aware that the children had lived with a maternal aunt before being placed with the Schwarzes.

As a part of her duties, she became involved with the supervision of A.J. and Patsy during the time that both children were living with Jessica and David.

The purpose of home visits was to monitor the case and to make sure that there wasn't any abuse or neglect going on in the home, and to inspect the physical surroundings to make sure the home was adequately kept, safe, and clean. She was to make unscheduled and unannounced visits, with the expectation that if something was going on, there wouldn't be a chance to cover it up.

"Most of the time when you visit the home, you try to get the family—the mother and the father and the children—there when you conduct. A lot of times it's done one-on-one because you want to talk to them to find out if there are things going on in the home that you should know about."

Sutherland discussed the need for counseling and therapy with the defendant, and Jessica told her that she had signed up A.J. for special classes in school and expressed a desire to get both of them in counseling. She agreed that A.J. needed extensive counseling and therapy.

"From my recollection, they appeared to have adjusted well to the new placement."

On February 20, 1991, Sutherland visited the Schwarzes because she had received a report from a protective investigator that "something" had occurred in the home. Because there had been an allegation of abuse, she was specifically looking for scars, bruises, or a difference in their attitude and behavior.

"You're looking for physical evidence in the home—all sorts of things."

Brown: And when you saw them, how did they appear?
Sutherland: It appeared that nothing was wrong.
Brown: They appeared fine, just fine?
Sutherland: Just fine.

On March 13, 1991, she had made a regular home visit and her observations regarding the children were that "everything appeared to be intact—the kids appeared to be okay." They were in counseling and therapy.

When she visited on May 7, 1991, she observed that A.J. "seemed very hyper, but for the most part—other than that—everything was fine."

Sutherland testified that, according to her notes, when she visited on August 16, 1991, the children had just eaten lunch and were playing outside in the pool, including A.J.

"Incidentally, did Jessica say any nice things about A.J.?" Brown posed.

"She said that he had done better in school despite the fact that he still has problems retaining information. She said he did better," Sutherland replied.

During an office visit with A.J. and Patsy on August 30, 1991, A.J. again was very hyper and disruptive.

Her observation on October 15, 1991, was that they both "looked well and healthy and are doing much better in school."

After his six-week hospitalization, she visited A.J. on April 13, 1992, and he told her he was "doing good" and that his behavior and grades were good and had improved.

"He told me that he didn't want to talk to his natural mother because she and her men friends had been mean to him in the past. He said they had beaten him with belts and belt buckles. He said he wants to remain with his dad."

Brown: Now, from the beginning of your supervision with him, up to this point had he told you anything like that about Mrs. Schwarz—Jessica?
Sutherland: No.
Brown: And had you seen any evidence of anything like that from Jessica Schwarz?
Sutherland: No.

When Sutherland made an unannounced visit to the Schwarz home on May 8, 1992, only A.J. and his stepsister, Lauren, were at the house. A.J. explained that his stepmother had gone to the store and would be right back.

A.J. told her that when he went to court on May 1, the judge in Broward County spoke to him in his chambers and told him that his natural mother was ordered not to see him—she had no visitation rights.

"He said that also applied to Patsy."

A.J. told her that he was doing fine and that there were no problems and she testified that she did not observe any scars or bruises that day.

She told the jurors that during the period of time that she was making visits to the Schwarz home, no one in the neighborhood—adult or child—had ever come to her and told her anything about any problems with A.J. And even though she had visited with Patsy on numerous occasions, sometimes outside the presence of Jessica, Patsy had never told her about anything improper that Jessica was doing to A.J.

In fact, when Patsy left the Schwarz home, Sutherland was the one who drove her away from the house and had talked to her during the ride.

> Brown: And she never once ever mentioned to you anything about Jessica Schwarz doing anything to that child, did she?
> Sutherland: No.

On cross-examination, Janie Sutherland said she didn't recall who Patsy's teachers were during the time she was supervising her, but that she had spoken to one of them on one occasion. Just prior to Patsy being moved out of the Schwarz home, Sutherland had picked her up from school and had a conversation with the teacher about Patsy being upset.

> Cupp: Prior to that, did you ever have a conversation with her teacher?
> Sutherland: I don't think so.
> Cupp: How about Andrew—who was Andrew's teachers during that time period?
> Sutherland: I don't remember.
> Cupp: Was there ever a time when you knew? At the

time that you were supervising Andrew, did you know who his teachers were?

Sutherland: I basically dealt with his therapist.

Cupp: So you never spoke with his teachers for any reason?

Sutherland: I may have. I can't recall at this time.

Cupp: Is there anything in your records that would refresh your recollection?

Sutherland: I don't think so.

Cupp: So, it's fair to say if it's not in your records, you never talked to them?

Sutherland: I may have. I don't recall.

Cupp: Wouldn't that be something that you would note in your records if you talked to a child's teacher to verify how they were doing, or if there were any problems you would note that—just like you would note when you go out to the home?

Sutherland: Yes. (She reluctantly admitted that some of her monthly "visits" were telephonic.)

Cupp: In fact, you could go an entire month without seeing the child if things were going along reasonably well. You could call up just to check in and see how everything was going; is that right?

Sutherland: I may.

Cupp: So, it's fair to say that the source of information for you in determining whether or not the child or children were doing okay, [it] would be the family, right? That's all you had to go on, was what Jessica said was going on?

Sutherland: No, home visits, and I talked frequently with their therapist or their counselor. (She admitted there was a period of time when A.J. was having a difficult time getting to counseling and he had missed quite a few sessions.)

Cupp: Isn't it fair to say that when A.J. would tell you about his wishes and wants, you really don't know

what the source of that information was—you don't know if that was him telling you his true wants, or somebody else telling him, "This is what you better say"?
Sutherland: No, I don't.

The next witness for the defense, Joan Wyllner, testified that she had been employed by HRS in several different positions for approximately 5½ years. In her capacity as a protective services officer, the management of A.J.'s case had been transferred to her, and as part of her duties, she visited the Schwarz home approximately once a month and kept records of her involvement.

When she arrived at the Schwarz home on August 20, 1992, she observed that the house was in a nice area and that there was a pool in the backyard and a security fence. In terms of cleanliness, it "appeared to be acceptable."

She visited again in September and October and saw no evidence that A.J. was being physically abused.

Brown: What are you looking for when you visit with a child?
Wyllner: Whether there's any indication of abuse, obvious neglect, whether the house is unsafe, if there's food in the refrigerator, if the child is receiving medical care, things along that line are things that we would look for.
Brown: And up to this date you haven't seen anything?
Wyllner: Nothing beyond our guidelines.

She continued her monthly visits and, on more than one occasion, she talked to A.J. about his feelings in regard to living with his father and stepmother.

"He wanted to stay with his father."

Even though the household, of course, included Jessica, he specifically said he wanted to be with his father—to stay with his father—and he did not want to have contact with his natural mother.

Brown: Did he ever mention anything to you about Patsy?

Wyllner: That he didn't want contact with either of them.

Brown: Now you've told us that Andrew indicated he wanted to be where he was. Did you get any indication that he was not wanted there?

Wyllner: I don't recall any specific statement like that, no, sir.

On cross-examination, Wyllner testified that the supervision of Andrew Schwarz was done as a courtesy to Broward County, where the case originated, and that her unit had him for a relatively brief period of time—approximately five or six months.

Cupp: It was not too long after you got into the case that you made it known, in a letter, you thought you had this situation figured out, right? You wrote a letter?

Wyllner: I wrote a letter requesting guidance from Broward.

Cupp: The point of your letter is you thought that protective supervision needed to fold up their tent and go home—these folks didn't need it?

Wyllner: I was reacting—that was the letter I wrote, yes, sir.

Cupp: And it accurately reflected your opinion—based upon your time with the case and dealing with the family—that you didn't think they needed protective supervision services any longer?

Wyllner: Given what I had in the file at the time, no, sir, I didn't.

Cupp: Because you-all have a pretty heavy caseload?

Wyllner: Yes, sir.

Cupp: If you can reduce it by one, you can spend more time with the others?

Wyllner: Yes, sir.

Cupp: By the way, had you reviewed anything about the Vero Beach hospitalization of A.J.?

Wyllner: I believe I had a copy of a report in the file.

Cupp: Did you review it?

Wyllner: I read it over.

Cupp: What did you learn from that; what do you remember learning?

Wyllner: I really don't recall any details about it other than he was on some kind of medication when he left Vero Beach.

Cupp: Did you also become aware that one of the big problems with his hospitalization was nobody was coming to see him?

Wyllner: No, sir, I don't recall.

Cupp: So you didn't read that?

Wyllner: I don't recall.

Cupp: Nobody made you aware of that?

Wyllner: I don't recall being told that.

Cupp: Did you learn that part of his problem was that his family was not coming up there participating in his therapy? Did you learn that before you wrote that letter?

Wyllner: I don't recall that.

Cupp: Do you think that would have been important to know?

Wyllner: I was going with what I understood at the time.

Cupp: Did you read his discharge summary?

Wyllner: I read over the file. I don't have any clear recollection of what specific things were included, no, sir.

Cupp: So, you don't know whether or not this little boy came out of Vero Beach as a pretty vulnerable kid? You don't know that? You didn't know it then and you don't know it now?

Wyllner: He was supposed to be in therapy, so I assume there were things to be done by the therapist, yes, sir.

Cupp: How were they doing in therapy during the six months that you had them? Were they going?

Wyllner: I believe they were. When I spoke with the

guardian, he said that they were going to counseling on a steady basis. I had been told, by Mrs. Schwarz, that she made arrangements for him to be seen in South County.

Wyllner didn't recall ever talking to A.J.'s guidance counselor, but said it was possible that she talked to his teacher, because she had spoken with "someone at school," but didn't recall who it was.

"Did you learn from Dr. Zimmern that he was prohibited—by Mrs. Schwarz—from speaking with A.J.'s guidance counselor? Did you learn that?" Cupp questioned.

Wyllner said no.

She then testified that in January 1993—when there was an allegation that the defendant had physically abused A.J.—she was transferring into another unit and was not seeing clients at that time.

Cupp: I'm not sure I understand. Were you the supervising worker or not?

Wyllner: I was still on the file as a supervision worker, yes, sir.

Cupp: What's the difference between a protective supervision and child protective investigator?

Wyllner: The investigator is the one that gets the abuse call and goes out and does the actual on-site investigation to determine whether the allegation is confirmed or not.

Cupp: And that wouldn't be your job—that would be somebody else?

Wyllner: That's somebody else's, yes.

Cupp: And you recall that this one in January—that worker was Barbara Black?

Wyllner: I believe so, yes, sir.

Cupp: And you know that because you talked to her before she went out there, didn't you?

Wyllner: I talked to her the day that she—yes.

Cupp: Before she went out?

Wyllner: Yes.

Cupp: And you told Barbara—before she went out—that this sounded like, or words to this effect: that there was probably nothing to it; that your understanding from dealing with the case was that Ilene—the biological mother—was always in the neighborhood stirring up [trouble] and calling in false reports. Didn't you give Barbara Black that type of information?

Wyllner: That was my understanding, yes, sir.

Cupp: You knew the biological mother to be Ilene?

Wyllner: I knew—yes, sir.

Cupp: Ma'am, do you recall when Barbara Black spoke to you, she told you that the person who called in the complaint was a person by the name of Ilene [*sic*], but she didn't know the last name? Do you recall that?

Wyllner: I—no, sir.

Cupp: You've had occasion to have seen this [abuse report], haven't you—the one that we are talking about regarding the January incident?

Wyllner: It was probably in the file. I haven't seen it since. The reporter information is not supposed to be on it when we get it. It's usually available to the investigator, but most of ours did not include it when we got the copy.

Cupp: If I hand you a copy of it that contained the information about the reporter, might that refresh your recollection as to who the reporter was?

Wyllner: Possibly.

Cupp (handing her the report): Just look at it in terms of the reporter information, if you will, ma'am?

Wyllner: It says, "Ilene."

Cupp: It says, "Ilene unknown"?

Wyllner: Yes, sir, spelled the way I understand the mother to spell her name.

Cupp: So you made an assumption, when Barbara Black called you, that the source of the report for these allegations of two black eyes and a suspected broken nose was the biological mother?

Wyllner: I don't recall what I thought, at the time.

Cupp: But that's what you told Barbara Black, isn't it?

Wyllner: That there had been earlier situations where the natural mother had tried to cause problems and was involved in court issues with the Schwarz family.

Cupp: And you didn't know that a neighbor—a new neighbor—moved in across the street by the name of Eileen Callahan?

Wyllner: No, sir, I didn't know the name of any neighbors.

Cupp: So you came to the assumption and you conveyed that to Barbara Black and she went out there that day with that assumption?

Wyllner: She went out there that day. What she thought, I don't know.

Cupp: But she spoke to you before she went out there?

Wyllner: Okay.

Cupp: You don't do this kind of work anymore, do you?

Wyllner: No, sir.

CHAPTER 20

He had a very low self-esteem. This is one of the things I was working on and A.J. wanted to be accepted so badly he would play the role of whatever you want him to do, to be accepted.

—Edwin Carpenter

The following day, August 30, 1994, the next witness for the defense was Edwin Carpenter, a Juvenile Family counselor with the Department of Public Safety, Division of Youth Affairs.

"We, as a service, are a family counseling service, voluntary, meaning that the client has to volunteer. They may enter or leave the service at any time. We go into the home or into the school or whatever is needed to work with the family with whatever problems we see. Basically, we're short term, three months, but sometimes we go beyond that. Volunteer means that even if they are referred, they have to agree to the counseling, or the service is not available."

He testified that no one who received this counseling was under a court order to be there, and that he had counseled Mr. and Mrs. Schwarz and A.J., having been in their home eleven times between May 21, 1991, and September 24, 1991. Also, he had seen A.J. at school on five different occasions, and he claimed that Jessica had not resisted his efforts to talk with the boy at school.

Carpenter stated that the conditions in the home were "very sufficient" and he had not observed any signs that A.J. was being abused.

> Brown: Did the Schwarzes pay for these services?
> Carpenter: No.
> Brown: Were there occasions when you talked with Andrew alone?
> Carpenter: Sometimes in the home we'd go to his room, other times in the living room, and then at the school I'd be dealing with him.

Carpenter explained that when he first started working with A.J., he made an agreement with him that he did not have to talk about anything that he didn't want to, but that if he did talk, he had to tell him the truth. The counselor explained to him that later he would have to tell the court what A.J. really wanted, so they would need to talk about things so he would know what to say.

A.J. told him that he wanted to live with his father; he did not want to go back to his natural mother because of "the way he was treated there." The counselor didn't think A.J. had told him about all the "bad things" that had happened while he was living with his natural mother because sometimes A.J. would say, "I don't want to talk about them."

> Brown: Did he ever—in that conversation—tell you that while living with Jessica Schwarz, bad things were happening?
> Carpenter: No.
> Brown: What else did he tell you, other than not wanting to live with his mom who did bad things to him?
> Carpenter: He said that he never felt loved. He felt his father loved him.
> Brown: What about his stepmother?
> Carpenter: He said she loved him in her own way. His

definition of love was taking care of him and he said,
"She takes care of me."

Carpenter suggested to the family that it would help A.J.
if they would show him physical affection—by hugging him
and getting close to him.

"I never observed this, but they would sit close to him
and put their arms around him."

When HRS asked the counselor to make recommendations, he suggested that the family have long-term counseling.

"Now, once you make the recommendation, do you know
who carries it through or who's supposed to carry it through?"
Brown queried.

Carpenter answered, "The family."

On cross-examination, Carpenter admitted that he did not
know what went on in the Schwarz home when he was not
there.

Cupp: Didn't it disturb you that one of the things that
you observed was A.J.'s definition of love—in regards
to his stepmother—was she takes care of him; did that
disturb you a little bit?

Carpenter: Yes, it did. Because, knowing what he had
told me about his previous family life, I thought he
needed more than just taking care of—but taking care
of was very important to him.

Cupp: He needed hugs and kisses?

Carpenter: He needed a lot of help with emotional—
maintaining his emotional balance.

Cupp: Did you ever hear the expression "Throwing
gasoline on a fire"?

Carpenter: Yes.

Cupp: Last thing [he needed] to be told by his stepmother is that she hated him?

Carpenter: That would be devastating to him.

Cupp: The last thing he needed to be told by his step-mother was that he was a useless piece of shit?

Carpenter: This would be devastating to him.

Cupp: The last thing he needed was to have his step-mother force him to eat a cockroach?

Carpenter: Yes.

Cupp: What would that do?

Carpenter: He had a very low self-esteem. This is one of the things I was working on and A.J. wanted to be accepted so badly he would play the role of whatever you want him to do, to be accepted.

Cupp: He wanted to be loved?

Carpenter: Yes.

Cupp: He wanted her to love him?

Carpenter: Yes.

Cupp: Did you see any evidence that she ever, in fact, loved him?

Carpenter: You'll have to define love because in A.J.'s terms—taking care of him—she loved him. I think she tried in what she defined as love.

Cupp: And again, the time period that you dealt with, I mean, you were wrapped up and done by September of 1991?

Carpenter: That's correct. (He had never seen A.J. in 1992 or 1993.)

Cupp: You don't know what the dates of these offenses are, do you?

Carpenter: I have no idea.

Cupp: Mrs. Schwarz didn't have to do anything as far as this counseling; all she had to do was be home?

Carpenter: That's correct.

Cupp: She didn't have to go anywhere, write anything down?

Carpenter: No.

Cupp: She didn't have to pay?

Carpenter: No.

Cupp: All she had to do was sit on the couch?

Carpenter: Correct.

Cupp: Isn't it true that they knew that what they told you—you were going to turn around and tell HRS?

Carpenter: Yes.

Cupp: So that everything that A.J. would tell you he knew would get back to Jessica, right?

Carpenter: Not necessarily. The rules of confidentiality would not allow me to tell the family what he told me in private. I would only tell in open court with a subpoena.

Cupp: Did you explain the rules of confidentiality to A.J.?

Carpenter: Yes.

Cupp: Do you think he understood you?

Carpenter: Yes.

Cupp: Do you think he believed you?

Carpenter: Yes, because at times he would say, "I don't want to talk about it," because he understood our contract with each other.

Cupp: Did he tell you that he didn't want to talk about things [in] reference to his stepmother and the home?

Carpenter: Sometimes he just wouldn't talk.

Cupp: Just wouldn't talk?

Carpenter: Yes.

Sandra Warren, who had been employed by HRS, Child Protection Services, for eighteen months, was the next witness for the defense. She explained that when visiting with children under her charge, she always checked to see if there were any visible marks on the child.

"We don't necessarily lift their clothing or anything like that every time we visit them, but we check to see if there's anything readily visible and then we just talk with them. It depends on what particular problem occurred that got us involved with the family as to what kinds of things we may be discussing."

Warren testified that she explains to the child—to the best of her ability—that what he says is going to be kept confidential and tries to ascertain that the child understands that.

When she first visited with A.J. on March 17, 1993, he was in his bedroom, lying on the bed, and she talked alone with him.

Brown: Did you talk with him about his natural mother and sister?
Warren: Yes. He told about his feelings about them. He told me that he did not like to talk about them, that he would feel sick when he would think about them.
Brown: Isn't it true that what he really said, "It makes me actually throw up"?
Warren: Well, in my notes when I made that reference, it's referring to when his mother is actually around.

She had participated in a meeting—a roundtable discussion—about the Schwarz family and A.J., and as a result of that meeting, a conclusion was made regarding Andrew Schwarz's placement with Jessica and David.

"It was felt that he should stay where he was at, with some changes in discipline and controlling his behavior and such. The child had indicated to those that were at this meeting that that's where he wanted to be."

According to the report from the March 26, 1993, meeting: "In the end it was decided that this is still the best placement for Andrew and that he's happy there and obviously loves them both very much."

Brown: Do you recall how many notes or how many notations in your file you made of bruises?
Warren: I don't recall how many.
Brown: Did you make any?
Warren: Yes. I know of one specific area that I made a

notation of a bruise. That would have been on March 17. He had bruises under his eyes and over the bridge of his nose.

Brown: Did you personally ask Andrew how that happened?

Warren: Yes. Something to do with some sort of a bike accident.

Brown: He had a bike accident and hurt himself; isn't that what he told you?

Warren: Yes, that's what he told me.

The "bike accident" happened on January 24 and, indeed, Dr. Richard Zimmern observed A.J. with two black eyes and a swollen nose on January 26. Sandra Warren saw the "bruises under his eyes and over the bridge of his nose" on March 17. Seven weeks later, the bruises were still visible.

Sadly—tragically—the cross-examination was notable because it showed—as it had with the previous defense witnesses, with the possible exception of Edwin Carpenter—how little the very people who were supposed to be protecting him knew about Andrew Schwarz.

Cupp: At the time that you entered A.J.'s life, do you know how many people—HRS, counselors, and doctors—he had seen by that time?

Warren: No.

Cupp: It was a bunch, wasn't it?

Warren: I have since learned that.

Cupp: Isn't one of the first things you do when you pick up a case is review—or try to review—what's occurred with the child prior to the time you get the case; you want to know the background, right?

Warren: That's correct.

Cupp: Who was the worker before you?

Warren: Joan Wyllner.

Cupp: Who was the worker before Joan Wyllner?

Warren: I don't recall.

Cupp: Do you know who Janie Sutherland is?

Warren: Yes.

Cupp: She's a supervision worker just like you?

Warren: She was, at that point.

Cupp: You didn't come across her name at some point?

Warren: I don't recall.

Cupp: Did you review the records?

Warren: I reviewed the records that were in the file.

Cupp: And who's Edwin Carpenter?

Warren: I don't recall.

Cupp: Do you know him as a counselor?

Warren: I've only recently met him, so at that time I did not know him.

Cupp: But you did not come across anything in the records, or did you know that A.J. had seen Edwin Carpenter?

Warren: Him specifically, no. Not that I recall anyway.

Cupp: Did you review the Vero Beach psychiatric records?

Warren: Yes.

Cupp: How was the counseling going with A.J., the family counseling, the individual counseling?

Warren: At the time I was involved with the case, it was not going at all—they were not going.

Cupp: Cause you any concerns?

Warren: Yes.

Cupp: Why?

Warren: Why what?

Cupp: Why did it cause you concerns?

Warren: Because according to what I had seen in the file, he needed to be in counseling—or being treated, I should say—at South County Mental Health.

Cupp: What about the family counseling?

Warren: I don't recall any—my feelings about it—at the time.

Cupp: Did you review the discharge recommendations by Dr. Uttley?

Warren: I don't recognize that name.

Cupp: Did you review the discharge summaries from the Vero Beach psychiatric hospitalization?

Warren: Yes.

Cupp: Do you recall what they were?

Warren: No.

Cupp: Do you know if any of the recommendations— were any of them being implemented by Mrs. Schwarz or by anybody?

Warren: I don't recall the recommendations, so I can't speak of them.

Cupp: Was he on imipramine, to your knowledge?

Warren: He had been. I don't believe he was at the time I was involved with the case.

Cupp: Why not?

Warren: Why wasn't he?

Cupp: Yes, ma'am.

Warren: There was a problem with Medicaid and communication between South County that was providing that for him and him being able to access it.

Cupp: So he just wasn't on imipramine?

Warren: To my knowledge, he wasn't.

Cupp: And he wasn't in family counseling?

Warren: To my knowledge, he wasn't.

Cupp: And he wasn't in individual counseling?

Warren: That I don't know.

Cupp: You were his protection supervision worker, weren't you?

Warren: Yes.

Cupp: That's your responsibility to know what's going on with the child?

Warren: Right.

Cupp: You don't know whether he was in individual counseling?

Warren: I had this case for a very short time. I spent
most of it trying to find the answers to those questions.
Cupp: Now, at this meeting when it was decided by the
powers-that-be that A.J. would stay where he was at,
Dottie Daniels was at that meeting, wasn't she?
Warren: Yes.

Cupp established that Dottie Daniels was a child protective
investigator supervisor. It was a child protective investigator's
responsibility to respond to and investigate calls that came into
the abuse hot line, which was not part of Sandra Warren's
duties because she was a protective supervision worker.

Cupp: But you have access to their reports, don't you?
Warren: Yes.
Cupp: And, in fact, one of the things that you have to
do when you get on the case, to properly supervise it,
is you have to be aware of any prior abuse complaints
and what happened?
Warren: That's correct.

Scott Cupp knew that one of the reasons it was decided at
the meeting that it was all right to leave A.J. in the Schwarz
home was that Dottie Daniels, Barbara Black's supervisor,
had stated—in no uncertain terms—that it was her opinion
that all the abuse complaints coming from the neighbors
were harassment. Also, she felt it was "going to cease," and
that it was directly as a result of the biological mother.

Cupp: Did you know Dottie Daniels to be Barbara
Black's supervisor, at that time?
Warren: Yes.
Cupp: Was Barbara Black at that meeting?
Warren: Yes.
Cupp: Was Barbara Black, child protective investiga-
tor, assigned to go out and investigate these allega-
tions that led to the black eyes and the bruised nose?

Warren: I don't know specifically what the allegation was at the time she went out.

Cupp: But you know her to be the investigator who went out on that particular call?

Warren: I don't know that.

Cupp: What counseling or what therapy or treatment was A.J. receiving for his bed-wetting problem?

Warren: I don't believe I've discussed that with anyone. I don't know.

Cupp: Nobody—Mrs. Schwarz never reported to you that she was having a problem with A.J. wetting the bed?

Warren: Not that I recall.

Cupp: That's something that you would note?

Warren: Yes, it would be.

Cupp: Why would you note that?

Warren: Because a child of that age—that might be an indicator of some other problems, something might be causing that.

Cupp: Like?

Warren: If it were something that happened on a regular basis.

Cupp: Like?

Warren: I don't—I'm not an expert in that field. I don't know.

Cupp: But you've received training in the area of child abuse, haven't you?

Warren: Yes.

Cupp: That's what you do. That's what you were doing at the time; you were dealing with abused and neglected children, correct?

Warren: Correct.

Cupp: Haven't you been taught that it's one of the hallmark indicators of abuse—if the bed-wetting is not tied to a physical problem?

Warren: Bed-wetting may be an indicator of a physical problem or possibly abuse problem.

Cupp: Assuming—assuming it's not tied to a physical problem, aren't you taught that's one of the hallmark indicators of stress on a child?

Warren: I can't recall if that was ever mentioned in any of my training.

Cupp: Okay. Is it fair to say from your involvement with Andrew that probably the most important thing in his life at that time was school?

Warren: I never discussed it in those terms with him. I really don't know.

Cupp: You didn't get that impression?

Warren: I don't know.

Cupp: But you did testify on direct that you were aware of the incident—the bicycle accident—and you spoke with Andrew about that?

Warren: What I knew of that accident was what Andrew told me.

Scott Cupp knew, in fact, that Barbara Black had made it known in writing that she had concerns about Andrew being able to tell the truth.

Cupp: You know that Barbara Black was indicted as a result of her activity?

Warren: I don't know what happened with Barbara Black.

Cupp: You don't know what happened with Barbara Black?

Warren: I did not follow that.

Cupp: No further questions.

Years later, when asked about Sandra Warren, Scott Cupp replied, "I couldn't pick her out of a lineup." But he remembered quite clearly what he was feeling as he cross-examined her: "Anger, disgust, utter frustration. If ever [in my opinion] one person in that inept agency personified their overall incompetence, it was her—only she was incompetence with an attitude."

CHAPTER 21

We tried to instill in the kids common sense and common decency even if we did not have too much money.

—Helen Woods

Lauren Cross, now almost twelve years old, was the next witness for the defense. Her testimony was intriguing and notable, but not surprising, in that she contradicted almost everything that over a dozen prosecution witnesses—neighbors and their children—had sworn was the truth. And many times, she spoke of A.J. in the present tense.

She did, indeed, attempt to paint the Schwarz family life as quite "normal" and emphatically rejected each of the abuse allegations against her mother. According to Lauren, Jessica did the cooking for the family, but sometimes Bear fixed biscuits and gravy for breakfast on Sunday. Her mom always cooked enough food for all the children, no one was denied any food, and A.J. was never put on a diet other than their regular meals. His food was not different from Lauren, Jackie, and Patsy's, and they ate as a family—in the kitchen.

Brown: Do you recall an incident when Gail Ragatz came to your home and your mother made Andrew sit on the floor near the cat litter box and eat his dinner?
Lauren: No, he never did that. He always ate at the table.

Brown: Did you ever see your mother handle a cock-roach?
Lauren: No, she doesn't like bugs.
Brown: Do you ever recall a time when A.J.'s mouth was taped shut by anyone in your house?
Lauren: No.

On and on, it went. All the children were allowed play-time—including A.J. Jessica—and sometimes Patsy or Lauren—helped A.J. with his homework.

Brown: Did Andrew have any toys?
Lauren: Yes, he had quite a bit of Ninja Turtles and re-mote control cars and trucks, and he had a big teddy bear thing or something like that and stuffed toys.
Brown: Were these the things that Andrew enjoyed playing with?
Lauren: Yes.

She said that A.J. had a bicycle but was not allowed to ride it to school.
"We tried it once but he almost got hit by a car and he's not too careful, so he walked."
Lauren admitted that sometimes she got in trouble with her mom. For punishment, Lauren would have to take a bas-ket of unmatched socks into her room and match them up, or a television show would be taken away for the night, or "just something simple like that." Jessica did not hit her—or A.J.

Brown: Now, when your mother talked to you when you got in trouble, how did she talk to you?
Lauren: Loud. She didn't talk, she yelled—well, not like bad or anything, but she wasn't calm either.
Brown: Did you ever hear her yell at anybody else?
Lauren: Yes. Everybody. Almost everybody yelled at each other once in a while in the house.

Brown: What about neighbors; did you ever see her yell at the neighbors?
Lauren: Yes.
Brown: Was she just a kind of person who yelled when she got upset?
Lauren: Yes.

Jessica got upset and yelled at A.J.—just as she did Lauren—when he didn't do his homework. Her mother was concerned about A.J.'s schoolwork and about him getting his work done.

"That's why she yells and tells him to do better."

Lauren said that when she had a chore to do—like cleaning her room—she had to stick with it until it was finished, but she was allowed to stop and eat dinner and then go back to her chores. And she claimed it was the same way with A.J.

Both David and A.J. cleaned the garage, and since A.J. liked to mow the lawn—and David had taught him how to use the weed whacker—the upkeep of the yard was A.J.'s responsibility. And, of course, she had never seen A.J. use household scissors to trim the yard.

They had a party for A.J.'s birthday in 1993 with cake and presents, and "we had his friends come over." He was allowed to invite anyone he wanted.

Lauren did not recall a time when it was raining and A.J. had to walk to school while she rode in her mother's car.

Brown: Did that ever happen?
Lauren: No, we all—she drove us. My mom drove us.
Brown: Would A.J. be in the car when it rained?
Lauren: Yes.
Brown: I want you to think about this question, and tell me if you ever recall coming home and Andrew running—or your mother ordering Andrew to run—down the street naked?
Lauren: That never happened.

Brown: Do you ever recall hearing your mother ordering A.J. to take off all of his clothes?
Lauren: No, she'd never do that; she never did.

And she had never seen her mother keep A.J. home from
school for punishment—or go to school to get him and bring
him home to do a chore. Lauren claimed that A.J. got sick more
than the rest of them because he was "thinner and skinnier."

Brown: Now, do you recall what kind of illnesses he had?
Lauren: Stomach virus. I think he had the flu once and
he had a stomach virus a lot. Sometimes he'd just go to
the bathroom and throw up.
Brown: Did he do that a lot?
Lauren: Yeah.

She had never seen A.J. wearing a T-shirt with any writing
on it—other than T-shirts that were bought with words im-
printed on them.

Brown: Lauren, I don't want to embarrass you, but I
want to ask you this question: did you ever hear your
mother say to Andrew, "I hate your fucking guts"?
Lauren: No.
Brown: Did you ever hear her say to him, "You're a
useless piece of shit"?
Lauren: No.

In reference to A.J. wetting the bed, Lauren said she did
not recall a time when her mother rubbed A.J.'s nose in the
wet sheets.

Brown: Did you ever see this happen?
Lauren: No.
Brown: Did Andrew ever tell you that it happened?
Lauren: No, because it never did.

According to the young girl, her mother tried to stop the bed-wetting problem by reading a home remedies book. When A.J. had to go to the bathroom, Jessica would tell him to wait for five minutes before he went—to strengthen his bladder.

Brown: How did you get your school supplies?
Lauren: My mother would take me out and buy them.
Brown: How did Andrew get his school supplies?
Lauren: Same way. We'd go together and we'd both have our list and we'd do his list and then go clothes shopping and then go home.
Brown: Now, Lauren, when did you first meet me?
Lauren: Today.
Brown: Have you discussed any of these matters— about which you have testified to—with your mother?
Lauren: No.
Brown: You understood the oath you took to tell the truth?
Lauren: Yes.
Brown: So help you God?
Lauren: Yes.
Brown: Have you told the whole truth?
Lauren: Yes.

Even though she was incarcerated, it seemed that Jessica Schwarz had the ability to control what her children told others about their home life—even under oath. The young girl was no doubt—if nothing else—the victim of her mother's intimidation. Not to mention the fact that Lauren had witnessed firsthand what her mother was capable of doing to a child.

The next witness for the defense was Jessica's mother, Helen Woods, who testified that she lived in Palm Bay with her husband and her two granddaughters, Lauren and Jackie. She and her husband had moved there two years earlier from Long Island, New York, where Jessica had grown up along with her older sister.

Mrs. Woods testified that she didn't think her method of discipline with her children was different from anybody else's.

"If the kids did anything wrong, privileges were taken away."

If they didn't finish their meal "properly" or eat as much as she thought they should, they did not get dessert or get to watch television. They had to go to their room, play there, and "that was it."

While Jessica was growing up, Mrs. Woods learned that her daughter wanted to become a truck driver.

"Did she realize that dream? Did she become a truck driver?" Brown asked.

Helen stated that yes, she did.

Like Lauren before her, Mrs. Woods described the Schwarz family and their lives as nothing out of the ordinary.

"A.J. was into Ninjas—the Ninja Turtles—and I myself bought him quite a few every birthday, Christmas; also [I got him] a wooden toolbox with little miniature tools that boys could use. He had a couple of board games, but I really couldn't tell you names of them because the kids always interchanged their toys anyway. He had trucks. He loved the little miniature cars and I had gotten him—for one of the birthdays or something—a carrying case for all of these little cars."

Jessica had also bought toys for A.J. and, "of course," she allowed him to play with them—and with other children. And A.J. had a bicycle. Both she and Jessica bought A.J. his school supplies, but "I think, by and large, it was Jessica who paid for most of the school supplies, but I did—even if it was just pencils—just to let him know that we cared."

Jessica cooked the meals and there was no scarcity of food.

"She cooked very balanced meals and lots of it. The biggest eater was Andrew."

> Brown: Did you ever witness Jessica feeding Andrew bread and water for dinner?
> Woods: No.
> Brown: Did you ever see your daughter playing with cockroaches?
> Woods: No, no, no way at all. First of all, we did not have cockroaches in our house. If I had spotted one, I'd have the exterminator there the next day. But I never saw her playing with any sort of bugs or cockroaches or whatever.

When Mrs. Woods stayed with the children for about a week while Jessica was in the hospital, A.J. walked to school while Lauren rode her bike, but if it rained, she drove them.

> Brown: During the time that you were in the home, did Jessica ever tell you to keep Andrew at home as punishment? At home from school, I mean?
> Woods: Definitely not, no.
> Brown: Did you ever see Jessica hugging Andrew?
> Woods: Yes, I have.
> Brown: How often did you see her hug him?
> Woods: Well, as I say, I wasn't a constant visitor down there and I can't say that it happened three times a day or anything like that, but I've seen her on occasions hug Andrew the way she hugged Lauren and Jackie. (She had heard Jessica yell at A.J. and the other children as well.)
> Brown: Did you ever hear her use profanity with the children?
> Woods: Certain words, yes.
> Brown: You have never seen Jessica rub Andrew's nose in urine-soaked linen, have you?
> Woods: Definitely no.

Brown: Do you recall, ma'am, Andrew, along with Jessica and the rest of the family, visiting your home Christmas of 1992?
Woods: Yes.
Brown: Did you have an opportunity to observe Andrew and the way he acted, talked, and things of that sort?
Woods: Yes.
Brown: Now, did your grandson walk like a zombie at that point?
Woods: No.
Brown: Did he act like a zombie?
Woods: No.
Brown: Was he lucid?
Woods: Yes.
Brown: Was he coherent?
Woods: Absolutely.

When questioned about her observance of A.J.'s table manners, she replied that "his table manners were fine," and that he did not "gulp down his food" as if he had been trained to eat in five minutes.

Brown: Did he eat lots of food?
Woods: He certainly did.

Scott Cupp started his cross-examination by asking Mrs. Woods about Jessica's upbringing.

Cupp: Your daughter did not grow up underprivileged, did she?
Woods: No, she did not.
Cupp: She didn't want for anything?
Woods: Oh, that's carrying it a bit far.
Cupp: Well, she was raised well?
Woods: Yes, she was raised well. We tried to instill in the kids common sense and common decency even if we did not have too much money.

Cupp: She grew up in Glen Cove, Long Island?

Woods: Yes.

Cupp: She lived in the same home her entire life? She wasn't moving around from place to place to place and she had one mother and she had one father?

Woods: Yes.

Cupp: She graduated all the way through the same school system?

Woods: Yes.

Cupp: She had two caring, loving parents? Who tried the very best they could to teach her right from wrong?

Woods: Yes.

Cupp: As far as you know, you did that?

Woods: Yes.

Cupp: Now, you've testified that on approximately five occasions you were in the Triphammer [Road] home. You went there approximately five times?

Woods: I believe so, yes.

Cupp: Over about a four-year span?

Woods: Probably.

Cupp: So, you only can tell us and tell this jury what went on when you were there, right?

Woods: Of course.

Cupp: You don't know what happened when you weren't there?

Woods: No.

CHAPTER 22

I may not be able to clearly define evil for you—not as a black-and-white statement lifted from the pages of a dictionary—but I can say without equivocation that I know it when I see it, and Jessica Schwarz will forever personify it in my eyes.

—Scott Cupp

"This was what I, Scott Cupp, knew about Jessica Schwarz. I knew that she had tapped a dark place inside of me that held every negative emotion I was capable of feeling. I'd experienced hate, loathing, anger, and vengeance, and I knew how detrimental that could be in extracting the truth. I knew that she had come to represent the very heart of evil in my eyes, which might have been a powerful motivator, but if it had blinded me to the facts and the nuances behind the facts—in the end—I would have hurt our case.

"The nefarious image of the woman was—above and beyond all else—directly related to the despicable abuses she had perpetrated, day in and day out, upon A.J., true—but it was more than that. It was the look on her face—part amusement, part vindictive, part raptorial—that conveyed the message that A.J. had gotten exactly what he deserved, and that she was just as happy as a clam to have been the one who saw to it. The psychological pieces that breed remorse did not exist in her.

"Jessica was a brute and a bully, but she wasn't stupid. Intimidation had become an art form for her. She had been successful at intimidating her powerfully built husband to such a degree that he had stood by and allowed her to throw his son around by the neck—and while she forced him to run down the street naked because he wasn't walking home from school fast enough to suit her.

"She had frightened her neighbors so effectively that most of them were afraid to call the police or social services—or anyone else—after hearing Jessica call her stepson names so denigrating you wouldn't address a dog that way. She had so intimidated this innocent ten-year-old—a kid whose biggest crime was a mischievous streak about the same size as any other ten-year-old boy's—that his IQ had dropped from 101 to 86 in less than two years.

"I knew that she—during that time—had destroyed a human being and had taken pleasure in it. I may not be able to clearly define evil for you—not as a black-and-white statement lifted from the pages of a dictionary—but I can say without equivocation that I know it when I see it, and Jessica Schwarz will forever personify it in my eyes.

"What I also knew was that the dark place inside of me was at war with the detachment, the calm, and the professionalism that had characterized my approach to every case I'd ever prosecuted. By the time Jessica took the stand that morning, the war had to be over—the dark place defeated, imprisoned, and silenced.

"I concentrated on my choice of tie, something conservative to go with the charcoal gray suit I'd laid out the night before, and let my mind replay the dream one more time. I knew it well by then, since it had robbed me of much needed sleep for the previous weeks.

I'm traveling by car with my family. It's a black night and the road is deserted. Torrential rain makes driving impossible. I'm as lost as I've ever been. We stop in front of a lonely Tudor mansion overgrown with vines and shrouded in darkness. I venture to the door. No one responds to my knock, so I push past the door and go inside. Not a soul; not a hint of light.

Sheets have been draped over the furniture and the drapes are drawn. I shiver. All at once, I glimpse a flickering light—like flames from a dying fire—coming from a nearby room. I follow it. The room is overwhelmed with chairs—hundreds of them—and the legs of the chairs form an impenetrable lattice.

Beyond the chairs, I see movement. A small, lithe shadow darting frantically in front of the fire. It's A.J. Trapped and inconsolable. When I realize the fire is dying out and the shadow is fading, I wake up. Every time. Even before I can call his name.

"'Okay,' I told myself, 'so you may not be able to call his name or reach out to him—but you can make sure his voice is heard.'"

Finally it was the moment Scott Cupp had been waiting for. Jessica Schwarz's direct testimony had been a marathon—lasting five hours—full of denials and, of course, an explanation for everything.

One of the more memorable moments was when Rendell Brown asked Jessica about the incident with Patsy—when the young girl had allowed the boys to come into the house to use the telephone. Jessica denied punching her with her fist, but she admitted slapping her once with an open hand.

"Well, part of her story was true—I had a rule when my husband and I weren't in the house—I said to all my kids, and this is just something I made up, I guess. I said, 'If somebody knocks at the door, I don't care if it's God handcuffed to a cop, if you didn't dial 911, or pray to God to come on down—don't open the door.'"

And her version of the Holiday Shop completely contradicted the testimony of Mary Idrissi.

"I gave him two dollars to go to the Christmas store. The things are very cheap, inexpensive; so, yes, that's considered a lot for that particular store. He bought a key chain for his father; it was gold—the color gold—with a black inset that said, 'Number one dad.' He bought me a Christmas angel candle and he bought Lauren a big red-and-white pencil that looks like a candy cane and then that's it. He ran out of money, so what he had done for Jackie was he made a home-made hanging ornament for the tree."

Jessica had testified on direct examination that A.J. had had a cat named Bud, but she claimed that "something" happened to it.

"I came in on the tail end of it, but I saw it happening. Bud was a little kitten—fit in the palm of your hand, just about—and Andrew was taking the cat and smashed its head into the wall, and after that, the cat just started hissing and scratching and biting at kids, so I gave it to a family with no children."

And then the final few minutes of her direct testimony with Rendell Brown—several times—referring to A.J. as Jessica's "son":

Brown: You indicated that many of the absences of Andrew Schwarz were unknown to you because nobody sent you reports?
Jessica: Right.
Brown: Did you ever keep him out of school to punish him?
Jessica: No, I did not.
Brown: Did you ever write, "I'm a worthless piece of shit, don't talk to me" on a T-shirt and make Andrew wear it?
Jessica: I never wrote on his shirt, and no, I never did write that. I never did write on anybody's clothes.
Brown: And you never—that scissors stuff never happened?
Jessica: No, no.

Brown: Did you ever make your son run down the street naked?

Jessica: No.

Brown: Did you ever rub your son's nose or face in any bedsheets—any urine-soaked bedsheets?

Jessica: No, I did not.

Brown: Did you ever say to your son, "I hate your fucking guts"?

Jessica: No.

Brown: Did you refer to him as a "useless piece of shit"?

Jessica: No, I did not.

Brown: Did you have any goals or aspirations as relates to your relationship with your son?

Jessica: Yes. I wanted him to be happy and stay at the house and just grow up there with us.

Brown: Did you ever come to a point where you just wanted Andrew out of the house?

Jessica: Yes.

Brown: Did you ever talk to anybody about that?

Jessica: Yes.

Brown: How was that resolved?

Jessica: They just left him in the house.

Brown: Did that upset you?

Jessica: It didn't make any sense to me, but it didn't upset me.

Brown: Where did you want him to be?

Jessica: I wanted him to stay with us in the house, but if that wasn't working, I wanted him—I felt he needed more than once-a-week treatment.

Brown: When you were talking to HRS about the treatment, did you specify to them what you wanted or what you thought he needed?

Jessica: At one point, yeah.

Brown: What was that?

Jessica: Hospitalization.

Scott Cupp reminded himself that if she had told the truth from the beginning, there would be no reason for a trial—and no chance for him to expose her for what she truly was.

It was one o'clock in the afternoon and the heat outside was oppressive and laden with humidity—typical West Palm Beach. Cupp was grateful for the air-conditioning circulating in the courthouse on North Dixie Highway—but a courtroom filled to the brim with people high on anticipation tended to negate the cool air.

He took his seat next to Joe Marx. Clearly, with the loss of his wife and unborn child, the last three months had taken a toll on Joe, but despite the turmoil, he had done his job well.

"Shall we do this thing?"

Joe nodded. "Take her down, chief."

Cupp scanned the defense table. Jessica was wearing the same flower-print dress; her puffy cheeks were blushed with makeup. She didn't look especially comfortable with either the dress or the makeup.

When Judge Colbath entered the courtroom, everyone rose in unison.

At 1:05 P.M., the jurors were escorted back into the courtroom, and as they took their seats, Cupp did his best to make eye contact, but they were more intent on Jessica's short trek back to the witness stand.

After the judge reminded her that she was still under oath, he nodded in the prosecutor's direction and Cupp positioned himself at the lectern.

"Tell us, Mrs. Schwarz, what was Andrew's favorite color?"

She hesitated and lifted her shoulders slightly in a dismissive shrug.

"Blue," she answered in a tone that suggested the lack of importance in the answer.

Scott looked her straight in the eye—the very last thing he wanted was for her to feel comfortable or confident. He wanted the jury to have a clear view of the woman behind the facade that her defense team had attempted to create with their direct examination.

Cupp: Your testimony to this jury is that at nighttime you would go in his bedroom and you would hug Andrew and kiss him good night?

Jessica: I never said I would go in. I said I would hug and kiss him good night.

Cupp: Every night prior to going to bed?

Jessica: Every night, yes.

Cupp: When you were growing up, is that the way your parents treated you?

Jessica: Hugging and kissing before [bed]?

Cupp: Yes.

Jessica: Yes.

Cupp: You weren't abused?

Jessica (a shade of red creeping into her cheeks): No.

Cupp: You weren't told that you were hated? (Every question was asked as if it had "like A.J. was" attached to it.)

Jessica: No, I wasn't.

Cupp: You weren't made to say things that demeaned yourself?

Jessica: No, I wasn't.

Cupp: You weren't made to say things that demeaned yourself in front of your friends? In front of your neighbors?

Jessica (her voice rising): No!

Cupp: You weren't given bizarre punishments? (He told himself to press—not push.)

Jessica: No.

Cupp: You were taught right from wrong?

Jessica: Yes, I was.

Cupp: Did your parents ever punch you?

Jessica: Yes.

(Cupp paused. A hush fell over the courtroom. It was certainly not the answer he had expected.)

Cupp (incredulous): They punched you?

Jessica (her cheeks flushing red): Punch? I thought you said "punished." I'm sorry. (She glanced at the jury, then back at Scott.)

Cupp: Did they? Punch?

Jessica: No!

Cupp: Did they swear at you?

Jessica: They swore.

(Now Cupp pushed.)

Cupp: To your face when you were nine years old? Did they swear at you and tell you, "I hate your fucking guts"?

Jessica: No! Neither did I.

Cupp: My question was: did your parents do that?

Jessica: No.

Cupp: Did your parents make you do yard work?

Jessica (shrugging): Yes.

Cupp: Did they make you go out with a little pair of household scissors and trim the lawn?

Jessica: No!

Cupp: Did they make you go around with a paintbrush and sweep every single blade of grass off the walk and back into the yard? Did they make you do that?

Jessica: No.

The slight rustling in the courtroom told Scott Cupp that everyone was thinking: *Then why did you make A.J. do that?*

Cupp: How much child support did you and your husband have to pay for Andrew before he came into your home?

Jessica: I didn't have to pay any.

Cupp: How much did your husband have to pay?

Jessica: I don't know.

Cupp: But he had to pay child support?

Jessica: I don't know.

Cupp: You don't know?

Jessica: I don't know what the whole situation was. I know that he owed money.

Cupp: And isn't it true that if Andrew went back to his original placement with his biological mother, that your husband would have to pay child support?

Jessica: No matter where Andrew lived, my husband would've had to pay, yes.

Cupp: When was A.J.'s birthday?

The sudden change in direction obviously surprised her. Jessica blinked and Scott could see her searching her mind for the date.

Jessica (finally): April 24, 1983.

Cupp: And he didn't go to school the day before his birthday, did he?

Jessica: To my knowledge, he did.

Cupp: In 1993?

A.J.'s birthday was on a Saturday that year, so his "special day" at school with his classmates would have been on Friday. Even though Mrs. Idrissi had testified quite the opposite, Jessica Schwarz insisted several times that "to my knowledge," A.J. had gone to school that day.

Cupp: Your testimony is that you sent A.J. to school that day?

Jessica: To the best of my knowledge, yes.

Cupp: How many other parties and school activities were there in his '92 to '93 school year—that you remember—I mean like special days, like Halloween, Christmas, field trips?

Jessica: Halloween, Christmas . . . I think there was the zoo, Thanksgiving, Easter. . . . There was also a carnival that the whole school was involved in.

Cupp: And isn't it true that, due to your instructions to Mrs. Idrissi at that open house, he was to participate in none of those?

Jessica: No, that's not true.

Cupp: That's just not true?

Jessica: That's just not true.

Mrs. Idrissi's earlier testimony had been so powerful and so emotional that the jury had very obviously been swept up in it, and Scott used that—intentionally pitting Jessica against her.

Cupp: Mrs. Idrissi is mistaken?

Jessica: Yes, she is.

Cupp: And she's mistaken because she doesn't like you?

Jessica: We didn't like each other.

Cupp: You couldn't get any cooperation from Mrs. Idrissi or—as you called her—"the maggot"?

Jessica (smugly): I never called her that. Didn't even recognize her that day.

Cupp: Well, Mrs. Idrissi was spoiling Andrew, wasn't she?

Jessica: Well, as she put it in her testimony, she changed the rules for him.

Cupp: So, Mrs. Idrissi—who has thirty children to educate—has the audacity to single your child out and spoil him, right? That's what she was doing?

Jessica: In essence, she was changing the rules for him.

Cupp: Isn't it true that she was trying to get A.J. to learn—trying to help him learn?

Jessica: No.

Cupp: Isn't it true that she was trying to compensate for what he wasn't getting at home?

Jessica: No.

Cupp: All the love and affection that Mrs. Idrissi was giving A.J. at school—he was getting that at home?

Jessica (without emotion): He was getting that at home.

Cupp: Uh-huh. This was a kid who just had this enormous thirst for attention and need to be loved, right?

Jessica: Right.

Cupp: So abnormal that even when he was in Vero Beach for six weeks—and you visited him twice—he's basically clutching at every nurse every time they come in, wants to be hugged, wants to be stroked, wants to be a kid?

Jessica: Yes, A.J. did that to everyone all the time.

Cupp: And to you?

Jessica: And to me.

Cupp moved away from the lectern. He took two steps toward the defendant and listened to the shuffling in the gallery behind him. His intention was to take the jurors and the spectators on a journey through the Schwarz household, where not a single picture of A.J. was ever hung on a wall or set on a desk or displayed on a dresser. Not one. Compared to dozens of pictures of the girls. Not a single one of his drawings from school on the refrigerator. There were no trinkets or souvenirs.

But Jessica had a different story.

Cupp: Oh, how many pictures of A.J. did you have hanging in your house in April of 1993?

Jessica: The hanging pictures?

Cupp: Okay, hanging, sitting up on a table, on your dresser, in the kitchen, on the refrigerator, anywhere in the house?

Jessica: Anywhere in the house?

Cupp: Yes, ma'am. If somebody walked in, how many would they be able to see?

Jessica: Two of them were in the hallway, one was in the living room, and the rest were in my photo album.

Cupp: So, your answer to my question is you had three?

Jessica: Yeah.

Scott then questioned her about A.J.'s bedroom—a room so barren that it had been described to him as "the dark side of the moon"—so drastically in contrast to the well-appointed rooms of Jessica's daughters that it made him embarrassed, angry, and resentful. The lack of pictures, the barren bedroom, the dearth of toys—all destined to help crush and break A.J.'s spirit.

"And you felt about A.J. as if he was your own son?" Cupp asked.

"As if he was my own," Jessica replied.

He asked her about A.J.'s nightly bed-wetting—a problem he had never exhibited before he arrived at Jessica's house. He quizzed her about the locks on A.J.'s bedroom door. He asked her why she prohibited the guidance counselor from speaking to A.J.

When she vehemently denied the accusations, he—struggling to minimize the sarcasm that he felt—said to the defendant, "This is a big conspiracy, isn't it?"

Jessica replied, "I don't know what this is."

Cupp questioned her about A.J.'s half sister Patsy and the incident that caused her to be taken out of the home for good. It, of course, began when Patsy allowed two boys inside the house without permission and it ended with a fist in her face.

Cupp: You've already testified that you've got a bad temper—or words to that effect?
Jessica: I don't remember saying that.
Cupp: Well, do you have a bad temper?
Jessica: I have a temper.
Cupp: And you're loud?
Jessica: Yeah.
Cupp: And you're crude?
Jessica: Yeah. I can be.
Cupp (calmly): So at the time this happened with Patsy, you were upset?
Jessica: Yes.

Cupp: You were angry.
Jessica: Yes.
Cupp: You lost your temper a little bit.
Jessica: Yes.
Cupp: And you balled up your hand into a fist and you punched her in the face.
Jessica: No, I did not.
Cupp: And her nose bled.
Jessica: No, it did not.

There was an edge of frustration and desperation in her voice, and the anger that Cupp wanted the jury to see crept to the surface as well.

Cupp (pushing): In fact, you knocked her down—you hit her so hard.
Jessica: No, I did not!
Cupp (glancing briefly at the jurors): Tell us. At the parenting classes you attended—were you taught to humiliate your child?
Jessica: No!
Cupp: Did they teach you that an appropriate method of punishment was to have your child wear a T-shirt with derogatory words on it?
Jessica: No.
Cupp: Did she go over bed-wetting—at all—at the parenting classes?
Jessica: I don't remember.
Cupp: You don't remember anybody ever telling you that a recognized method is to take the child's head and rub his nose into the urine-soaked sheets—like a dog?
Jessica (her face red with anger): I didn't even do that to my dogs. I didn't do it to my dogs or my children.
Cupp: You didn't do it to your dogs—you just did it to A.J.
Jessica: I didn't do it to Andrew!
Cupp: Isn't it true that the pets got treated better in your house than Andrew?

Jessica: No.

Cupp: Did they tell you to use nudity as a punishment? Has anyone ever told you that that's a recognized way to punish a child?

Jessica: Absolutely not.

Cupp: Or making him walk to school in the rain while you give another child a ride?

Jessica: I never did that, so I wouldn't know what it was used for.

CHAPTER 23

*We always remembered how Corporal Hopper
pointed out later to us that she noticed rather quickly
that morning that something didn't feel right to her inside the home. It was like A.J. hadn't "lived" there.*

—Scott Cupp

From there, Scott Cupp delved into A.J.'s six-week odyssey
at the psychiatric hospital in Vero Beach, so physically and
emotionally whipped that the doctors, fearing for his life, ordered around-the-clock supervision. After acknowledging
how extraordinarily traumatic that must have been for A.J.,
Jessica admitted that she and his father went to visit the fragile nine-year-old a total of two times—one of those being the
day they dropped him off.

When Cupp made it clear that the hospital staff at Vero
Beach literally begged Jessica and David—the boy's own father—to come visit him more often, the emotion in the courtroom was palpable. And when he threatened to use the
records to prove that they refused to come to the hospital to
pick A.J. up after his discharge, the tension running through
the room was like an electrical current.

Cupp revisited the perverse practice of keeping A.J. out
of school as a form of punishment. He'd already established
that out of the forty-two days that A.J. was absent during his
tumultuous third-grade year—Thursday was a given. Thursday

was recycling day on Triphammer Road, and a half-dozen neighbors had already testified to the number of times they witnessed A.J. out at 5:00 in the morning, picking up cans for Jessica.

He didn't expect Jessica to admit that A.J. was forced to get up at 4:30 in the morning to collect cans for her bene-fit—that wasn't the point. Cupp wanted the jury to hear her lie in the face of the witnesses they had already heard from. He wanted them to experience her arrogant attitude toward A.J.'s repeated absences. He wanted them to feel her smugness.

> Cupp: Never made it to school on a Thursday, did he?
> Jessica (flippantly): Looks like he didn't.
> Cupp: There were a lot of cans out on those Thursdays, huh?
> Jessica: Yep.
> Cupp: And A.J. was out there collecting them, wasn't he?
> Jessica: Not to my knowledge.
> Cupp: But he didn't make it to school those days. You sent him, though, right?
> Jessica: I sent him to school.

The defense team had attempted to paint Jessica Schwarz as a woman possessed by her affection for children and ani-mals, but Scott Cupp attacked her claim that the Schwarz house was a hangout for all the neighborhood kids by show-ing just how few of their names she even knew—except for the ones who had testified earlier.

When Jessica denied trying to prevent HRS workers from talking to her children, Cupp asked, "Isn't it true that you threatened A.J. about talking to anybody from HRS about anything that went on in your house? Threatened him in front of your neighbor Beth Walton?"

"No, I didn't threaten him in front of anybody," she replied curtly, her body language revealing her arrogance. She couldn't conceal it—but Cupp sensed that she really didn't want to.

Cupp: When A.J. had the incident with his eyes and nose—you didn't see it happen?

Jessica: No, I didn't.

Cupp: Shortly after he came into his home, his nose literally started getting big in front of you? And that struck you as funny?

Jessica: Well, it just sort of looked funny and I did laugh. (Incredibly, she appeared to be fighting off a grin even as she spoke. Cupp plunged ahead.)

Cupp: And he didn't cry?

Jessica: No, he wasn't crying and there was no blood.

Cupp: And his nose was—your words—getting bigger in front of your face?

Jessica: Yes.

Cupp: In fact, whatever hit him, hit him so hard that the next morning you literally had to wash his eyes to get them open because he could not open them—isn't that what you told us earlier?

Jessica: I don't remember saying I was washing his eyes open—but they were black in the morning.

Cupp: And you couldn't get them open?

Jessica: I didn't say that.

Cupp: Do you remember giving a statement about that at another time?

Jessica: No, I don't remember it.

Cupp: If I showed you the statement, would it refresh your recollection?

Jessica: It might.

Scott Cupp, not wanting to break the momentum, made a quick decision to move on—for the moment.

Cupp (staring at her): And isn't it a fact that the reason why you finally took A.J. to the doctor was that the detective who came out to the house told you, "You better get that kid to the doctor"?

Jessica: No.

Cupp: No. (He repeated her denial to underline yet another lie, spoken under oath.) Detective Calloway didn't have all the information, though, did he?

Jessica: I don't know what you mean. He got all the information—from A.J., mainly.

Cupp: Did he talk to Jackie?

Jessica: Yes. He talked to Jackie—alone, as a matter of fact.

Cupp: After you told Jackie what to say, right?

Jessica: Absolutely not. You don't tell Jackie what to say. Jackie says whatever she wants.

Cupp: Isn't it true that A.J. and Jackie went across the street to Eileen Callahan's house? And when Ms. Callahan saw his eyes and nose and asked him what had happened, it was Jackie who said—

Rendell Brown objected, saying it was hearsay, and Cupp withdrew the question. The defense attorney's timing was good—good for the prosecution. It left the jury filling in Jackie's words.

Cupp then produced the statement that Jessica had given to Detective Michael Waites on May 2, 1993, in which she told him about the incident with A.J.'s black eyes. He handed the statement to her and asked her to read a portion of it to herself.

Cupp: And you told him his eyes were so black and blue that you had to wash his eyes out?

Jessica: I said they were really black and they were really swollen. I didn't remember having to wash his eyes open, but if I said it, I did it.

Cupp: And they really hurt?

Jessica: Yes.

Cupp: And he didn't cry?

Jessica: No, he didn't. He wasn't struck with anything. He hit—he fell into the bicycle. No one struck him in any way, shape, or form.

Cupp: You never struck him?
Jessica: No.

Candace Ahern had testified earlier that Jessica had laughed at the condition of A.J.'s nose and eyes and made fun of him in her presence, but when Cupp questioned Jessica about it, she denied it.

Cupp: You didn't laugh at him in front of her and call him "shit for brains"?
Jessica (nonchalantly): Not in front of Candace Ahern. (Her answer couldn't have been more perfect for the prosecution.)
Cupp: How about not in front of Candace Ahern?
Jessica: Yes.
Cupp: And you called him "shit for brains"?
Jessica: And HRS called me about that and I told them.
Cupp: And that didn't happen in front of Candace Ahern? That happened a different time?
Jessica: I don't really remember.
Cupp: You testified—on direct—that he was hiding food in the garage and he never told you why. He didn't have an explanation?
Jessica: He wasn't admitting to anything. I asked him if he was the one hiding the food.
Cupp: And didn't you say that he denied that there was food there or said, "What food?" That's why you took him around to show him?
Jessica: Yes.
Cupp: And you—of crude character, allowed—did you say sometimes you're abrasive? Some people think you're abrasive?
Jessica: Oh, yes.
Cupp: And you were angry. Here's this kid opening up the food and he's laying it around—hiding it in the garage. You were angry, weren't you?
Jessica: I wasn't angry.

Cupp: Calm? You calmly just rested your hand on his neck and showed him here and showed him there? That's Jessica?

Jessica: I wasn't crazy. I was just walking—look here, look there.

Cupp: You'd never picked him up by his head and dropped him?

Jessica: No.

Cupp (with measured sarcasm): Not Jessica?

Jessica: That's right.

The buzzing in the gallery suggested strongly that the spectators—at least—didn't believe her, and Judge Colbath was forced to quiet them with a sharp crack of his gavel.

Cupp: Your testimony—so I'm clear—in reference to Richard Zimmern . . . when he drove up to your house on A.J.'s birthday, A.J. was not trimming the sidewalk with scissors?

Jessica: That's exactly right.

Cupp: He was not?

Jessica: No, he was sweeping with a broom—a full-sized broom.

Cupp (pointedly): Dr. Zimmern is mistaken?

Jessica: Absolutely.

Cupp: I guess he's just getting old and senile?

Not surprisingly, Rendell Brown strenuously objected and Scott Cupp quickly withdrew the question, knowing the point had already been made.

"Isn't it true," Cupp continued, "that—after you were all interviewed by the police in May—you told the girls, 'Don't tell them anything. I could go to jail'?"

Brown quickly came out of his chair, protesting, "Your Honor, I'm going to object—"

But before he could finish, everyone in the courtroom heard Jessica say, "I told Jackie that."

The defense attorney was stunned. Everyone was stunned.

Cupp (quickly continuing): And where was Lauren?

Jessica: She was there.

Cupp: She was standing right next to you?

Jessica: Yes.

Cupp: Your testimony is that you felt equally fond of all three children—Lauren, Jackie, and A.J.?

Jessica: Right.

Cupp: Do you think maybe A.J. was hiding food because he was not getting enough to eat?

Jessica: Absolutely not.

Cupp: You weren't giving him a limited amount of time to eat? Is that what you were using the timer for?

Jessica: I was using the timer for bed-wetting when he first moved into my home.

Cupp: When A.J. was placed on the imipramine—when he came home—how long was it before he started throwing it up?

Jessica: I really don't remember.

Cupp: And then you took him off it?

Jessica: If he threw it up, I took him off it until he felt better.

Cupp: But he never had a problem tolerating it for six weeks while he was in Vero Beach, did he?

Jessica: I guess not, if that's what they say.

Cupp: Isn't it true that you told Dr. Zimmern that you didn't think the imipramine was helping A.J. and you took him off of it?

Jessica: No. I told him about the throwing up.

Cupp: That was never a point of contention that Dr. Zimmern thought he should be on the imipramine? Was that something you disagreed with him about?

Jessica: No, I didn't disagree about him being on the

imipramine. I just took him off of it until he stopped throwing up and felt better.

Cupp: Did you also tell Dr. Zimmern that you didn't think the counseling was helping A.J.? That he didn't need counseling—he needed discipline?

Jessica: He asked me a point-blank question. He said, "Is Andrew getting any better with everything that's going on in the home, in school, and in counseling?" And I said, "It gets better and it gets worse, but the overall picture—I think he needs more help."

Cupp: You didn't tell Dr. Zimmern that you didn't believe in counseling?

Jessica: I told him I didn't believe in it for me, but I would participate.

Cupp: Oh, I see. During the 1992 to 1993 school year with Mrs. Idrissi, he was not on imipramine during that year, was he?

Jessica: Yes, he was.

Cupp: Your testimony is that he was on imipramine during his third-grade year with Mrs. Idrissi?

Jessica: Yes, I think so anyway.

Cupp: You're not sure now?

Jessica: Well, I'm about 100 percent sure, but on and off. Again, it was always on and off, so I really don't remember the exact date.

Cupp: Wasn't that the time period when you said that Dr. Ukuedojor wouldn't prescribe it?

Jessica: What I had originally said was that I was getting stuck with having to find someone to prescribe this.

Cupp: And Ukuedojor prescribed it?

Jessica (rambling): He did. Nobody was doing the blood levels is what it was. He had to have blood levels, blood taken and levels—however they do it—on a monthly or weekly basis. That much I don't really remember, but nobody wanted to take the responsibility for taking the blood; so in essence, they turned it around and said if we don't take the blood we can't prescribe the pill, so I had called Dr. Uttley and begged him for the stuff—

Cupp (interrupting): Ma'am, was he or wasn't he on imipramine?

Jessica: He was on and off, on and off. That's all I tried to tell you.

Cupp: No further questions.

Cupp was emotionally drained after the cross-examination. A local reporter later referred to Jessica as being "hammered away at."

Usually, when a defendant chooses to testify, there is some redirect by the defense attorney—to clean things up a bit. It was extremely significant that Rendell Brown chose not to try to salvage any damage done to Jessica on cross. He knew that if he did any redirect, Scott would get another shot at her on re-cross. By asking no more questions, he was telling the prosecution—and more important, the jury—that he wanted her off the stand.

After the defense rested, Joe Marx called Corporal Bobbie Hopper to the witness stand as the prosecution's only rebuttal witness.

Immediately after she was sworn in, Brown asked to approach the bench, his concern being that the witness had been at the Schwarz home on the day A.J.'s body was found.

"I don't know what she's going to say."

Marx assured the judge and the defense attorney, "I don't plan on going into that. I'll keep my questions very narrow."

Corporal Hopper testified that she had been employed with the sheriff's office for fourteen years.

Marx: Listen to my questions very carefully and just answer the question. On May 2, 1993, did you have an opportunity to enter the Schwarz residence?

Hopper: Yes, I did.

Marx: While you were present in the Schwarz residence, did you have an opportunity to go into Andrew's room?
Hopper: Yes, I did.

When Marx prompted her to describe the room, she told him that Andrew's room was a small room off the kitchen area that appeared to be a utility room.

"In the room there was a bed on the far wall; there was a dresser next to it. On top of the dresser were plastic bags and I don't know what was in them. They were all tied up and piled on the dresser. At the foot of the bed, there was a lot more of these plastic bags. There was a pair of sneakers on the dresser and probably a ten-inch plastic police car."

Marx: Was it nicely decorated?
Hopper: Absolutely not. It was . . . it was very depressing.
Marx: Was it barren?
Hopper: There was nothing in there. It was just the bed and a toy.
Marx: Did you have an opportunity to go into the girls' bedrooms? Could you tell me what you saw there?
Hopper: Complete opposite. They had printed bedspreads, matching curtains, TV, Nintendo, toys, games. It was like two opposite ends of the world.
Marx: While you were in the Schwarz residence, did you see pictures on the walls and on the tables of the two girls?
Hopper: There were lots of pictures on the walls and around the residence.
Marx: While you were in the Schwarz residence, did you see one single picture of Andrew Schwarz?
Hopper: No, sir, I did not.

CHAPTER 24

This boy couldn't tell anybody anything. He had nowhere to run—nowhere to go. His whole life was a living hell.

—Joseph Marx

On Thursday, September 1, 1994, Jessica Schwarz, clad in a printed dress topped by a white cardigan sweater, listened sullenly as Joseph Marx gave the closing arguments for the prosecution.

Ilene Logan, who had been kept out of the courtroom because her name appeared on the state's witness list, was allowed to be present for the closing arguments.

David "Bear" Schwarz was on the defense witness list, but he was never called to the stand; in fact, he did not attend the trial at all. As soon as it started, he disappeared. He would later claim that he did not want to testify because he was concerned that the prosecutors would "misrepresent" his real feelings and imply that he was afraid of Jessica.

The prosecution never intended to call him as a witness. Scott Cupp knew that was exactly what Rendell Brown wanted—so he could "lead him by the nose" on cross. David was a wild card for both sides, and a card that neither wanted to play—despite any posturing.

The atmosphere in the packed courtroom was electric and, not surprisingly, the media was present in full force.

When he was interviewed for his job, Joe Marx had been asked what he saw himself doing in five years. He answered, "I see myself giving the closing arguments in the biggest murder case you've got." Ironically, it was five years later—to the day—that he did just that.

As he faced the jury, he felt the pain and anger of his own tragic, personal loss—only months earlier—because of senseless violence. He struggled to push those thoughts and feelings away as he focused on the matter at hand.

"Last night, when I was staying up thinking about what I was going to say—and crumpling up papers—I had a recurring thought and it was this: That in today's society we've come to accept violence as a way of life. We just accept that's the way it is.

"We turn on the TV when we get home and we turn on the news. This person has been shot. This person has been killed. This child has been kidnapped. And we just accept it because we can't do anything about it.

"It's hard to believe that people can be so cruel to one another. Sometimes this thing we call a trial—this search for truth and justice—is an ugly process.

"But the sad part of the story—and what's unfortunate—is that it's true and you can't turn your head and you can't change the channel.

"But you see, there's some good news here. Because this time it's your chance, as citizens and as jurors, that you can do something. It reminds me of an old movie with Faye Dunaway and William Holden called *Network*. And everybody sticks their head out the window and shouts, 'I'm mad as hell and I'm not going to take it anymore!'

"And this is your chance. You send this defendant a message that you're mad as hell and you are not going to take this anymore. You're not! This is your opportunity.

"During the trial, you heard eighteen different people come into this courtroom and tell you that Andrew Schwarz was a loving little boy, a boy starved for love, a boy starved for attention.

"You heard Mrs. Idrissi, a twenty-two-year veteran of the Palm Beach County school system. Mrs. Idrissi is a beautiful woman who cares about children. She got choked up during her testimony. She cared about Andrew Schwarz.

"Several people got choked up during their testimony. The funny thing is, only one person didn't get choked up at all—the defendant, cold and emotionless.

"You see, Andrew Schwarz was desperate to please. Dr. Rahaim told you that. Several witnesses told you that—desperate to please.

"As described by the defendant—this little 'liar' and this little 'thief' came to school during Christmastime . . . and Mrs. Idrissi told you about the Christmas story and that he came to school when all the other kids were excited and happy about buying Christmas presents. . . . And he came to school with no money. So what did she do? She gave him money.

"Now, what did the little 'liar' and 'thief' do? He took the entire amount of money and bought presents for Mrs. Idrissi.

"Emotional abuse—the system of degradation of another—a course of conduct taken by the defendant against Andrew, designed to reduce his self-concept to the point that he considered himself unworthy of friendship, unworthy of love, and unworthy of protection.

"Emotional abuse is just as deliberate as physical abuse.

"'You're stupid.' 'You're a worthless piece of shit.' 'I hate your fucking guts.' She might as well have punched. It's as deliberate as a gunshot. Emotional abuse scars the heart and damages the soul.

"This little boy's spirit was broken. He was ten—ten years old—and his spirit was broken.

"Let's talk about Mr. Brown's defense in this case—or should I say defenses? Let's start with the first one. His client did it—but she didn't know any better. She couldn't help herself. She's a tough woman trucker, educated from a background where she learned discipline.

"Well, is that what we heard? Her own mother took the

stand and told you, 'We taught her right from wrong, she comes from a somewhat privileged background, and she has a high-school education.'

"Now, ladies and gentlemen, you don't need a college education to raise a child. What you need is a heart.

"So, try another one. A.J. was a bad kid, brain-damaged, and uncontrollable. The defense claims that everybody is lying. The only person who is telling you this kid is brain-damaged and uncontrollable is this woman. The only person.

"Eighteen people told you Andrew Schwarz was a good boy—never a discipline problem.

"Back on September 9, 1992, Dr. Zimmern wrote, 'Why is Andrew so cooperative in school—and so rotten at home? Something is wrong here.' There was something wrong. The defendant was lying! The whole world is wrong and Jessica Schwarz is right. Don't buy it. Don't have your intelligence insulted.

"But, most importantly, Dr. Rahaim took the stand. Dr. Rahaim doesn't know anybody, never saw Andrew, doesn't know the defendant—an expert. He told you there's absolutely no evidence in all the stacks of documents and records that he reviewed—no evidence that there was brain damage. None. Zero.

"This whole question of imipramine became comical. It became a joke.

"The defendant couldn't get her story straight. Yes, he was on it. Well, sometimes he was on it—when he wasn't throwing it up. Mr. Cupp got up on cross-examination and said, 'Now, Mrs. Schwarz, isn't it true you couldn't get a prescription?' 'Oh, well, this woman wouldn't give it to me, and Dr. Uttley washed his hands of me. I couldn't get it—but he was on it.'

"'But, ma'am, didn't you tell HRS and Medicaid you wouldn't pay for it, so you couldn't get it?'

"'Well, yes, but I was giving it to him.'

"And then she says she gave it to him, but he threw it up.

That's why he didn't go to school. But the funny thing is, the Vero Beach records show that he was on the imipramine and there was no evidence that he threw up. This is a joke—it's funny.

"On top of all of this—if that isn't enough for you—she tells Dr. Zimmern, 'I'm not giving him the imipramine.'

"Let's assume for a minute that this kid was the worst kid in the world. Let's assume that he was brain-damaged. Let's assume that he was retarded. Let's assume that he was a special child. Assume it.

"Does he deserve to be treated that way? Does he deserve that? Nobody deserves that—and certainly not a ten-year-old boy.

"This boy couldn't tell anybody anything. He had nowhere to run—nowhere to go. His whole life was a living hell.

"Let's try another defense. It's HRS's fault. It's the counselor's fault. It's Dr. Zimmern's fault. It's everybody's fault—but hers.

"So we go to the next defense. This is the best one. She just—flat out—didn't do it.

"The final defense: This is one big conspiracy. People who didn't know each other—veterans of the school system, retired pediatricians, doctors, neighbors that she knew, neighbors that she didn't know, pest control people, friends, enemies—they all got together somewhere over on Triphammer Road. They all got together, got their stories together, and this is all one big conspiracy.

"There's an old saying in the law: 'When the law is on your side, you pound the law. When the facts are on your side, you pound the facts. When neither one is on your side, you pound the table.'

"When this trial started, Mr. Brown walked over and told you, as the defendant sits here, she's innocent—cloaked in this veil of innocence. He was right. She was—absolutely—but after nine days of trial, we slowly removed that veil. And what did we find? A monster. That's what we found—a monster—a person who is manipulative, a bully intimidator, and most of all—a liar. That's what we found.

"She was devoid of any emotion when she spoke about Andrew—a stone.

"When you go back there with the verdict form, it's a hard job that you have to do. You're sitting in judgment of another human being. This is your opportunity to do the right thing. Don't spend one second feeling sorry for this woman. Don't spend one second feeling sorry for Lauren. You're doing her a favor. And don't feel sorry for that defendant because you're not doing anything to her. She did this to herself. She didn't give a crap who was watching. She didn't care. She told you, 'I'm abusive. I'm crude—but I'm not rude.'

"Ladies and gentlemen, when you go back to the jury room, don't think about her. Don't feel sorry for her. You're not doing a thing to her. She did it to herself.

"Thank you."

As Joe Marx sat down, he felt that it had gone well—that he had connected with the jurors and that they would do the right thing. Touched by his powerful and emotional words, many people in the gallery were crying.

After a short break, Rendell Brown gave the closing argument for the defense.

"Mr. Marx said when the law is on your side, you argue the law. When the facts are on your side, you argue the facts, and when neither is on your side, you bang on the table.

"Well, let's extend that a little bit further—there's an extension of that—because of what we've seen in this trial. There's another one that says this: 'When you bring a person into court accused of a crime against a child, the jury is expected to come in with sympathy for the child.'

"So, when you're prosecuting regarding a child, appeal to the emotions of the jury. And that's precisely what the state has sought to do throughout the trial. It's culminated in an argument that went something like, 'If you convict Jessica Schwarz, you'll rid the country of violence on the streets.'

"That's an appeal to nothing that came forward in this case. That's an appeal to your emotions and that is asking you—as jurors—to violate the law.

"Mr. Marx stood here telling you to get mad—show your anger. His Honor is going to instruct you that sympathy, bias, prejudice, have no place in this trial. He will tell you that. Further, he will tell you that the burden of proof is upon the state—not to evoke emotions—not to evoke sympathies—but rather to prove guilt of each and every material element of each and every crime charged, beyond and to the exclusion of every reasonable doubt.

"And when you don't have those proofs . . . when your evidence has failed . . . when your witnesses have obviously failed . . . then you get up here and you say, 'Well, there's a little child involved, feel sorry for him, convict her, evidence be damned.' That's the argument you heard.

"I knew I could represent the truth to you and then stand here proudly, as I do, now knowing that I wouldn't have to argue for you to get emotional. I wouldn't have to ask you to feel sorry for Jessica Schwarz. All I want you to do is look at the evidence and be fair. That's the law and I work within the law.

"We knew it wouldn't be easy. We knew you were going to hear some things that you weren't supposed to hear. And then we were going to ask you to do something that is close to humanly impossible—forget about the fact that there are other proceedings and there are other trials—and focus on the proofs in this case and this case alone.

"Andrew was a young child. That evokes sympathy, but there is no place in this trial for sympathy—that's a violation of that solemn oath you took.

"Most of you admitted that you had—at some point or another—seen news articles or television stories, or whatever, about these allegations. I said to you, ladies and gentlemen, can you do this? It's not going to be easy, but can you do this? Can you sit here; hear the facts—because I know that after you hear the facts, you're going to decide that Jessica Schwarz is not guilty of the crimes charged. But can you hold your head high, square your shoulders, look squarely into the eyes of your husbands and your wives and your friends and your coworkers and your neighbors, and say, 'I found her not guilty because the state failed to prove her guilty'?

"'I found her not guilty because I know the facts. Facts come not from the newspaper—but from this stand—and all of the stuff that you think you know from reading a newspaper just isn't facts. The facts are what I voted on and my conscience is clear. I did the right thing. I sent the lady home to her daughters because she's not guilty of the charges—under the laws of the state of Florida guaranteed to us by the Constitution of the United States—and the state of Florida—as well.'

"And I asked you those questions because, ladies and gentlemen, that's not an easy chore, but you've got to do it—because if you can't make the system work, the system can't work. If you let the system fail, you fail the entire system, the country, everything. It does not avail you in the least to convict an innocent person to satisfy your husbands or your wives or your neighbors or your employees or your coemployees or your employers or anyone else.

"Do the right thing—follow the law. Say to the state of Florida, 'You as representatives of the law are not going to make me break the law by violating my solemn oath and finding a not guilty person guilty.'"

Rendell Brown held up the school picture of A.J. for the jury to see once again.

"The state is very proud of this photograph of this boy. I want you to look at the photograph for what it can help you with. This is a picture taken of Andrew Schwarz at school. I beseech you to show me a mark on this boy or show me there was makeup used to cover a mark. We all know that if a child is brutally beaten and bruised—as these witnesses have said he was—even if the marks heal, the kinds of marks we're talking about will ultimately leave a scar—a permanent scar. Take it back there with you and study it. This is how we test the evidence.

"Ours is not an argument of conspiracy. Things like this can happen when rumors start to run rampant. You've got a bunch of neighbors . . . it's been a hotbed of conversation. I'm not going to trash these kids. I'm going to tell you this way. Children hear rumors, see a playmate on TV. The thought is, that's the way to get some attention: 'I'll go them one better.'

"The [HRS] workers went there—announced at times—unannounced at times. They talked to the child sometimes in Jessica's presence—sometimes out of her presence.

"When you hear the fact that there were various HRS workers—the people who were sent there on unfounded reports . . . I think the evidence says seven or eight occasions—never once founded—never once any real problem. Who do you think those calls were coming from? The same neighbors—whose truth the state seeks to vouch for—kept sending these people there. Police kept going there—can't find a thing there. What in the world is going on?

"So how is it so difficult to understand that they are here lying—if they would lie and tie up these hot lines about abuses that simply weren't going on? Why is that so difficult to understand and to believe?

"Jessica had an obligation to train this child how to function and live in society.

"There's no way in the world Andrew Schwarz—given the problems and situation he had—could have gotten these grades by himself. Jessica Schwarz worked with that child, and I think she did a tremendous job, for him to get these kinds of grades—given the problems and facts of illnesses and the times he missed from school.

"State talked about Jessica Schwarz and, well, she didn't break down and cry—she wasn't emotional. What you see is what you get because that's what she is—and she didn't get up here and try to pretend that she's something that she is not. She was just the way she was because that's Jessica Schwarz—she hurts inwardly, not outwardly.

"Did they prove she was trying to help this child with an education? Or was she trying to maliciously punish? Was she right to punish? She has more than a right. She has an obligation like everybody. If we're going to stop that killing that Mr. Marx talked about, if we're going to stop the kidnappings that he talked about, if we're going to stop all of these ugly things, we're going to start with children Andrew's age and start letting them learn that when you do things—you're going to be punished and not rewarded. That's what Jessica sought to do. She had an obligation to do that. Every parent in society has that obligation and that's what she did—no hatred, no ill will—simply doing what she was taught to do. Get his attention when he does something wrong because society won't tolerate it.

"Can you look at this evidence as presented and decide within your heart and within your soul—beyond and to the exclusion of every reasonable doubt—that it was not done for educational purposes? The things that they did do—making him stay on task—making him go back and do his chores until he got it right . . . if that was malicious and ill will and with hatred, then go ahead and convict if that's what you call that. Go ahead and convict her.

"But if you find what the truth points out here was real— that this lady was trying to do what all of society needs to start trying to do again—then you've got to find her not guilty. She didn't do anything to hurt this child.

"Don't abrogate the law. Don't make a mockery of our laws that our forefathers sat down and thought out to apply to every individual whether it happens to be a tall, slim, attractive, gorgeous lady—or a two-hundred-pound truck driver. Everybody has a right to be presumed innocent until proven guilty by good and competent evidence—and sympathy is not good and competent.

"Untruths and half-truths are not good and competent evidence, and that's what you must determine within yourselves.

"Somehow I'm convinced that you heard what I heard and that your memory is probably far better than mine, and I'm not going to insult your intelligence by going through all of those contradictions and falsehoods and the like.

"You knew it wasn't going to be easy. I knew it wasn't going to be easy, but you vowed to do the right thing. You vowed to do it in spite of whatever others outside this courtroom might feel. You said you understood that the only facts that anybody knows would be the facts that you would hear from this stand and this courtroom and this trial, and that's what His Honor is going to tell you as well.

"If you follow the law and if you do the right thing, you'll have no choice but to find Jessica not guilty. When you do the right thing, justice will have been accomplished in this courtroom, and Jessica Schwarz will have these shackles— that were unlawfully placed upon her—removed from her.

"Thank you."

The hushed courtroom listened intently as Scott Cupp spoke passionately to the jurors in his powerful rebuttal.

"The first thing I want to discuss with you is Dr. Rahaim, HRS, and the Child Protection Team.

"Dr. Rahaim has been treated extremely unfairly—extremely. What you did hear is that on February 23, the first time that Dr. Rahaim—in his capacity as a consultant to the Child Protection Team—had any contact with this situation, he stated in no uncertain terms that this is a target child in this situation. Dr. Rahaim feels that the child is living in exactly the wrong situation.

"Among the recommendations was that HRS, in consultation with the Child Protection Team, determine whether the child is in an appropriate placement with his natural father and his stepmother. And if you remember Dr. Rahaim's testimony, what he was stating is that therapy—family therapy—individual therapy—is not a cure-all. There are times when what you need to do is take the kid out of the home.

"Family therapy?

"All you've heard and all you will hear about David Schwarz is contained in a few signatures, where he signed a few reports. There was no family. This was David. This was Jessica. David was never there. And if any of you think for a minute that if we brought David Schwarz in here, that he would do anything other than do what Jessica Schwarz did . . . I think it's interesting to note that the defense didn't call the defendant's husband. Not even her husband came in.

"What family? It's appalling. It's disgusting that those words—'family,' 'mother,' 'stepmother'—those words shouldn't have even been used in this entire trial because they did not apply. This was not a family. She was no mother—you all know that.

"Mr. Brown mentioned how all that Mrs. Schwarz wanted to do was to train the boy up the right way—to grow up in her home and become a law-abiding member of society. Every once in a while, a trial comes along that teaches us something different. You know what we've all learned? This has been a lesson in what's wrong with our society and this has been '101, How We Train Criminals.'

"Because you know what? In a few short years, Andrew J. Schwarz was going to be a citizen's worst nightmare. He was going to be the accident that came into somebody's house and poured acid on somebody's head—or murdered somebody's spouse while she sat there and watched. And citizens like yourselves would then fill this courtroom, clamoring to me as a prosecutor: 'Nail him, he's sadistic. He's unfeeling. Look at him sitting there. He doesn't care about anybody but himself.' Who trained him?

"That's what trained him! She trained him how to be uncaring about other people, about himself, sadistic. He got a real good course in sadism. Maliciousness. It's sickening.

"I asked you very few questions in jury selection. One of the questions I asked you—because I was concerned about it then and I'm still concerned about it—that one of the biggest difficulties with this case is believing, being open to believe that there are people like that out there among us that can do these sorts of things. And nobody wants you to feel sorry, so I won't even use the word 'child'—that there are people out here that can do this to 'people.'

"We just don't want to have a place for that in our minds. How can anybody do this stuff? And you hear the charges and people are shaking their head and they are going, 'My God, this stuff can't go on. This doesn't go on—it's got to be exaggerated.' But I asked you all, and you all answered affirmatively, 'Would you be open to the possibility that, unfortunately, day in and day out in our community—not other places that you see on CNN—but right here in our communities, this stuff can and does go on?'

"How do Mr. Marx and I show you bruises? This case isn't about bruises. You're not going to hear one charge that A.J. was beaten. His psyche was battered, bruised—ripped to shreds. How do I come in here and show you a picture of this kid's soul? How do I show you a picture of his spirit?

"We did it by bringing people in here. Not a bunch of cops and not a bunch of people that I've got strings on, and certainly not a bunch of people from HRS. Because—make no mistake about it—the system failed this boy horribly. And you did learn—as I warned you in the beginning—to keep your eye on the ball. There are other trials and other cases."

Scott Cupp pointed at Jessica. "This is about that!

"Those are other proceedings—those are other trials. But you did learn that at least one person is under a grand jury indictment—not by Mr. Marx and myself. But from people out of the community who come in—like yourself—but that's not what this case is about.

"In opening, I made a reference to A.J.'s life inside the asylum. I misspoke. In an asylum, there's hope. This was a concentration camp. There was absolutely no hope.

"Thank you."

Before Judge Colbath charged the jury, Joe Marx asked if it would be all right for him to go ahead and leave. When the judge gave his permission, Marx—feeling very strongly that he had done what he came to do—walked out of the courtroom, down the hall, and out of the courthouse.

While the jurors deliberated, Scott Cupp waited—relatively calmly—alone in a hearing room, reading newspapers and "just waiting." After 5½ long hours, word came that they had arrived at their verdicts.

The courtroom was again packed when the clerk read the verdict on count one—that Jessica Schwarz had maliciously punished Andrew Schwarz by forcing him to eat food from a bowl placed next to a cat's litter box. There was a heart-stopping moment when a resounding "not guilty" filled the room.

Cupp would later say that he couldn't describe how he felt at that moment because he was "numb." He stated, "My brain was getting ready to handle a complete acquittal!"

Michael Waites, sitting on a bench in the rear of the courtroom, dropped his face into his hands, his heart sinking.

Jessica Schwarz remained indifferent and unaffected. She stood between her attorneys, devoid of all emotion, as the verdicts were read on the remaining charges.

"Guilty!" Six times. She was found guilty on all the remaining charges—four counts of aggravated child abuse and two counts of felony child abuse—and faced the possibility of seventy years in prison.

Jessica Schwarz merely glanced at Rendell Brown and shook her head, and as she was escorted from the courtroom—handcuffed and flanked by deputies—she averted her eyes and declined to make any comment to the media.

Neighbors of the Schwarz family, on Triphammer Road and the surrounding area, breathed a collective sigh of relief.

Everyone was more at ease—especially the children—knowing that the neighborhood "bully" was safely behind bars.

When Scott Cupp talked to Joe Marx by telephone and told him the news, Marx was "just thrilled out of [my] mind."

On Friday, December 9, 1994, at her sentencing hearing, a very frustrated Jessica Schwarz informed Judge Walter Colbath, "I never did these things. I never hurt him. I never hurt anyone."

Rendell Brown asked the judge not to exceed the nine-year sentence recommended by Florida's sentencing guidelines.

However, Scott Cupp requested that the guidelines be exceeded and a forty-five-year sentence be imposed on Jessica Schwarz.

The judge declared that only a "monumental conspiracy" by A.J.'s friends, neighbors, and teachers would make her story believable, and then sentenced her to thirty years in prison. He also ordered that—after her release from prison—she was to be on probation for fifteen years, and that she pay a $5,000 fine to a child abuse organization.

CHAPTER 25

It's no mystery that she killed A.J. She probably enjoyed it.

—Scott Cupp

In order to get a conviction for second-degree murder, it would not be necessary for the state to prove that Jessica Schwarz intended to cause A.J.'s death. And they only needed to seat a six-member jury, instead of the twelve required for a first-degree murder charge.

Scott Cupp felt that the jury instructions for second-degree murder in this case were quite appropriate:

1. The victim is dead.
2. The death was caused by the criminal act of the defendant.
3. There was an unlawful killing of a victim by an act imminently dangerous to another and demonstrating a depraved mind without regard for human life.

An "act" includes a series of related actions arising from and preformed pursuant to a single design or purpose.

An act is "imminently dangerous to another and demonstrating a depraved mind" if it is an act or series of acts that:

1. a person of ordinary judgment would know is reason-ably certain to kill or do serious bodily injury to another;
2. is done from ill will, hatred, or an evil intent;
3. is of such a nature that the act itself indicates an indifference to human life.

A first-degree murder charge would have forced the state to prove premeditation; and all the evidence was circumstantial. Cupp felt that asking a jury to convict on first-degree murder would really be pushing it.

The point became moot, however, when both sides agreed to "waive jury." Defendants have the right to have their cases decided by a jury of their peers, but if a defendant wants to waive that right—and the state agrees—the case is tried by a judge, who then sits as both the finder of fact and decider of law.

Rendell Brown had approached Scott Cupp after the abuse trial and said he may want to waive a jury. He seemed to think that Cupp would automatically not agree to it, but Cupp told him to give him some time to think about it. It had advantages and disadvantage for both sides. The big one for Brown would be that he wouldn't have to worry about not calling Jessica to testify. She had done horribly. Her demeanor alone cried out, "Spite, ill will, and evil intent"—just what the jury instruction on second-degree required.

In a case such as this, the defense runs a huge risk in not having the defendant take the stand and look at the jury and tell them she didn't do it. Judges, however, are trained to make decisions by simply following the law and instructions—regardless of whether or not the defendant testifies. Judges are looking only to whether or not the state proves its case beyond and to the exclusion of every reasonable doubt.

Scott Cupp based his decision to agree to the waiver on who the judge was to be and took a calculated gamble. Karen Martin would be the judge hearing the murder case. New to the circuit bench—having spent time in county court hearing misdemeanor cases and issues of less severity—she had most recently served a rotation in juvenile court. Cupp's concern was that the pressure on her would be tremendous.

A.J.'s murder trial would be her first in "prime time," and she proved to be more than up to the task.

Jessica Schwarz's nonjury trial for murder and witness tampering began on Monday, March 20, 1995. It would seem that her attorneys weren't as concerned about her impressing anyone with her appearance this time around; instead of sundresses, she simply wore her blue jail-issued "uniforms."

The defense chose not to give an opening statement, but Scott Cupp promised—in his opening—to present evidence to the court to show that Jessica was, indeed, responsible for A.J.'s death.

Circuit court judge Karen Martin allowed—over the protests of Rendell Brown—the state to present much of the testimony about Jessica's abuse of A.J., after Joe Marx successfully argued that it showed she had a motive to kill him.

However, the prosecution was not allowed to use the fact that she had rubbed A.J.'s face into his urine-soaked sheets. Or the fact that she kept him home from school as a form of punishment. Or that she forced him to trim the lawn with household scissors.

Ironically—considering that a jury of her peers had already convicted the defendant of the same abuses—Judge Martin considered them to be "inappropriate parenting skills." Judge Walter Colbath had cited the abuses as "barbaric and grotesque."

Many of the witnesses were the same—and their testimony very similar—as those presented at Jessica's trial on the abuse charges. The huge difference now being, of course, that no one had to be careful not to mention the fact A.J. was dead.

The judge heard testimony from several neighbors who said that the young boy was a good swimmer—and that he could easily stand up in the four-foot-deep, aboveground swimming pool.

There was chilling testimony from Catherine Turner, the neighbor who lived behind the Schwarzes, that during the night that A.J. died—between one and two o'clock in the morning—she had heard a young boy cry out, "I won't do it again! I won't do it again!"

Laura Perryman, Serena Perryman's mother, told the judge that Jessica had said to her—at least four times—that she was going to kill A.J.

"She told me she was going to kill A.J. I told her she couldn't really mean it. The more I told her she couldn't mean it, the more cold-bloodedly she said it."

Her voice broke as she tried to describe the tone of Jessica's voice: "It wasn't like anything I'd heard before. She said she just couldn't take it anymore. She told me A.J. was bad."

Laura Perryman had been so troubled by the conversation that she made it a point to avoid Jessica from then on.

Dr. James Benz's testimony for the defense had to be dealt with—and not just neutralized. Scott Cupp knew that Dr. Joseph Burton's opinion had to supercede Benz's.

The prosecution couldn't afford a tie. There's an old baseball axiom that a tie goes to the runner. In a criminal trial, a tie goes to the defendant in the form of a not guilty verdict, so Benz had to be discredited.

Cupp accomplished that by setting it up on cross-examination to be able to call Dr. Philip Colaizzo in rebuttal to show that the nonsense that Benz claimed happened at the infamous meeting in his office after A.J.'s autopsy was just that—nonsense.

Brown saw where the prosecution was going with Benz and tried to stop it by objecting to Cupp asking Benz about the "threats." By then, it was too late.

Scott Cupp would later say, "I would be lying if I didn't admit my personal satisfaction in Judge Martin allowing me to make Benz stand and demonstrate how that nameless, faceless police detective yelled at him during the meeting."

Dr. Colaizzo, of course, had also been present at the meeting with Dr. Benz and had been seated only a few feet from him.

Cupp: At any time during this meeting, did this event take place: Did anyone—in a loud voice, in speaking to Dr. Benz—scream, "Come on, God damn it, you know this woman killed the kid! God damn it, what the hell is wrong with you? You know that!"
Colaizzo: No, it didn't happen.

It came as no surprise that Brown did not call Jessica to the witness stand, claiming later that she wanted to testify, but he didn't think it was "merited," given the state's case.

On Tuesday, April 11, 1995, Judge Karen Martin—after reviewing written arguments—announced the verdicts in the case of the *State of Florida* v. *Jessica Schwarz* to a packed courtroom.

She began with the witness-tampering charge. Florida statutes define witness tampering as knowingly using intimidation or threat to another person with the intent to cause or induce the person to withhold testimony from an official investigation or proceeding, or to testify untruthfully in an official investigation or proceeding.

"In this case, based on the evidence, I find that Jessica Schwarz and her two daughters were waiting in an interview room at the police station while the father was being interviewed about the death of Andrew Schwarz.

"While they were waiting in the interview room, the defendant picked up her four-year-old daughter, held her at face-to-face level, and asked her, 'Do you want Mama to go to jail?' The four-year-old responded, 'No.' And the mother said, 'If you tell them anything, Mama will go to jail.'

"The video shows the mother contradicted the statements

the child is making and telling her, 'Don't tell these people any-thing. Just say I don't know. You don't talk to nobody anymore.'

"Then on her way out of the police station with the rest of her family, a police officer heard the defendant say again to the two girls, 'I don't want you talking to these people anymore.'

"Later that same day, when the police officer came to the defendant's home with an HRS representative to remove the two daughters from the defendant's custody, the defendant, in the presence of the police officers, said to the two girls, 'Don't tell these fucking assholes anything. They are not your friends.'

"Based on the law and all the evidence regarding witness tampering, I find beyond a reasonable doubt that the defendant, Jessica Schwarz, intended to cause her four-year-old to withhold testimony and testify untruthfully, and that she used intimidation and threat to do so.

"I do find beyond a reasonable doubt that Jessica Schwarz is guilty of witness tampering."

Judge Martin proceeded to give an excellent and detailed synopsis of the case—and of the evidence that she had con-sidered—pertaining to the second-degree murder charge.

A.J. was found dead floating midway between the top and the bottom of a four-foot-deep, aboveground swimming pool in the backyard of his home. He was naked and his body was covered with bruises and scratches—thirty to forty bruises and scratches. Rigor mortis had set in.

The body was autopsied the next day and again four days later. Both medical examiners were very well qualified. They both concluded that the immediate cause of death was drown-ing. Both made efforts to determine whether the drowning was from natural causes, suicide, accident, or homicide.

Both autopsies revealed bruises and scratches of varying ages on Andrew's body, abrasions on the right side of his nose and the left corner of his mouth. Palpable swelling was above his left ear, three bruises at various other locations were on his scalp.

"And when the scalp was peeled back—called reflected—during the autopsy, it revealed four areas of subcutaneous bruising extending from the skin surface to the galea. There was obvious hemorrhage in the galea."

It went on and on: a crescent-shaped laceration behind each ear, two areas of bruising inside his upper lip, bruises underneath his chin—on each side. A bruise on the right side of his chest, a scratchlike abrasion of the left side of his chest, two bruises on his abdomen. Bruises on his back and multiple bruises on his buttocks, a scratchlike abrasion on his right hip.

"On the arms, the upper left arm at least three bruises within one to two inches of each other with deep acute hemorrhages extending to the underlying musculature; a scratchlike abrasion on the left forearm."

Abrasions and scratches on his left wrist. A scratchlike abrasion on his right forearm and a small bruise on his left elbow.

Large areas of bruising on the back of his right thigh—extending from below the buttocks to his midthigh. Abrasions on his right calf. Bruises on his left thigh. A bruise below his left knee. An abrasion and bruise on his right lower leg and scratchlike abrasions on both his ankles.

"Both doctors concluded, after the autopsy, that Andrew had been physically abused, and both wrestled with the question of whether his injuries were connected with a homicide."

Dr. Benz concluded that he could not state with any degree of medical certainty whether Andrew's death was an accident, a suicide, or a homicide.

Dr. Burton concluded—without any doubt—had A.J.'s body been found in any circumstance other than a pool and water, the case would have been certified a homicide. Because the body was found floating in water, it complicated the issue of determining if A.J.'s death was, in fact, a homicide.

"He reported that the injuries to the scalp were sufficient—in and of themselves—that they could have caused the death in someone of Andrew's age and size."

A.J. did not die from natural causes or suicide.

"Dr. Burton testified there was nothing in any of Andrew's medical history to indicate any natural causes such as blackouts or seizures which might have precipitated such a drowning."

There was no evidence that Andrew committed suicide.

"Dr. Burton testified that committing suicide by drowning oneself in a pool or bathtub is virtually unheard of in children of this age."

That left the remaining question of whether A.J. died as a result of an accident or a homicide.

When A.J. went to bed on May 1, 1993, he seemed to be fine and there were no scratches or abrasions seen on his face. The next morning, he was dead—floating naked in the swimming pool—and there were abrasions on his face.

According to Dr. Burton, "the fingers of a person" caused the crescent-shaped lacerations behind each ear, and a recent scratch on his chest was "fingernaillike."

The bruises on his upper inner thighs were recent.

"As to the bruise on the upper aspect of the left arm, he testified it would have taken a lot of pressure to force that much blood out of the tissues on the left arm.

"And in his autopsy report, Dr. Burton states that the pattern of bruises on the scalp could in no way have been caused by some type of accident. He stated they were multiple—involving all four quadrants of the scalp."

The bruises were approximately the same age—a few minutes to a few hours old.

The abrasions by his mouth, on his nose, behind his ears, and the bruise beneath the left arm were "consistent with someone having held his head with the hand placed behind and possibly another hand across the nose and then being held submerged until he aspirated enough water to become unconscious and die."

The other possibility was that the numerous bruises to the head "could have resulted in unconsciousness and—in an attempt to cover the act—Andrew's body could have been placed in the pool in an unconscious state; he would have aspirated water and drowned."

Dr. Burton indicated there was some swelling of the brain, which could either have been caused by punches or blows to the head—or from the drowning.

"Dr. Burton testified that he had done—I think it was—twenty to forty thousand autopsies and his specialty is working with children.

"Dr. Burton was not able to say with any degree of a reasonable medical certainty that either one of these scenarios was exactly how Andrew came to his death, but the injuries were consistent with either one."

So it became necessary to look at whether any of the recent injuries could have been caused by an accident rather than at the hands of another person. Some of the injuries that A.J. had were definitely older and were not considered.

"The injury to his buttocks could have been caused by a whipping which he supposedly got some days before, a week before.

"The injuries under his chin were consistent with an incident which neighbors observed several weeks prior to his death: Andrew was picked up by the head and neck and swung from side to side with his arms flopping like a rag doll—and was seen to have been picked up by his [step]mother.

"Dr. Burton testified that the injuries to his head could not have been caused by accident. And all of these scratches and bruises could not have been explained by accident.

"Then there's the issue of why was Andrew in the pool in the middle of the night in the first place and why was he naked?"

Had A.J.—as the defense suggested—slipped out of the house to swim alone naked in the middle of the night? Because he was so busy with chores that he didn't have much chance to swim? Was he naked because he didn't want Jessica or David to discover that he had been out swimming in the middle of the night?

"There's no question that this child was constantly made to do chores. But let's examine what was happening the day before the evening that he died."

Jessica and David and the rest of the family had gone to Sunfest and A.J. was left home alone for the day. A neighbor saw him playing in the front yard. If he had chosen to do so, he could have gone swimming at any time that day.

"It makes no sense that he would go out naked in the middle of the night, on a very cold night, in the dark to swim.

"Andrew had never been known to swim naked. And then there's the testimony that nakedness was used as a form of punishment and humiliation in the family.

"Neighbors had seen Andrew forced to run naked down the street. It was obvious that he was embarrassed in trying to cover himself—and crying.

"Then there was the expert testimony of Dr. Rahaim that for a child who had been repeatedly humiliated and punished through nakedness, it would be a terrifying experience to swim naked in the middle of the night.

"So, it is possible? Remotely. Is it reasonable? Not at all.

"So based on the physical evidence alone and the surrounding circumstances, I find beyond a reasonable doubt that the corpus has been proven in this case."

The judge then proceeded to the issue of who had done this and why.

It was obvious from numerous witnesses' testimony that Jessica Schwarz was the disciplinarian in the family. They reported seeing her slap A.J. on the back of the head—and punching him on the head and face. And they testified to seeing her force him—as a form of punishment—to go naked.

"Her motive? The record is replete with testimony that this [step]mother despised this child; that she considered him nothing but trouble."

Laura Perryman had given the chilling and frightening testimony that Jessica had told her that she just couldn't take it anymore—couldn't take A.J. anymore—and that she was going to kill him.

"The neighbor tried to tell her, 'you don't mean that, you cannot mean that,' and the neighbor reported that she became more and more cold-blooded in her insistence that she was going to kill him—as though she had made a business decision. But that happened in December of '91 or [early] '92 and Andrew died in '93.

"Why after a year to a year and a half would Andrew be purposely drowned?

"The record is also replete with evidence that Andrew was becoming a bigger and bigger problem to his stepmother."

At the scene—the morning after the drowning—Bear had been grief-stricken and in tears; he was inconsolable. Jessica's reaction—as described by the police officers—had been "cool and uninvolved."

"It's not in any way reasonable that either one of the [other] children would have committed this offense nor do I find it reasonable that this would have been done by the father.

"At the most—according to the evidence—the father occasionally disciplined the child by spanking him on the behind. He was never known to belittle this child, to punish this child by punching him in the top of the head or on the face, to cause the child to go naked or to humiliate him in any way.

"I find the conclusion that this death was not an accident is inescapable; find that the state has proven beyond a reasonable doubt the elements of this offense:

"That Andrew Schwarz is dead.

"That the death was caused by the criminal agency of Jessica Schwarz.

"And this killing was done by an act imminently dangerous to Andrew and evincing a depraved mind regardless of human life.

"And it makes no difference which of the scenarios of Dr. Burton apply. It's clear that this child was beaten, that this child was either unconscious—perhaps semi-unconscious—when taken to the pool and held underwater. This child did not go into the pool on that night of his own volition.

"So I'm finding you guilty as charged."

Overcome with emotion, Scott Cupp's eyes filled with tears as he laid his head down on the table in front of him. Later—outside the courtroom—he told reporters, "Maybe now, A.J. has some peace."

The proof that the strategy with Dr. Benz had worked was evident in Judge Martin's findings-of-fact. She had barely referred to Benz at all and her verdict was replete with references to—and an almost total reliance on—Dr. Burton's opinions for her conclusions.

Benz's performance in A.J.'s case was the beginning of the end of his career as the chief medical examiner in Palm Beach County.

Scott Cupp would later comment, "In many ways, it was sad to watch over the next several years—but in the end, he did it to himself."

On Friday, July 28, 1995, Judge Martin listened to four hours of testimony at Jessica Schwarz's sentencing hearing for the murder of A.J.

Strangely enough, even though Jessica's parents, Edward and Helen Woods, both claimed that they believed their daughter was innocent, neither one of them asked the judge to show her mercy. Showing very little emotion, they testified that there was no alcoholism or drug abuse in their family and that Jessica had not been an abused child.

According to Mr. Woods, "There is nothing in her past. Nothing reaching a level of such destructive reaction."

Lauren Cross, Jessica's twelve-year-old daughter, cried openly as she told the judge, "If you put my mother away, you'll be locking up an innocent mother and let the real killer run loose."

During almost an hour and a half on the witness stand, Jessica berated her former neighbors, the prosecutors, and even the media for "wrongfully" convicting her.

When Rendell Brown asked her if she had ever cried, she—after thinking about it for several moments—replied, "When my kids were born, when a friend died . . . when A.J. died."

On cross-examination, when Joe Marx questioned her about her abrasive personality, she admitted that she had a "loud mouth," but she claimed she was not violent or threatening.

Marx reminded her of a comment she had made to him during a recess about his wife, Karen Starr Marx, who had been murdered the previous year.

"Do you remember saying, 'Why don't you join your wife? I'll see you out on bond'?"

Jessica Schwarz admitted that she remembered, but she denied that she was threatening him.

She also denied killing A.J. and insisted that she couldn't feel remorse for something she hadn't done.

On Friday, August 4, 1995, Judge Martin imposed the longest prison term possible—under Florida sentencing guidelines—on Jessica Schwarz. A forty-year sentence that would have to be served after she finished her thirty-year prison term for the abuse—seventy years total.

Schwarz's attorney had asked the judge not to sentence her based on her attitude:

"It's easy to understand her indignation because she did not do what she is accused of doing."

Joe Marx—referring to Jessica's daughters—had implored the judge:

"Do them a favor and put her in jail and keep her there as long as possible. Protect these children from her."

EPILOGUE

> *Many had questioned why no indictment for first degree. Immediately after the trial, I was very sensitive about that question. I guess I was still reeling from the reality that she was actually convicted and would be going off for seventy years on a case that in the beginning was dead in the water. Very few thought she would be convicted!*

—Scott Cupp

In April 1997, Scott Cupp, who had been responsible for handling the prosecution of Barbara Black, the HRS worker who had been indicted for threatening Eileen Callahan, announced that Black would not face criminal charges.

The pretrial intervention agreement required only that she perform community service, once a month for six months.

"It sat on the back burner until after Jessica's trials. By that time, it was decided that the point had been made and going after Black may have been overkill and treating her like a scapegoat. I don't know if that was right or not—but that's what we did."

After leaving the Palm Beach State Attorney's Office in 1999, Cupp opened his own practice in LaBelle, Florida—a beautiful little town on the banks of the Caloosahatchee River—twenty miles from Fort Myers. In 2002, he returned to prosecution and is presently chief of felony for the Lee County Office for the Twentieth Judicial Circuit.

(Everyone who was interviewed insisted that the arrest and successful prosecution of Jessica Schwarz was a team effort. However, they all agreed that if Scott Cupp had not insisted on a second complete autopsy, Jessica Schwarz would have gotten away with murder.)

Joseph Marx stayed with the state attorney's office until March 2000, then—after having his own private practice for a few years—he was appointed to a judgeship by Governor Jeb Bush in 2003. On August 1, 2003, he took over as county court judge for the Fifteenth Judicial Circuit in Palm Beach County.

He is married to Judge Krista Marx and has three step-children.

Michael Waites continues in law enforcement as an investigator for the state attorney's office.

Chris Calloway is now a sergeant with the PBSO. Jimmy Restivo has since passed away from a heart attack.

Dr. James Benz continued as the medical examiner for Palm Beach County until 1996. He has since retired and lives in Indiana.

Dr. Joseph Burton has Emeritus status with his office in Georgia and has his own consulting firm.

Near the end of the first trial, David Schwarz surfaced by phone, late one night to one of the investigators. He was alone somewhere in a motel room in another state—drunk and incoherent. That was the last Scott Cupp ever heard of him.

Jessica Schwarz's appeals have run their course. The convictions in both trials were appealed to Florida's Fourth

District Court of Appeals and were upheld, and the Supreme Court of Florida declined to hear them. Her current projected release date is December 3, 2034—subject to review.

As of this writing, she is incarcerated at the Broward Correctional Institution. She is middle-aged with graying hair—and unrepentant.

AFTERTHOUGHTS

by Carol J. Rothgeb

Jessica Schwarz—through intimidation and misguided, twisted loyalty on their part—was able to control her children and her husband. Very much the way William K. Sapp—serial killer and the subject of Hometown Killer—*controlled his mentally challenged, and childlike, accomplices.*

—Carol J. Rothgeb

Three days before I was asked to join Scott Cupp in this project, I was talking to a dear friend of mine about the possibility of writing another book. We were discussing a case in which a stepfather murdered his two stepchildren. I made the remark that I didn't think I could write one about natural parents killing their child, but maybe I could deal with writing one about a stepparent.

Then I got the phone call. I was hesitant at first. The editor sent me all the information that he had at that time. When I looked through the material, I was immediately touched by this young boy's tragic death, and—even more so—by his tragic life.

There's a young boy about A.J.'s age who catches the school bus across the street on the corner, about one hundred feet from my house. I can see him clearly out my kitchen window in the mornings. For whatever reason, his mother drives him to the bus stop.

She pulls up across the street, and if the weather is nice, the little boy crosses the street to wait for the bus. If the weather is bad or just plain cold, the boy waits in the car until he sees the bus coming down the street, then gets out and crosses over to the bus stop. Either way, his mother waits until the bus comes before pulling away.

So, what I see when I look out my window is a loving mother who cares about her child. For all I know, it is his stepmother, but whoever is driving the car cares what happens to the little boy.

Indeed, a poignant contrast to A.J.'s life.

Only Jessica Schwarz knows the whole story of exactly what happened in the wee hours of Sunday, May 2, 1993, between the times when Ron Pincus Jr. saw A.J. walking his dog and when Bear found his lifeless, bruised body in the aboveground swimming pool.

One can only imagine what the infraction of the rules might have been that so aroused Jessica's anger and rage that she could beat a child nearly to death with her bare hands and fists. And then hold the slender ten-year-old boy's head underwater until he stopped struggling for his very life.

As sad and demeaning as A.J.'s life was—he struggled to survive.

If he would have lived to adulthood—still living under the same miserable circumstances—one can only wonder what would have become of him. It's fairly common to read or hear of murderers—serial killers, especially—who were severely abused as children. Sometimes it's hard not to have compassion—at least for the children they were.

And what if A.J. had been removed from Jessica and David's house and placed in a loving foster home and received the help—and hugs—he so desperately needed? What if just one more neighbor would have called the authorities? So many "what-ifs" and "if onlys" . . .

Most parents worry about what will happen to their children as they venture out into life—into the world. Going to school. Going to play at a friend's house. The mothers and fathers admonish them over and over again not to talk to strangers. Not to accept a ride from someone they don't know.

And then there are the children who have no safe place—whose spirits are damaged or broken—who have no one to turn to for help. Their caregivers—the ones who feed them and clothe them and give them a roof over their heads—are also their tormentors. Surely these children spend their days—and their nights—in the presence of evil.

AFTERWORD

by Scott H. Cupp

I always found it curious that in the aftermath of the convictions and sentences—amid all the many words written and spoken about A.J., Jessica, and HRS, the state agency responsible for his care at the time of his murder—no one other than myself speculated about what A.J. would have been like had he survived to become a young man. No one.

When the proposal for this book made the rounds, the publishers who rejected it sounded a consistent theme. Child abuse is just too painful a subject. Yes, it is. It's the kind of pain that creeps into your dreams. It's the kind of pain that makes you weak. It's the kind of pain we in America persist in refusing to deal with.

Maybe it touches something in us that we lack the courage to think about and to speak about. A.J.'s story not only touches that, it *slaps* it. Maybe what A.J. touches in us are thoughts that, for reasons largely unknown to us, we are ashamed of. Maybe we secretly harbor a relief that he did not survive to become a young, angry man. A man we would certainly have to deal with. That would be easy, though. Then we would be dealing with the behavior, not the person.

Perhaps he touches in us things about our own childhood that are too painful to go back to. Maybe he touches something in us that we fear there have been times in our lives we know we were perilously close to slipping into. The worst of ourselves. And we can't figure out how those times happened. Or what is locked inside us that we can't seem to get to. And then it passes. Maybe it's the same thing I sensed was present during the trial, from being in the presence of Jessica Schwarz.

Ask again—how would A.J. have turned out had he survived the relentless physical and psychological pounding he received? What kind of citizen would he have looked like? A.J., the boy, would have been a prohibitive favorite to become A.J., the man, filled with substance abuse, physically violent to those in his life, and worse. It would not be much of a stretch to see him as a relentless killer.

The child protective system in Florida, as I suspect is the case in most states, has been broken for decades. Children are being murdered and sexually and physically abused by their parents. Children being cared for by the state are being murdered and sexually and physically abused, and this, too, has been so for decades. Nothing is changing.

The court system bends over backward in attempting to keep children in their present placements—even after they have been proved to have been abused. This started many years ago when the focus on "rights" took prevailing importance. It was seen that parents had rights. Rights not only to retain custody of their children after it had been proved that they had burned them with cigarettes or placed them in hot water or engaged in sex acts with them, but they also had the right to expect the state to "teach" them to stop doing those things and become better parents.

They had the right to insist that a court order the state to submit a case plan that would show how—over a period of many months—the state would make it so they could retain custody of the very same children they had abused. If at the time of expiration of the plan there were still problems and the children were still not safe with their parents, the case plans could be extended if the parents could show that the state hadn't provided them enough services or hadn't taught them properly how to be a safe parent.

This continues today. The present trend is called "reasonable efforts." The courts are applying the system of laws laid down by legislatures, which means the people—you and I.

When any adult, including and especially a parent, intentionally and willfully causes the kind of harm previously mentioned, shouldn't they automatically forfeit any "right" they had concerning the child they have abused? Why bother to "teach" someone not to have sex with his child, or not to place a lit cigarette against his child's skin, or allow her boyfriend to have sex with her children? The law's overemphasis on the biological link between parent and child should more easily give way when it is clearly established that parents have abused their children. This will, in the long run, strengthen the concept of family. The law must begin sincerely to apply "the best interest of the child" standard.

When children are finally removed from the people who have harmed them, why are they placed within a system that too often has been shown not able to do much better? The foster care system is broken. Some have suggested that orphanages should again be used. It is clear that far too many children are left in abusive places, and far too many children stagnate in the purgatory of foster care. Centralized schools or homes would allow social services to be given displaced children in an effective and efficient manner. We can and must do better.

My purpose in writing this book is that A.J. helps to begin the debate anew. For everyone who met him—or had to deal with his tragic and senseless death—I can think of no better epitaph.

ABOUT THE AUTHORS

Carol J. Rothgeb is the author of *Hometown Killer*. She lives in Springfield, Ohio.

Scott Cupp has prosecuted many high-profile criminal cases. His articles on child advocacy have appeared in the *South Florida Sun-Sentinel, Palm Beach Post, Miami Herald,* and elsewhere. He lives in LaBelle, Florida.

MORE MUST-READ TRUE CRIME
FROM PINNACLE

<u>BOOK YOUR PLACE ON OUR WEBSITE</u> <u>AND MAKE THE</u> <u>READING CONNECTION!</u>

We've created a customized website just for our very special readers, where you can get the inside scoop on everything that's going on with Zebra, Pinnacle and Kensington books.

When you come online, you'll have the exciting opportunity to:

- View covers of upcoming books
- Read sample chapters
- Learn about our future publishing schedule (listed by publication month *and author*)
- Find out when your favorite authors will be visiting a city near you
- Search for and order backlist books from our online catalog
- Check out author bios and background information
- Send e-mail to your favorite authors
- Meet the Kensington staff online
- Join us in weekly chats with authors, readers and other guests
- Get writing guidelines
- AND MUCH MORE!

Visit our website at
http://www.kensingtonbooks.com